SAVILE ROW

The Master Tailors of British Bespoke

James Sherwood

With photography by Guy Hills
Foreword by Tom Ford

With 445 illustrations

For Simon Hesling

Cover: Handcrafted peaked lapels and pearl
stitch buttonhole, Chittleborough & Morgan.
Photograph by Samuel Clark.
Page 1: Chalk and pins still life.
Pages 2–3: Detail of Queen's Royal Lancers mess
dress tunic tailored by Dege & Skinner for 'The
London Cut' exhibition, Florence, in 2007.
Pages 6–7: Savile Row portrait shot by
Jude Edginton for *Times Luxx* magazine
(left to right): Richard James, Alan Bennett
(Davies & Son), Edward Sexton, Frederick
Willems (Gieves & Hawkes), Anda Rowland
(Anderson & Sheppard), Nick Hart (Spencer
Hart), Patrick Grant (Norton & Sons), Guy
Hills (Dashing Tweeds), Patrick Murphy
(Huntsman), John Hitchcock (Anderson &
Sheppard), William Skinner (Dege & Skinner)
and Kathryn Sargent (Gieves & Hawkes).
Page 11: Anderson & Sheppard stock model shot.
Page 12: Tom Ford cover of *The Rake*, Issue 7.

First published in the United Kingdom in 2010 by
Thames & Hudson Ltd, 181A High Holborn,
London WC1V 7QX

This compact edition 2017
Reprinted 2022

Savile Row © 2010 and 2017 James Sherwood

Designed by Samuel Clark
www.bytheskydesign.com

British Library Cataloguing-in-Publication Data
A catalogue record for this book is available from
the British Library

ISBN 978-0-500-29261-7

Printed and bound in China by C&C Offset
Printing Co. Ltd

Be the first to know about our new releases,
exclusive content and author events by visiting
thamesandhudson.com
thamesandhudsonusa.com
thamesandhudson.com.au

FSC
www.fsc.org
MIX
Paper from
responsible sources
FSC® C008047

Contents

Preface   10

Foreword by TOM FORD   12

INTRODUCTION
The Development of the Form Divine   14

Chapter 1
ROYAL SAVILE ROW
Monarchs who Ruled the Row   28
– – EDE & RAVENSCROFT   40
– – HENRY POOLE & CO.   50
– – HUNTSMAN   60

Chapter 2
THE BEAUX ON THE ROW
Men who Led Fashion   72
– – DAVIES & SON   84
– – HARDY AMIES   90
– – MARK POWELL   98

Chapter 3
SAVILE ROW AT WAR
Tailoring for Heroes   106
– – DEGE & SKINNER   116
– – GIEVES & HAWKES   122
– – NORTON & SONS   132

Chapter 4
SAVILE ROW IN HOLLYWOOD
Aristocrats of the Silver Screen   138
– – ANDERSON & SHEPPARD   152
– – HAYWARD   160
– – KILGOUR   168

Chapter 5
SAVILE ROW REVIVAL
The New Establishment   176
– – OZWALD BOATENG   186
– – RICHARD ANDERSON   194
– – RICHARD JAMES   200

Chapter 6
SAVILE ROW IN FASHION
The Row Renaissance   208
– – EDWARD SEXTON   218
– – SPENCER HART   230
– – TIMOTHY EVEREST   236

GENTLEMEN'S REQUISITES   242
BARBERS & PERFUMERS, HATTERS,
SHIRTMAKERS, SHOEMAKERS,
UMBRELLA, WHIP & STICKMAKERS

ANATOMY OF A SUIT   254
MAKING A SUIT   260
SAVILE ROW CLOTH DIRECTORY   268
THE LANGUAGE OF SAVILE ROW   270
CONTACTS   272
ACKNOWLEDGMENTS   276
BIBLIOGRAPHY   276
PICTURE CREDITS   278
INDEX   280

'It's unthinkable that world renowned destinations such as Savile Row, which is synonymous with quality tailoring, could become indistinguishable from any other high street around the world'

WESTMINSTER CITY COUNCIL
LONDON EVENING STANDARD (2016)

PREFACE

When I wrote *Savile Row: The Master Tailors of British Bespoke*, first published in 2010, it was a love letter to the craft of bespoke tailoring and the culmination of an intense period of collaboration with the supremely talented ladies and gentlemen who work on and around the Row. The book captured a moment of great optimism for the future of British bespoke tailoring that has, in many respects, been fulfilled.

The mission of the Savile Row Bespoke Association, founded in 2004 'to protect and develop the art of bespoke tailoring', has been accomplished. In 2004 the shortfall of apprentices necessary to revitalize the craft had reached a critical stage. Walk down Savile Row today and you will see in showroom windows and basement workshops many of the sixty-two tailors and cutters who graduated from SRB's hard-won apprenticeship scheme and learned their trade from the master tailors. Thanks to a sustained campaign of global exhibitions, BBC documentaries and international press coverage, British bespoke tailoring is once again at the pinnacle of excellence, and the leading firms report an average of two requests per day from students pursuing a life on the Row.

Fears voiced in 2010 that bespoke tailors might be priced out of the street they have called home since 1846 have not been realized. In November 2016 Westminster City Council designated Savile Row one of five Special Policy Areas protecting London streets with unique historic character. The firewall policy in place for the Row states that new stores may only open if they do not replace bespoke tailoring uses, that new tenants should sell 'bespoke, unique, limited edition or one-of-a-kind products' and that they should be complementary to the character and function of the quarter.

I have long believed that the system of listing historically important buildings should be extended to businesses over a century old that constitute the crown jewels of London retail. The 'golden mile' of tailors surrounding Savile Row that would qualify include Anderson & Sheppard, Davies & Son, Dege & Skinner, Ede & Ravenscroft, Henry Poole & Co., Huntsman, Kilgour, Meyer & Mortimer and Norton & Sons. The aforementioned tailors stand tall and firm in 2016 but Westminster Council's Special Policy Areas announcement does endorse the importance of preserving bespoke tailoring in the central London landscape.

Above: Crosshairs trained on the window of Anderson & Sheppard, one of several tailors in the area to have dressed men of distinction for over a hundred years.

History was made in 2012 when the first female head cutter on the Row, Kathryn Sargent, left Gieves & Hawkes to open her own business on Hanover Street and subsequently took a temporary lease on the Row in 2016. The First Lady of Savile Row opens the door to a new bespoke business model tailoring 50 per cent for men and 50 per cent for women. 2012 also saw the opening of Anderson & Sheppard's magnificent if modestly named haberdashery at No. 16 Clifford Street providing every gentleman's requisite bar the bespoke suit. The Prince of Wales's Royal Warrant was conferred on Anderson & Sheppard in 2014.

But the strength of London's bespoke tailoring trade does not lie solely with the monoliths of Savile Row. Some of the most creative work produced in London comes from the bespoke ateliers of mavericks such as Edward Sexton (Knightsbridge), Timothy Everest (Spitalfields), Sir Tom Baker (Soho), Mark Powell (Soho) and Connock & Lockie (Bloomsbury) whose elegant 'Dickensian hipster' Georgian townhouse on Lamb's Conduit Street opened in 2016. Perhaps the most impressive stars to emerge since I wrote *Savile Row* are Thom Whiddett and Luke Sweeney, who have traded as Thom Sweeney since 2009 from a whip-smart bespoke townhouse on Weighhouse Street and a ready-to-wear flagship on Bruton Place. The most unexpected – if welcome – return is Carlo Brandelli who, as of 2014, is once again creative director of Kilgour.

Of course the future for bespoke tailoring lies in the hands and minds of the young under-cutters and tailors who are honing their craft on and around the Row. It is entirely plausible that, within the next few years, some may take inspiration from the Tommy Nutter–Edward Sexton story and bring a new Peacock Revolution to London men's tailoring. Thanks to the apprenticeship boom on the Row the troops are in place, though no one has yet risked leading the charge. I sincerely hope we see bespoke tailors teaching designer fashion a lesson in the near future and that I will be there to write the dispatches when they do.

James Sherwood

The topography of Savile Row has changed since 2010, though the controversial 2012 opening of Abercrombie & Fitch's children's store at No. 3 did not – as predicted – open the floodgates to other global brands seeking to annex the prestigious Savile Row address. The fashion brands who chose the Row for their men's flagship stores have good reason to position themselves here. Lanvin is the oldest surviving Parisian couture house and the only one to maintain a bespoke tailoring department, founded in 1924.

Alexander McQueen, opened at No. 9 in 2013, was a perfect fit because the late designer famously apprenticed at Anderson & Sheppard and Gieves & Hawkes: an association that made generations of fashion students respect Savile Row. In an elegant and authentic gesture, McQueen quietly established a bespoke department in the basement of No. 9 directed by former Hayward head cutter Ritchie Charlton. Norton & Sons owner Patrick Grant, meanwhile, made a confident step from bespoke to fashion in 2014, opening a flagship for the contemporary men's concept brand E. Tautz, of which he is creative director, on Duke Street in Mayfair.

'English gentlemen's tailoring, and in particular the tailoring of Savile Row, really set the standard for the way the stylish 20th-century man dressed. This English style, in fact, became the international style for well-dressed men all over the world, and this influence has not waned even in today's more casual world. I suppose that when it comes to men's clothes I am an Anglophile and if I did not design my own men's collection, *I would have virtually my entire wardrobe made on Savile Row.*'

TOM FORD

INTRODUCTION
The Development of the Form Divine

Of all handicrafts, that of tailoring appears to be the most successful in modern *arts*—in the way of making (*coining*) money, we might compare it to witchcraft. The march of refinement has made rapid strides in this particular *walk* of scientific improvement. There is now no longer a *tailor* to be found in the classic region of St. James's. No! they are one and all *professors of the art of cutting*,

"The development of the form divine."

'O f all handicrafts, that of tailoring appears to be the most successful in modern arts – in the way of making (coining) money, we might compare it to witchcraft. The march of refinement has made rapid strides in this particular walk of scientific improvement. There is now no longer a tailor to be found in the classic region of St. James's. No! They are one and all professors of the art of cutting.' So said satirical London society journal *The Town* on 7 April 1838, in an issue preserved in the Henry Poole & Co. archives. *The Town* went on to describe the art and craft of bespoke tailoring as 'the development of the form divine'.

Though *The Town* mocked this burgeoning cult of bespoke tailoring within the golden mile of Mayfair that surrounds Savile Row, reverence for bespoke – the pinnacle of men's sartorial elegance – has persisted into the 21st century. Although much abused of late, the word 'bespoke' refers only to a suit tailored for an individual on an exclusive basis: a process by which the customer is measured by hand, his pattern cut by hand and the garment sewn by many hands, with an average of three intervening fittings. The entire process takes around fifty-two man hours, requiring three

months from order to delivery, and it varies little from the craft described in 1838.

That these 'professors of the art of cutting' have continued to colonize the same golden mile for over two centuries is little short of a miracle. The roots of the Row were planted in 1667 when the 1st Earl of Burlington, Sir Richard 'the Rich' Boyle, acquired a Piccadilly mansion from Restoration poet Sir John Denham. In 1718, the 3rd Earl of Burlington (also named Richard Boyle) began constructing Burlington House, a Neo-Palladian palace inspired by his grand tour, which replaced Denham's more modest mansion. The street we now recognize as Savile Row (named for the 3rd Earl's wife, Lady Dorothy Savile) is built over the orchards that were planted behind Burlington House. The house itself survives as the Royal Academy of Arts.

Like many grand designs conceived on the Row, the Earl's took him to the brink of bankruptcy, forcing the sale of the lands where Savile Row, Bond Street and Conduit Street now stand. In 1733, James Douglas, the double Duke of Queensberry and Dover, completed the Giacomo Leoni-designed Queensberry House on this plot (now Abercrombie & Fitch), where the poet John Gay lived and died. The *Daily Post* reported that

Above: Cover story of *The Town* (1838) satirizing the cult of the bespoke tailor.

Opposite: A Savile Row streetscape (left to right): Huntsman, Dege & Skinner, Kilgour and Gieves & Hawkes.

'A man cannot make love with any conviction unless he is wearing a coat cut within half a mile of Piccadilly.'

TAILOR & CUTTER, c. 1920

'a new pile of buildings is going to be carry'd on near Swallow Street … which is to be named Saville Street.' These buildings – including the Gieves & Hawkes flagship at No. 1 Savile Row – stood on the west side of the Row; the east was still part of Queensberry's garden.

Burlington House was the centre of a glittering circle of ducal palaces under construction on the Piccadilly, Park Lane and St James's Street axis, of which only Spencer, Apsley and Burlington Houses survive. The location was chosen for proximity to the Royal Court at St James's and, later, Buckingham House, which was acquired for the Crown in 1761. It was this fashionable world that drew tailors, bootmakers, perfumers, wigmakers and jewellers to Piccadilly and Mayfair. A typical rags-to-riches tale of 1760, reminiscent of Gay's *The Beggar's Opera*, sees Thomas Hawkes come to London to make his fortune with five pounds in his pocket. Having found employment on Swallow Street with an intemperate velvet cap maker called

Mr Moy, Hawkes took advantage of his patron being permanently 'on the cod' (drunk) to pay court to the customers. By 1771, Hawkes had set up his own shop on Brewer Street, and counted the Dukes of Portland, Marlborough, Leeds and Grafton as customers. By the time he died in 1809, Hawkes & Co. had earned the Royal Warrants of King George III, Queen Charlotte and the Prince of Wales.

Until 1848, Savile Row was a street of doctors (before the profession migrated to Harley Street, from where they still practise). The tailors colonized streets surrounding the Row such as Sackville, Cork, Conduit, Hanover, Princes, Bond and Maddox Streets. Great tailoring names that rose to prominence in the late 18th century, such as Jonathan Meyer, Mortimer, Flights, Adeney & Boutroy, Stultz, John Weston and Schweitzer & Davidson, were primarily military tailors and almost exclusively Jewish immigrants. It took the violent reigns of terror unleashed by a French Revolution and a British Beau to initiate the cult

Above: Gold-embroidered velvet smoking caps cut in a style that would have been familiar to Thomas Hawkes's customers in 1771, made today by James Lock & Co.

Opposite: Regency cartoonist James Gillray lampoons the wedding of the Prince of Wales (later George IV) to Princess Caroline of Brunswick in 1794. George 'Beau' Brummell was one of only four supporters, strongly suggesting that the single natural head of hair not bewigged (just visible at the right-hand side of the drawing) could be a previously unidentified portrait of the Beau.

The BRIDAL-NIGHT.

of the dandy, which led Regency men's fashion and went on to serve as the foundation of the contemporary suit.

The French Revolution of 1789 heralded the death of decadent 18th-century aristocratic court dress, which was tailored in silks, brocades and velvets loomed in France. The birth of British bespoke tailoring was inspired by 'honest' English country gentlemen's riding attire cut from native wool cloth. It was this English equestrian tailoring that supreme dandy George 'Beau' Brummell elevated to an art form a decade later. Bespoke houses that opened during the Beau's lifetime, such as Meyer & Mortimer (1801), Davies & Son (1804), Henry Poole & Co. (1806) and Norton & Sons (1821), still survive to this day.

The year 1848 was a landmark in bespoke tailoring. Henry Poole, on inheriting his family firm in 1846, converted a stable block backing onto the Row into a showroom with an entrance at No. 32 Savile Row. By 1951, Poole's grand Savile

Row façade stretched from No. 36–39. Thus Poole earned the title 'Founder of Savile Row'. Henry Poole played host, paterfamilias, sartorial oracle and confidante to the monarchs and men who ruled and built the British Empire. A watercolour survives from 1855, when the firm erected an audacious gas-illuminated eagle-and-coronet light show above the façade of No. 36–39 to celebrate Napoleon III's state visit to Queen Victoria (and to his tailor, Henry Poole).

Henry Poole & Co. was a cornerstone of Savile Row, and it remains so today, despite the demolition of No. 36–39 in 1961 to make way for a car park. Along with Dege & Skinner, Welsh & Jefferies, Maurice Sedwell and Anderson & Sheppard, Poole's is one of the few remaining firms on the Row to make only bespoke suits. It may be incomprehensible to young men today, but before the Great War of 1914–18 bespoke tailoring was a thriving national industry, patronized by all strata of the class system. A Henry Poole & Co. bespoke

The Gieve Life-Saving Waistcoat, exhibited in the Gieves & Hawkes archive at No. 1 Savile Row. The inflatable rubber ring tailored inside a neat blue worsted waistcoat was patented at the turn of the 20th century.

Ambassador's court coatee tailored by Gieves & Hawkes's bespoke workroom and embroidered by London's oldest and finest hand-embroiderers, Hand & Lock (founded 1767). The house made an identical model for Michael Jackson in 1989.

suit would have cost circa £6 in the Edwardian era:
roughly the annual wage of a lowly house servant or
labourer. But the sheer volume of tailors in Britain
allowed even the poorest to alter a hand-me-down
or order a Sunday best suit. The *Tailor & Cutter*
journal analysed the 1900 census and estimated:
'In England & Wales there are 237,185 tailors of
whom 117,640 are female. Of these London finds
employment for 38,801 males and 41,270 females.
13,156 of the males are foreigners the larger
number of whom are either Poles or Russians.
791 male tailors are aged between 10 and 14. 1065
are 75-years and upwards. 1594 male tailors are
recorded in lunatic asylums and 379 in prison.
20 are returned blind and 569 deaf and dumb.'

The Great War not only culled two generations
of the nation's finest, it also toppled monarchies
and dealt a near-death blow to the ceremonial,
court and military dress that was bread-and-butter
trade to Savile Row. Just as a coronation such as the
King of Tonga's in 2008 can underwrite a year's
trade for Gieves & Hawkes's military head, Mr
Garry Carr, so the rituals of Edwardian court life
could bankroll Huntsman, Davies & Son, Poole's,

Gieves & Hawkes and Welsh & Jefferies, who made
court dress, liveries, ambassadors' coatees, naval
full dress and tunics for the royal household, with
sufficient trade to spare. Other firms could survive
making mourning dress alone.

The old world did not expire in 1918. But that
year did mark the passing of the age of certainty
for bespoke tailoring. The old idols had been torn
down, with princes usurped by film stars as objects
of worship. Three houses capitalized on silver screen
magic, painting portraits in cloth of screen gods such
as Valentino, Astaire, Chaplin, Gable and Grant.
Anderson & Sheppard, Huntsman and Kilgour,
French & Stanbury were arguably the greatest
Hollywood co-stars never to be credited. It was their
suits that seduced Greta Garbo, traded wisecracks
with Mae West and smouldered as Marlene Dietrich
smoked. These houses starred in more Oscar-
winning productions than Katharine Hepburn.

The Second World War culled another
generation of bespoke customers but, crucially,
also heralded the triumph of ready-to-wear over
bespoke tailoring. Hawkes & Co. managing director
George Ballingall had introduced 'immediate wear'

to the Row in 1929, and by 1948 ready-mades were outselling bespoke.

The demise of formality and the ever-decreasing number of occasions that required formal dress inevitably damaged the bespoke trade. However, the superiority of bespoke was never disputed. In 1952, Hollywood's best-dressed star, Douglas Fairbanks Jr, declared: 'Savile Row has recaptured tailoring supremacy of the world.' The coronation of HM Queen Elizabeth II in 1953 boosted morale in the Row's workrooms and allowed the ceremonial departments of bespoke houses to show off their craft. Foreshadowing the present Savile Row Bespoke Association of tailors, in the late 1950s and early 1960s Row giants united as the Men's Fashion Council and led men's style with presentations at the Savoy Hotel that introduced innovative cuts such as the 'Flare Line' or the 'Slim Line'. But, inevitably, the 1960s 'Youthquake' stole attention from traditional bespoke tailoring and put the focus

firmly on the new fashion boutiques of Carnaby Street and the King's Road.

Two houses were responsible for giving Savile Row the hip replacement it so desperately needed. In 1967, Douglas Hayward opened a tailoring shop on Mount Street and brought style icons such as Michael Caine, Terence Stamp and Steve McQueen back to the discreet charm of hand-cut clothing. In 1969, Savile Row *enfant terrible* Tommy Nutter and his partner Edward Sexton opened the most louche, wild and happening bespoke pleasure palace on Valentine's Day, and went on to dress The Beatles and The Rolling Stones, and sundry aristocrats, kings of finance, and queens. Nutter has been praised by Timothy Everest, Ozwald Boateng and Richard James, Savile Row's New Establishment tailors, for inspiring them to open houses in the early 1990s that combined bespoke craft and directional fashion.

Though initially not welcomed by the old guard, this New Establishment – whose number

Above: Anderson & Sheppard's wall of patterns at No. 32 Old Burlington Street.

Opposite: 'The London Cut' exhibition in the British Ambassador's Residence, Paris, July 2007.

was strengthened by Carlo Brandelli at Kilgour, Soho tailor Mark Powell, Nick Hart and former Huntsman head cutter Richard Anderson – resuscitated great British bespoke after a decade in which men's style had been dominated by fashion houses such as Giorgio Armani, Comme des Garçons and Jean-Paul Gaultier. In fairness to the grand old men of Savile Row, the bespoke trade has never been antipathetic to fashion; rather, it is the presumption that ready-to-wear with a designer label can be priced higher than handcrafted unique masterpieces that rankles. Bespoke tailoring is the high-water mark that sets the Row apart. Why, they reason, would a man choose to buy a garment not chosen, developed, amended and fitted to his own tastes, physique and expectations? This is the fundamental question. The Savile Row Renaissance of the 21st century is the answer.

In 2004, the Savile Row Bespoke Association was established to protect and promote the craft of bespoke tailoring. In 2006, the master tailors of Savile Row were invited to show a major retrospective, 'The London Cut', by Florentine men's fashion foundation Pitti Immagine Uomo in the Duke of Aosta's private apartments in Palazzo Pitti: palatial staterooms that had not been opened to the public since the Italian royal family fled the country in 1946. The world of men's style is once again focusing on Savile Row. All the values bespoke tailoring holds dear – craft, respect for the past, trust that quality will never be compromised – are the values that strike a resounding chord with society today. Savile Row bespoke tailoring is made in England, largely within a square mile of the street itself. It is carbon neutral, with a blank passport and few footprints when compared with designer imports. It respects the creativity of the customers, whom designers choose to overwhelm. There is no greater sartorial pleasure, and none more addictive, than commissioning a suit that you admire and aspire to own, and then displaying it to invite admiration and aspiration from others.

Kilgour Spring/Summer
2005 advertising image
shot by Nick Knight, with
creative direction by Carlo
Brandelli and art direction/
modelling by Peter Saville.

Edward Sexton bespoke
chocolate houndstooth
suit with yellow
double-breasted vest,
photographed in Tuscany
for *The Rake* in 2009.

Chapter I

ROYAL SAVILE ROW

Monarchs who Ruled the Row

Preceding pages, left:
Satirical *Vanity Fair* cartoon by
Hay (1888), titled 'Eddy', of
Prince Albert Victor wearing
a patrol jacket of the 10th
(Prince of Wales's Own)
Royal Hussars. The posture,
not to mention the jauntily
angled cap, gently pokes
fun at the dandy, dissolute
heir apparent.

H istory has proved that
the better dressed a Prince of Wales, the less
suited he is to the throne. Of all the British royals
to patronize Savile Row, the greatest sartorial
names have indeed been ill judged by posterity.
When dandiacal monarch King George IV died
in 1830, *The Times* reported that 'there was never
an individual less regretted by his fellow creatures
than this deceased King'. When jovial King
Edward VII, arguably Savile Row's greatest patron,
finally reached the throne in 1901, he reigned
for only nine years. His narcissistic son and
heir Prince Albert Victor, Duke of Clarence and
Avondale (otherwise known as Prince Eddy), died
prematurely, aged twenty-eight. Eddy's brother
King George V's peacock of an eldest son, Edward
VIII, later the Duke of Windsor, abdicated before
he had even been crowned, for the love of American
divorcee Mrs Simpson, in 1936.

And yet we have these magnificent Princes to
thank for endorsing Savile Row's great tailoring
houses with their Royal Warrants, and setting
fashions in men's tailoring that endure to this day.
King George IV may have been the most sartorially
incontinent of princes – leaving a wardrobe valued
at £15,000 on his death (the equivalent

of approximately £1,200,000 today) – but without
his patronage when Prince Regent, a fashion
leader such as Beau Brummell would not have
been able to elevate fine tailoring from a trade
to a royal prerogative.

It is not coincidental that the beginning
of Savile Row's reign as monarch of men's style
coincided with the French Revolution of 1789.
Summing up his legacy, Brummell declared:
'I, Brummell, put the modern man into pants,
dark coat, white shirt and clean linen. I dare say
that will be sufficient to secure my fame.' As the
Duke of Windsor pointed out in his 1960 memoir
A Family Album, Brummell's legacy was revolutionary:
thanks to him, 'all men now dress more or less
alike'. It was a subversive crusade when commoners
dictated to princes such as the Regent. In an equally
audacious example of lèse-majesté, the Prince
Regent attended Brummell's morning levee at
No. 4 Chesterfield Street, where the fashionable
world would gather to watch the Beau dress. The
levee was a major court ritual before
the Revolution, during which court attended the
ruling family at their morning toilette; thus the
Beau was supplanting a very potent divine right of
kings. Scant surprise, then, that the Prince Regent

A heroic, not to mention
idealized, portrait of King
George IV when Prince
of Wales, *c.* 1790, after
a miniature painted by
Richard Cosway.

swatted Brummell like a fly, precipitating his social and financial ruin, in 1816.

As the Regent grew fatter, he banished Brummell's rules of severe cut and fit from court and returned fashion to pre-Revolutionary excess, a style embraced by his equally corpulent brother, who was crowned William IV in 1830. The unsung hero of 'Brummellism' in the British royal family was German Prince Albert of Saxe-Coburg-Gotha, who married Queen Victoria in 1840. He was also responsible for bullying his son Bertie (later Edward VII) sufficiently to trigger a lifelong addiction to bespoke tailoring. In a letter drafted by the Prince Consort (quoted in *A Family Album*), Queen Victoria writes to her son and heir that 'dress is a trifling matter which might not be raised to too much importance in our eyes', adding, 'we do not wish to control your own tastes and fancies which, on the contrary, we wish you to indulge and develop. But we do expect that you will never wear anything extravagant or slang.'

Is it any coincidence that the Prince of Wales placed his first order at Henry Poole & Co. in 1860: a year when Prince Albert's health and influence over his son were failing? To the despair of his widowed mother, Bertie's extravagant wardrobe was indeed sartorial slang that went on to have worldwide influence. As the Duke of Windsor later recalled, 'My grandfather unquestionably had a wider influence on masculine fashions than any member of the Royal Family since George IV. He was a good friend to the tailors of Savile Row; consolidating the position of London as the international sartorial shrine for men as already Paris was for women.'

As King Edward VII, Bertie introduced the dinner jacket, white dress waistcoat, velvet smoking jacket, loden shooting suit and the homburg and Coke (bowler) hats to male attire, as well as initiating the tradition of leaving the lowest button of a waistcoat undone to accommodate his paunch. Marriages of Queen Victoria's family to every royal household in Europe also resulted in an influx of

The Royal Family in 1846 by Franz Xavier Winterhalter. Prince Albert wears 'new style' court dress tailored to the design commissioned from Henry Poole & Co. by Queen Victoria in 1839, a year before her marriage to Prince Albert.

Prince Eddy strikes a pose on his grandmother's Scottish estate Balmoral (c. 1890), sporting sartorial anomalies for country attire such as what appears to be a badger's head sporran, wing collar and flamboyant tie knot. On other occasions, Prince Eddy was photographed wearing spats with his kilt.

On the occasion of a visit by his nephew Kaiser Wilhelm II to Sandringham House in November 1902, King Edward VII wears an Inverness cape tailored by Henry Poole & Co. in the Glenurquhart cloth he made fashionable and rechristened Prince of Wales check.

'Dress is a trifling matter which might not be raised to too much importance in our eyes.'

A LETTER DATED 1851 FROM QUEEN VICTORIA TO HER SON, THE FUTURE KING EDWARD VII (PROBABLY DRAFTED BY PRINCE ALBERT)

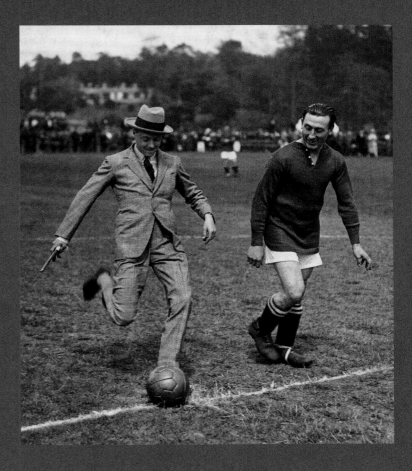

Right: The Prince of Wales kicks off a charity football match in 1921 with evident glee and gusto. The sporting Prince was also a keen golfer, steeplechaser and womanizer.

Opposite, from top left: Photographed in 1911, the seventeen-year-old Prince of Wales wears a three-piece suit probably tailored by his father's choice, Davies & Son. However, the two-button, single-breasted coat worn with a tightly knotted tie would not look out of place in contemporary London, but for the white wing collar.

Throughout the 1920s and early 1930s, the Prince of Wales led the world of men's style. The Fair Isle sweater and cloth flat cap pictured here were just two of the trends he initiated.

For Royal Ascot and the Derby, the Prince of Wales's black morning coat tailored by Scholte was edged with jazzy grosgrain trim, and Prince Edward preferred a louche spotted silk bow rather than the conventional tie or cravat.

Exceptionally conservative, King George V refused to give up the Victorian frock coat and black silk top hat of his youth and continued wearing this uniform until his death in 1936. The King heartily disapproved of Prince Edward's sartorial experiments, such as flannel trousers with turn-ups worn with a navy blazer and tobacco suede shoes for town.

foreign royalty to Henry Poole & Co., including the Crown Princes of Prussia, Denmark and Russia, and the Kings of Belgium, Spain and the Hellenes.

The Prince lost prematurely to Savile Row was Edward VII's eldest son, Prince Eddy. But for conspiracy theories linking him to the Jack the Ripper murders (unlikely) and the Cleveland Street male brothel scandal of 1889 (more than likely), Eddy would be a mere footnote in history. However, scandal and his sudden death from influenza in 1892 made him a cult figure not dissimilar to the late Diana, Princess of Wales. Like the Princess, Eddy was a cause célèbre and fashion plate in the burgeoning British newspapers and pictorial journals of the era, such as the *Illustrated London News*.

Photographs and sketches including the 'Spy' cartoon for *Vanity Fair* demonstrate Eddy's dashing, decadent demeanour and instinctive appreciation of fashion that went beyond royal protocol. As his biographer Andrew Cook relates in *The King Britain Never Had* (2006), 'The way Eddy dressed is the

clearest indication of his interest in life outside Royal circles. In mufti, he wore high collar and big cuffs in the "masher" style of the 1880s,' which led to his nickname, 'Collars & Cuffs', in the journals of the day. Mashers, or swells, were cocksure men about town, and Prince Eddy – with his hooded eyes, waxed moustache and knowing smile – was a right royal masher. By all accounts an indolent, fashion-conscious young man with little grasp on his destiny as future king, the monarchy may have been fortunate that the title Prince of Wales and prospective bride Princess May of Teck passed to his brother, Prince George, on his death.

Thus the arch-conservative King George V inherited the throne in 1910. The King's severity towards his son Edward's attire had much the same effect as Prince Albert's disapproval of Bertie's. It drove him away from the King's tailor, Davies & Son, and towards Scholte, one of the Row's great revolutionary cutters. When F. P. Scholte died aged eighty-three in 1948, the *Tailor & Cutter* saluted 'one of London's greatest tailors for nearly half a century who made one of the greatest changes in men's fashion that has ever been introduced when he began using drape at the end of the last century'. Originally a military tailor, Scholte was the godfather of the London Cut: a high-waisted, close-fitting but softly draped lounge suit promoted by Edward. It is a cut still championed by Anderson & Sheppard. In his chapter of the *Family Album* titled 'Father', Edward, Duke of Windsor, characterizes George V's sartorial reign in a concise paragraph: 'On domestic occasions, when I dined with my father, we would always wear a white tie and tails and the Garter Star, though when he himself had no guests he would relax so far as to wear a dinner jacket. In the daytime, of course, whenever I visited my father, I would have to put on a morning coat.'

Edward, then Prince of Wales, chose to declare his independence from his oppressive father through dress. His taste went on to have worldwide influence. As *Cloth & Clothes* magazine declared in 1953, 'The uncrowned Edward VIII as Prince of Wales was the undoubted style leader of the younger set in the rather flippant Twenties. He probably has had more influence on the unusual in present day trends than anyone in the world.' The Prince was an early adopter of the double-breasted four-button coats that had evolved from Edward VII's reefer, and demanded side vents to allow for comfort and movement. His trousers followed the fashion for wider, looser legs, in contrast to the Edwardian drainpipe. Much to Scholte's relief, Prince Edward never went so far as to wear the heavily pleated, turned-up 'Oxford bags' that became a brief fad amongst varsity students in 1924.

The Prince's taste in clothing reflected his somewhat rackety, dynamic life in the 1920s. He circumnavigated the globe as an ambassador of British style. He flew his own plane, drove his own Hillmans and danced nightly at the Café de Paris or the Embassy Club. Instead of traditional regal sports such as shooting and horseracing, the Prince preferred golf, steeplechase and sea bathing off the coast of Biarritz. He banished the stiff stud collar in favour of shirts constructed complete with soft collars and cuffs. Contrary to popular belief, Prince Edward loathed formal dress and would subtly subvert it at any given opportunity to annoy his father.

It was Prince Edward who finally set the blueprint for what we know as the black tie dinner jacket. He, like all society men, wore evening tails with 'boiled' (read 'stiff'), bibbed evening shirts for most of the 1920s. But in the 1930s, the Prince revived a midnight blue short jacket that had been cut by Henry Poole & Co. for Edward VII for private dinners, and had Scholte cut a copy that he wore in public with a white waistcoat similar to his grandfather's. The only sartorial coup de théâtre he denied initiating is – somewhat ironically – the Windsor tie knot. As he says in *A Family Album*, 'The knot to which the Americans gave my name was a double knot in a narrow tie. It is true that I have always preferred large knots as looking better than small ones.' However, the Prince's distinctive knots were achieved with an extra thickness of material rather than dexterity, much to the disappointment of the website forums who now spend hours debating the art of the Windsor knot.

On accessories, the Prince excelled, toning his tie, socks, shirt and handkerchief with his suit, though never matching. His eye for balancing checks, spots and stripes is still considered masterly by Savile Row. When his remarkable wardrobe was auctioned by Sotheby's in 1997, long after his death, it was noted that many of the suits he wore in later life had been cut by Scholte in the 1920s and 1930s. He was way ahead of the curve in the 1920s, wearing tobacco suede lace-ups with grey flannel trousers and navy blazer in town. His eye for tartans, tweeds and sports clothes is faultless to the point that relaxed elegance emerges as his true legacy to men's style.

When Edward VIII was forced to abdicate, the most influential man to have graced Savile Row was exiled from Britain. The newly titled Duke of Windsor lost everything except his sense of style. As men's tailoring journal *The Outfitter* concluded on 19 December 1936, 'The sartorial world has certainly lost its most dominating personality but let it not be thought that by this great depravation we will be without style leadership. The new King [George VI] might have taken as his prototype his late father, for he has the same extreme good quiet taste.' *Cloth*

Prince Philip, Duke of Edinburgh, photographed in Admiral's full dress uniform tailored by Gieves Ltd, in the Green Room at Windsor Castle (1987).

Thirty-year-old bachelor Prince Charles photographed in 1979 on Smith's Lawn (at Guards Polo Club in Windsor), having just left the Royal Ascot race meeting, hence his charcoal grey Anderson & Sheppard bespoke morning tails, and carnation boutonnière worn by the Windsor men at the royal meeting.

A twenty-one-year-old Prince William wearing white tie tailored by Gieves & Hawkes, photographed for the September 2003 cover of *Vanity Fair* by Mario Testino.

& Clothes in 1953 christened Queen Elizabeth II's father 'the impeccable monarch', but he never reached the heights of sartorial excellence achieved by his brothers the Duke of Windsor and the equally chic Prince George, the late Duke of York.

Neither, it must be said, did the Queen's consort, Prince Philip. In October 1952, *Men's Wear* quoted Fred Stanbury, co-chairman of Kilgour, French & Stanbury, as saying, 'The Duke of Edinburgh does not want to be a style leader. The art in tailoring is to make the customer – not the suit – look his very best.' Tailored by Teddy Watson at Hawes & Curtis, then Watson's undercutter John Kent, Prince Philip has progressed quietly and elegantly as a Savile Row man for over fifty years. At the side of the Queen at all great state occasions, resplendent in Gieves-tailored Admiral's full dress, His Royal Highness is a magnificent sight.

The present Prince of Wales's relationship with Savile Row has been diffident; possibly because the shadow of the dapper Duke of Windsor still loomed large over the the royal family in his formative years.

The tailoring fraternity expected a champion of flamboyant Windsor style and received instead a careful, sometimes contradictory man. In 1971, a young Prince Charles attended a Savile Row white tie dinner wearing a sports jacket in response to industry criticism of his style. Prince Charles did indirectly follow in his great uncle's footsteps by choosing the Anderson & Sheppard cut (a scion of Scholte tailoring) and recently returned to the house after a period being tailored made-to-measure by Turnbull & Asser. His military tailor is the grand old house of Welsh & Jefferies. While minor members of the royal family such as the late Lord Louis Mountbatten (Prince Charles's mentor) and Prince Michael of Kent display flamboyance worthy of the Duke of Windsor, Prince Charles, like his father, enjoys bespoke tailoring while not resorting to what Queen Victoria famously called 'slang' attire. All eyes on Savile Row inevitably rest on heir apparent Prince William and his rather more rakish younger brother Prince Harry. Though discretion prevents me from naming the house, it is satisfying for British bespoke tailoring that one of their number has taken the measure of Princes William and Harry in 2009. Equally gratifying was Lord Freddy Windsor's pride in his Hardy Amies bespoke morning tails cut for his 2009 wedding to Sophie Winkleman. Though it is unlikely a Prince will ever again lead fashion, the young royals' support for Savile Row is most welcome.

EDE & RAVENSCROFT

-- ESTABLISHED 1689

The lineage of royal robe makers Ede & Ravenscroft can be traced back to 1689, the year William and Mary were crowned, and the house has tailored coronation robes for every British monarch since, up to and including Queen Elizabeth II. But the name Ede was not connected to the firm until 1811, when apprentice Joseph Ede was indentured to William Webb of the Strand, who held the Royal Warrant for King George III. Ede & Ravenscroft hold the most detailed, historically important British royal ledgers of all Savile Row houses, including the 1761 records of George III's coronation robe (which survives in the Royal Ceremonial Dress collection at Kensington Palace) and the orders of sixteen dukes and forty-six earls.

Joseph Ede would have been sufficiently schooled by 1821 to be one of the twenty-seven tailors who worked on the official orders for the coronation of King George IV. The sixty years that had elapsed since George III's coronation necessitated new robes for the nobility and liveries for the officers of state. Detailed engravings of the coronation produced in 1826 bear testimony to the artistry of London's greatest robe maker.

William Webb's son Frederick headed the firm for the coronation of William IV in 1831 but, as it was only a decade after his brother's show-stopping pageant, the lion's share of the robes and the coronation mantle itself were simply renovated. In 1834, Frederick Webb sold his ailing family business to Thomas Adams, uncle of Joseph Ede, and the firm was christened Adams & Ede. Ede was appointed robe maker to William IV and, three years later, to his niece Queen Victoria.

Adams & Ede's importance as tailors to the Victorian Church, state and monarchy is indicated in Joseph Ede's mid-19th-century day books (reproduced in Ede & Ravenscroft's 1989 book *Robes of the Realm*). Listed are a rich damask state robe for the Rt Hon. the Speaker of the House of Commons (1838), a rich green velvet mantle of the Most Ancient and Most Noble Order of the Thistle for His Grace the Duke of Montrose (1845) and twenty-seven mourning cloaks of superfine black cloth for the funeral of the Duke of Wellington (1852). Quarterly accounts were sent to Buckingham Palace and the Lord Chamberlain's Office.

In 1868, the firm moved to Nos. 93 and 94 Chancery Lane under the name Ede & Son,

Baroness Thyssen, former fashion model Fiona Campbell-Walter, poses outside the Mayfair Hotel in new style peeresses' coronation robes, distinctively trimmed with scalloped fur, designed by Norman Hartnell for the 1953 coronation of Queen Elizabeth II. Tailored strictly according to protocol, a Baroness's train is a yard (90 cm) in length with ermine edging of 2 inches (5 cm).

Preparing for the Coronation of the King and Queen
In London and in Devon.

MAKING CORONATION ROBES FOR THE PEERS

Lace Now being Woven for the Queen's Coronation Robes

DRAWN BY F. MATANIA

Skilful fingers are now busy making the ermine and rich velvet robes and coronets for the coronation at Messrs. Eede, Son and Ravenscroft, at whose premises this picture has been especially drawn. One of the two uppermost views above, on the left, the pillow on which lace is made with the numerous pricked pattern bobbins and a finished piece, while on the right are seen little girls engaged in the work. The lower view shows a finished piece of Honiton lace, the work is being turned out at the Lace School at Shaldon, a pretty little village on the South Devon coast.

Opposite, from top left:

Opposite, from top left: The 1937 coronation of King George VI and Queen Elizabeth, pictured here with the Princesses Elizabeth and Margaret Rose.

A 1911 feature in the illustrated weekly journal *The Sphere* depicting Ede, Son & Ravenscroft's workshops preparing robes and coronets for the coronation of King George V.

The coronation robes of King George V and Queen Mary, adapted from those tailored less than a decade before for the previous reign.

The coronation robe tailored for Queen Alexandra in 1902 is shown to magnificent effect held by Her Majesty's six page boys, who are dressed by Henry Poole & Co.

where it has remained ever since. The greatest contribution of the 'son', Joseph Ede, to the family firm before his premature death aged twenty-six in 1871 was to marry Rosanna 'Rosa' Ravenscroft. It was this formidable, emancipated woman who would hold the reins of the house for the next sixty years. She united Ravenscroft, a wig-making business founded in 1726, and Ede & Son, bringing the highly respected (and lucrative) international legal robe and wig-making business to the firm she directed. As a mark of respect to her late husband, the house was named Ede, Son & Ravenscroft until 1921 (a decade before her own death).

Like Joseph Ede before her, Rosa Ede was perfectly placed on the death of Queen Victoria in 1901 to tailor almost entirely new robes, sixty-three years having passed since the last coronation. In a ledger index for the 1902 coronation of King Edward VII, which is held in the Chancery Lane archive, the firm records tailoring coronation robes for (in order of precedence): King Edward, Queen Alexandra, Princess Charles, Princess Victoria, Prince Charles, the Prince of Wales, Prince Christian, the Duchess of Fife, the Duchess of Connaught, Princess Margaret of Connaught,

Princess Patricia of Connaught, Prince Victor Christian, Prince Philippe of Saxe-Coburg, Princess Louise, Duchess of Argyll, the Duke of Connaught, the Duke of Cambridge and Princess Beatrice of Saxe-Coburg.

Black-bordered letters were sent out from Ede & Son to all peers of the realm, beginning: 'We venture to write asking if we may have the honour to put your Robe and Coronet in hand.' Someone, possibly Rosa Ede herself, hand-writes on the proof copy of the letter: 'Send out March 1901 2 months after the death of Queen Victoria', suggesting that the letter was drafted just days after the old Queen died. A collection of letters to and from the royal households gives a fascinating insight into the special relationship between the royal family and Ede & Son. In reply to a letter from the Hon. Sir William Carrington enquiring, 'Would you kindly let me know for the Prince of Wales's information if the velvet for His robe is English or French. His Royal Highness hopes it's English,' Ede & Son writes, 'The coronation robes of the plushest English crimson silk velvet lined with white silk and trimmed with choice Minerva will not exceed

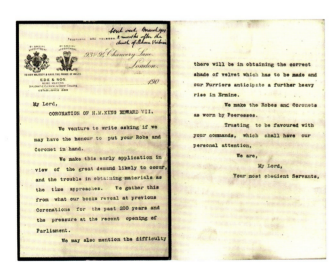

Letter printed on black-bordered Ede & Son mourning paper offering the peerage the firm's services as robe maker for the coronation of King Edward VII, following the death of Queen Victoria in January 1901.

A collection of correspondence dated 1905 between Rosa Ede and Miss Knollys, dresser to Queen Alexandra, concerning a request by Mrs Ede for Her Majesty's signature on a portrait of Her Majesty robed and crowned.

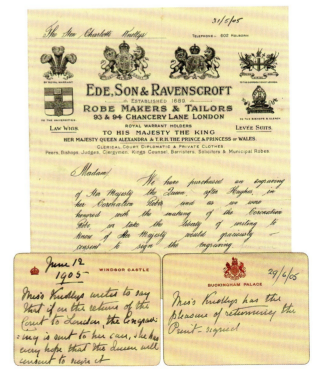

the sum of seventy-five Guineas. The above will be made strictly to regulation and the velvet and silk will be made on the same looms as we are making for His Majesty The King's robe.'

Characters to emerge in the 1902–3 letters include Queen Alexandra's fearsome dresser, Miss Knollys, who writes from Windsor Castle on 31 January 1903: 'The Queen wishes the real ermine on her coronation train to be taken off at once and sent to Her Majesty at Buckingham Palace and replaced by imitation ermine preparatory to its being exhibited to the public either at the Tower or some other place.'

The coronation robes of King Edward and Queen Alexandra were returned to Ede, Son & Ravenscroft for renovation to the gold lace embroidery, before making a second appearance at the 1911 coronation of King George V and Queen Mary. As *Robes of the Realm* says, 'There was little robe making to be done prior to this coronation,' except for the Garter robes worn by the Prince of Wales (later the Duke of Windsor). Business was brisker when King George VI was crowned in 1937,

as the house's coronation ledgers prove. It is the handwritten notes that accompany the 1936 orders that fascinate. Robes for the little princesses Elizabeth and Margaret Rose were edged with fourteen ermine skins but 'no spots on both robes'. The Duchess of Gloucester's coronation robe was made with 'mock edgings' rather than costly ermine. Under Lord Louis Mountbatten's order, the tailor notes: 'make an allowance for large epaulettes', and the firm is instructed to 'make calico shape of robe edge with cloth showing width of fur – also cape' for the robe of Queen Elizabeth (later the Queen Mother).

Queen Elizabeth II commissioned a purple velvet coronation robe and a crimson parliamentary robe from Ede & Ravenscroft on her accession in 1952. The house also tailored the coronation robe of the Duke of Edinburgh. It appears the Queen shows every indication of living as long as her mother. Thus the coronation of King George VII (as it is whispered Prince Charles will be styled) would be the longest hiatus in succession in the history of the British monarchy.

Above, left: An engraving of Queen Alexandra's coronation portrait, dedicated to Rosa Ede in 1905 and subsequently her prized possession, now takes pride of place in the Chancery Lane shop.

Above, right: Ede & Ravenscroft director Albert Batteson (far left) shows VIP guests of the house an Earl's coronet and tabard worn by an officer of the College of Arms (bottom left), c. 1953.

Opposite: Queen Elizabeth II leaves Buckingham Palace robed in crimson velvet to attend her coronation on 2 June 1953. In a charming aside, the Ede & Ravenscroft archives record a charge of £9 to make a 'mock robe' for rehearsal at Westminster Abbey.

Left: The doorway of Ede & Ravenscroft at No. 8 Burlington Gardens flanked by the company's Royal Warrants as robe maker to the Queen, the Duke of Edinburgh and the Prince of Wales.

Above: The majestic interior of Ede & Ravenscroft at No. 93 Chancery Lane.

Ede & Ravenscroft retains the aristocratic aura of British bespoke tailoring for the Autumn/Winter 2009 collection shot by Lorenzo Agius on Earl Spencer's Althorp estate in Northamptonshire. Opposite: Vintage check worsted flannel suit with claret wool Melton waistcoat. Following pages, left: Wool and cashmere Viceroy flannel suit. Following pages, right: Pure wool covert coat worn with chalk-stripe suit.

The constitutional changes in 21st-century Britain will challenge Ede & Ravenscroft's head of ceremonial dress, Mr Chris Allan; not least the abolition of hereditary peers, the possible introduction of an elected House of Lords, dress reforms in the judiciary and Prince Charles's indication that he would wish for a multi-faith coronation. But reform rather than continuity requires new robes, and who better to design them than Ede & Ravenscroft? In recent years the Labour peers ennobled in the House of Lords are invariably seduced by ermine trim. Similarly, the Rt Hon. the Speaker of the House of Commons John Bercow, elected in 2009, wears the black-and-gold-trim gown worn by his illustrious predecessors at state occasions, even though he chose a plain black academic gown for when the House is sitting.

Ede & Ravenscroft is unique amongst Savile Row houses in that it has retained its position as premier tailor to the legal profession and robe maker to the royal household. It stands for continuity while the fortunes and specialities of other houses wax and wane. When Ede & Ravenscroft opened an outpost at the top of Savile Row (No. 8 Burlington Gardens), the house established itself as a bespoke tailor, though head of bespoke Philip Thomas works from Chancery Lane. Where they excel is evening dress. As Thomas says, 'Putting on a dinner suit or evening tails does make you feel like a million dollars. It's easy to put on a pair of jeans, isn't it? There's no satisfaction or pride in that. Once you've worn a handmade suit you won't go back, I can promise you that.'

Ede & Ravenscroft is the only house on the Row that can kit a chap out in white tie from black silk top hat to black patent leather slippers as bespoke, made-to-measure or immediate wear. Not only do they sell stiff collars, dress studs, collar tabs and stud-collar shirts, they have an infinite variety of all of the above. The shops, with outposts in university cities Oxford and Cambridge, are run like traditional gentlemen's outfitters: they will not allow a fellow to leave unless he is dressed correctly.

HENRY POOLE & CO.

-- Established 1806

N o firm on Savile Row has been, nor ever will be, granted as many Royal Warrants 'of any note' as Henry Poole & Co.: forty to date, not including the non-regnant princes, royal dukes and consorts listed in the company ledgers, who would bring the tally closer to one hundred. For this, Henry Poole & Co. has to thank the man whose name remains above the door. The rise of Henry Poole from court tailor to man about town, fêted by monarchs, politicians, literary lions and bankers, has no equivalent in the 20th century. It is a tale of social mobility that would make modern comparisons – with fashion designers Yves Saint Laurent or Gianni Versace, for example – appear reticent. In 'Old Pooley's golden age between 1860 and his death in 1876, the firm was tailoring an average of twelve thousand bespoke orders per annum for the men who ruled the civilized world.

Secreted in chairman Angus Cundey's office at No. 15 Savile Row is a single surviving copy of 'Poole's Ladies' & Gentleman's Polite Assistant and Useful Remembrancer for 1849', which contains a detailed almanac, 'The Sovereigns of Europe'. By the 1870s, Poole's dressed them all, including the royal families of England, France,

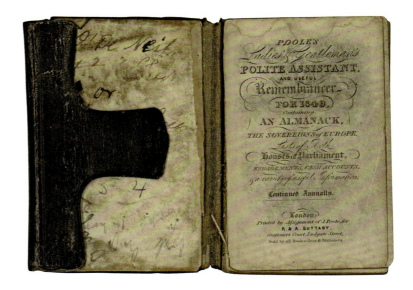

Russia, Austria, Germany, Belgium, Italy, Portugal, Sweden and Norway, Brazil, and Egypt. His first Emperor was Napoleon III of France, when the then exiled Prince Louis Napoléon, nephew of thegreat Bonaparte, was living at the Brunswick Hotel in Mayfair; in 1846, he ordered nothing more regal than a superfine black frock coat costing six pounds, sixteen shillings and sixpence. A man of fashion, if not influence, Prince Louis was fortunate to encounter Poole's client, the banker Baron Mayer de Rothschild, who assuredly stood most of a £10,000 fighting fund (to which

Above: 'Poole's Ladies' & Gentleman's Polite Assistant and Useful Remembrancer for 1849'.

Opposite: Franz Xavier Winterhalter's magnificent coronation portrait of Emperor Napoleon III (1852) displays the handsome military tailoring that earned Poole's its first Royal Warrant in 1858.

Far left: 'Old style' court dress, still tailored by Poole's for High Sheriffs of the Counties, who retain the Georgian style of lace jabot and cuffs instead of wing-collar dress shirt and bow tie.

Left: 'New style' court dress approved by Queen Victoria in 1839, as tailored by Poole's.

Henry also contributed) in order to restore empire rule in France.

Henry Poole was not, however, a self-made man. His father and company founder James Poole was first recorded in 1806 running a draper's shop in Everett Street. James volunteered to fight in the Napoleonic Wars and, as Stephen Howarth's *Henry Poole: Founders of Savile Row* (2003) tells it, he and wife Mary tailored his personal kit 'to such a high standard that others, including officers, asked for their own to be made by the same hands'. James Poole, military tailor was sufficiently successful to

hold an account with Coutts & Co. in 1819 (who remain the firm's bankers) and to sign a lease on the grand Neoclassical, John Nash-designed No. 171 Regent Street in 1822. In 1828, James Poole & Son moved to No. 4 Old Burlington Street, a property that backed onto Savile Row.

It was James Poole who made the firm's first introduction to royal circles. In the infancy of Queen Victoria's reign, the monarch signalled a break with her thoroughly despicable Hanoverian uncles (notorious philanderers, spendthrifts and blackguards) and demanded that Georgian court

British livery watercolour (*c.* 1860s) illustrating the breadth of work tailored by a livery department such as Poole's, from state livery for household servants to undress stable jackets for the most junior lad in the mews.

dress be modernized. James Poole submitted designs that were accepted in 1839. All gentlemen who attended court levees and balls were thus required to wear court dress designed if not tailored by Henry Poole & Co., which consisted of black velvet single-breasted tailcoat and breeches with white satin waistcoat.

James Poole's greatest contribution to the family firm was giving his son Henry his head in early Victorian society. His 'high-stepping pair and mail-phaeton [carriage]' were a familiar sight on Rotten Row in Hyde Park. He was also a welcome guest at country house parties hosted by the Earl and Countess of Stamford (where he allegedly marked up a presumptuous fellow guest's ill-fitting suit with billiard chalk). James kept Henry's feet on the ground by sending him on a debt-collecting trip, as the earliest letter from Henry in the company archive relates. Henry's exasperation is clear – 'Why give credit to such a man Hunt of Cork St whom everybody knows to be such an unprincipled sharp & scamp?' – as is how much his parents indulge him: 'Have you seen my young horse? Is he regularly exercised?'

As those close to our present royal family know, horses are a failsafe entrée into the highest society. When jockey Jem Mason won the inaugural Grand National on Lottery in 1839, he was already an intimate of Henry Poole. This friendship is akin to a Savile Row tailor today being pally with David Beckham or Frankie Dettori. Mason was fêted as one of the great sportsmen of the age and, not unlike Mr Beckham, was already carving out a career for himself as the glass of sporting fashion. His affiliation to the house of Poole's brought the firm a reputation as sporting as well as military tailors, which was fortuitous, considering that England had entered a period of relative peace after the French wars.

In 1846, James Poole died and Henry rang the changes by reversing his father's Old Burlington Street emporium and making its Savile Row entrance the principal gateway to his privileged world. In an act of ostentation, Henry commissioned fashionable architect Lewis Cubitt to construct a grandiose Italianate façade for Henry Poole & Co. at No. 36–39 Savile Row in 1851, while inside Henry furnished what was essentially

Below, left: The earliest letter signed by Henry Poole to his father James in the company archive (c. 1830s).

Below, right: Henry Poole & Co.'s letterhead, ablaze with the house Royal Warrants printed from the original engraved plate, first cut c. 1880. The house boasts four Emperors, seven Kings, one Queen Empress, five Princes, three Grand Dukes, one Viceroy and a Shah.

Opposite: Though King Edward VII is remembered in history as a rotund, jolly monarch, when he first visited Henry Poole in 1860 he was the slim, elegant buck about town seen in this portrait, aged nineteen.

Above, clockwise from left: Lewis Cubitt's grand, Italianate Savile Row façade for Henry Poole & Co., unveiled in 1851 and tragically pulled down in 1961.

The palatial interior of Poole's showroom at No. 36–39 Savile Row, photographed in the 1930s. Clearly visible is the oval portrait of Napoleon III, a wooden carving of his Imperial eagle and the set of jockey scales used to weigh customers who gained disproportionate weight in between fittings. The scales survived and are on display in the present shop at No. 15 Savile Row.

One of Poole's spectacular façade decorations of Nos 36–39, dressed to celebrate the coronation of King Edward VII in 1902.

a gentlemen's clubroom that would host Prince Bertie's (the Prince of Wales's) Marlborough House set within the decade.

Poole already had an Emperor on his books, and the firm's remarkable livery trade was helped in no small part by his annual visits to Napoleon III's court at the country palace of Compiègne, for which he tailored green-and-gold uniforms. Not only was Poole favoured by the Emperor's brother, Prince Jérôme, he also tailored fashionably close-fitting black riding habits for the Empress Eugénie that brought the house to the attention of Empress Elisabeth of Austria (who had to be sewn into her riding habit), her sister ex-Queen Marie of Naples and Catherine 'Skittles' Walters (a courtesan who counted the 8th Duke of Devonshire amongst her beaux), who would be measured-up astride an artificial horse christened Bucephalus.

The celebrated actress Lillie Langtry was another infamous customer. Mrs Langtry became mistress of the Prince of Wales in 1877 and did not become a customer of Henry Poole until 1885, so the romantic notion that their affair blossomed behind the doors of Henry Poole & Co. is just that. Equally romantic is a story told by

the Duke of Windsor in his *Family Album*, recording his grandfather's introduction to Henry Poole. Allegedly, the eighteen-year-old Prince Bertie attended a play in which French actor Charles Fechter played an adventurer. 'The adventurer's coat was a mass of rents and patches, but the acute Royal eye quickly noticed that the garment was well cut, and at the end of the play he [Prince Bertie] sent for the actor and asked him for the name of his tailor. The answer was Poole.' Suffice to say, Bertie must have had X-ray vision in addition to his acute royal eye.

The Prince of Wales found his way to Henry Poole in 1860 (a year after Fechter was first recorded in their ledgers), and, according to the Prince's 1964 biographer Philip Magnus, the tailor 'served as a kind of post office in helping him keep in touch with friends'. In other words, Bertie used Henry Poole & Co. to conduct his varied affairs. It is hard to imagine Bertie as a Lothario when one ponders pictures of him as King Edward VII. But one must remember that he was sixty years old when his mother Queen Victoria died. Portraits taken during Henry's lifetime show that the Prince was a slender young man, and Poole's

Clockwise from top left: Tailors labour to complete no fewer than five ambassadorial coatees in Poole's livery department at No. 21 Clifford Street (now Richard James Bespoke).

In the 1930s, the present chairman's father Sam Cundey compiled a photograph album of Poole's key staff members, photographed at No. 36–39 Savile Row. The chap photographed is head of the packing room; his immaculate appearance is testimony to the standards of dress set by the founders of Savile Row.

Such was the stature of the grandest Savile Row tailors that they owned tailoring workshops off-Row, such as Poole's three-storey King Street (now Kingly Street) premises that employed over seventy journeymen tailors.

waisted, skirted, double-breasted frock coats show off an admirable figure.

It is with no little pride that Henry Poole & Co. chairman Angus Cundey retrieves the Prince of Wales's order books of 1865 to prove definitively that the house was the father of the silk dinner jacket. In 1865, Prince Bertie commissioned a short smoking jacket to be worn at Sandringham. In 1886, he met New York financer James Potter and – enjoying the company of his pretty wife, Cora – invited the couple to weekend at Sandringham, where short coats for evening had become the rule. Legend has it that Potter consulted Henry Poole & Co., who made him the correct attire, although no records for Potter can be found in the archive. However, the royal invitation may account for the appearance of a short smoking jacket worn by a certain Mr Potter at the Tuxedo Club that has since sparked endless controversy about the origin of the dinner jacket.

Though Poole's under Henry took justifiable pride in its royal custom, it would be churlish not to mention other gentlemen who patronized the house and who are not without merit: Wilkie Collins,

Anthony Trollope, Charles Dickens, Prime Minister Benjamin Disraeli, the Earl of Cardigan and Prince Bismarck (the Iron Chancellor), to name a few. But just as royalty elevated Henry Poole & Co., so it was to bring the company to the brink of bankruptcy, resulting in Henry's premature death. The last surviving letter from Henry Poole in the company archive, dated 8 October 1875, was written eight months before his death. It records, 'There will be nothing much to leave behind me when I have worked for a Prince and for the public & must die a poor man.'

The catastrophic state of the company's finances (making a profit of £47,600 on sales of £182,000 in 1874) was due to the system of patronage given in exchange for unlimited credit, and, one suspects, Henry's own largesse. Henry's heirs, sister Mary Anne and cousin Sam Cundey, were forced to write off £10,000 in bad debt, including the account of the Prince of Wales, who was less than amused when approached for retrenchment. The lease on the Regent Street property was sacrificed and auction house Christie's sold Poole's 'Valuable collection of watercolour drawings' in 1877. *Vanity Fair* marked his passing with the words: 'So poor Poole is dead. He was quite a noteworthy figure in this Society of ours ... he patronized most of the crowned heads of Europe and the greater number of the nobility and gentry of these blessed islands, and knew more realities of figure and finance than half the people who give themselves airs ... [he was] one having no need to be ashamed of his trade. Perhaps this helped to make him the great man he was.'

The death of Henry and the Prince of Wales's displeasure did not diminish Henry Poole & Co.'s royal progress. 'Grandmother of Europe' Queen Victoria's children and grandchildren had married into every European royal dynasty, placing London at the centre of the social and ceremonial spider's web for what the old Queen called 'the Royal mob'. Tailors both military and civilian flourished as royal relatives and their households paid court to Queen Victoria and, after 1901, King Edward VII, who restored his Royal Warrant to Henry Poole & Co. a year later.

The continued success of the firm was thanks entirely to Sam Cundey, who, the *Tailor & Cutter* said, 'had for 46-years been Mr Poole's other self to all customers'. On his death in 1883, son Howard Cundey took the reins. If a quote can encapsulate a man's life's work, then the *Tailor & Cutter* of 1897 provided it: 'On being asked to what particular quality or feature he attributed the phenomenal position of the business which had made the name of Poole a household word amongst gentlemen of fashion in Europe and America, Mr Cundey replied that he thought much of the success of a first-class West-End business depended upon the power of showing that it is possible to be both a tailor and a gentleman.'

The *Tailor & Cutter*'s 'Noble Tailoring Establishment' feature of 1893 offers a fascinating insight into the grandest firm on Savile Row. Henry Poole & Co. engaged twelve cutters and a workshop of over three hundred tailors. The cut is described meticulously:

'This firm has a special style and character of their own, so that cutters in the West End have no difficulty in recognizing Messers Poole's coats in the street. They can tell their coat from the lapel, collar and turn, and from other features of the garment. While it is now the almost universal practice to line coats throughout, many coats continue to be made in Messers Poole's with no back lining, having the old fashioned buggy. In making, thinness and neatness is their ideal rather than the thick sewing or very much of it. The shoulders of their coats are very rarely built-up, but a character is given to the shoulder by the cut of the coat and sleeve head, aided of course by judicious manipulation.'

The Henry Poole cut – the techniques of which are still passed down to strikers by head cutter Philip Parker – became world famous under the patronage of the Maharaja of Mysore (1881), the Maharaja of Cooch Behar, who ordered over 1,000 suits (1887), the Maharaja Gaekwar of Baroda (1905), the Shah of Persia (1906) and the Khedive

A Henry Poole & Co. bespoke suit with the correct system of white baste stitches clearly visible. When a tailor adds superfluous baste stitches to impress a customer (a trick used in the window displays of made-to-measure tailors on the west side of Savile Row), it is called 'flash basting'.

The official 1921 photograph of Crown Prince Hirohito of Japan (far left) and Edward, Prince of Wales (second from left), suggests that though Henry Poole & Co. tailored superlative white tie for the visitor to the Court of St James's, Hirohito was as yet unschooled in the sartorial rule that not an inch of white waistcoat should show beneath the tailcoat.

of Egypt (1910). Poole's royal service continued in the 20th century when, on the evening of 3 March 1921, Crown Prince Hirohito of Japan sailed on a 16,000-ton battleship on a six-month tour of Europe. A tailor from Poole's was sent out to meet the ship in Gibraltar and take measurements for Western civilian and military clothes for the Prince to wear on his official visit to the Palace of St James's. Prince Hirohito's measurements were cabled back to London and a complete wardrobe was waiting for him on his arrival only three weeks later.

Poole's skill as court and livery tailor has endured. Every monarch from King Edward VII to Queen Elizabeth II has appointed the house as livery tailors to the royal household. The house suffered arguably the greatest tragedy in the firm's history in 1961 when the lease on its magnificent flagship expired. 'Westminster Council came along and did a compulsory purchase order to build a car park on the glorious Henry Poole building,' recalls

Angus Cundey. 'Henry Poole had been there for 150 years. The car park lasted just thirty before it was demolished. It was a scandal.'

It is one of Mr Cundey's greatest achievements that in 1982 he returned Henry Poole & Co. to No. 15 Savile Row, after two decades in exile on Cork Street. 'I remember visiting my father [Sam] in his hospital bed and saying, "Father, I'm moving the company back to Savile Row." I got the most enormous smile, and three days later he died,' says the man now titled Godfather of Savile Row. Today, Henry Poole & Co. employs without doubt the greatest court and livery tailor of his generation, Mr Keith Levett, who can be seen from the street in his basement workshop constructing scarlet-and-gold state coachman's liveries for the Royal Mews, identical in cut and quality to those tailored by the house in 1902, some of which are still in commission. What better advertisement for the longevity of Henry Poole & Co. tailoring, and the skill of its craftsmen?

Opposite, clockwise from top left: The façade of Henry Poole & Co. at No. 15 Savile Row, home to the firm since 1982.

Head of ceremonial tailoring Keith Levett tailoring a full state footman's coat. Models of this coat tailored by the house in 1902 for King Edward VII's footmen are still in service to the royal household.

A collection of liveries tailored by Poole's for the royal household (left to right): full state footman's coat (1902), full state walking groom's coat (1937), full state coachman's coat (1996), full state postillion's coat (1999) and Royal Ascot postillion's coat (2010).

HUNTSMAN

-- ESTABLISHED 1849

Established in 1849, Henry Huntsman's eponymous tailoring firm is one of the most auspicious bespoke houses on Savile Row. While Henry Poole & Co., Gieves & Hawkes and Anderson & Sheppard can credit royals, the armed forces and Hollywood as the foundation stones of their respective businesses, Huntsman had the power to attract people who count in every field at every point in its illustrious history. As head cutter Patrick Murphy says, 'Huntsman has this grand aura about it. The reputation was huge. It was the biggest and most expensive tailor on the Row. When I first started twenty-five years ago, my dad was in the workshops at Huntsman. It had an authority. As an apprentice at Alan Bennett across the road, I remember watching all the chauffer-driven cars gliding up to No. 11 Savile Row and the smartest men, accompanied by women smothered in furs, would get out. It meant something in those circles to have a Huntsman suit, even if a gentleman was otherwise loyal. As head cutter I feel responsible to the generations who have gone before me.' As well he might.

The Huntsman cut is as distinctive on Savile Row as Anderson & Sheppard's limp look, or its total antithesis, the Kilgour, French & Stanbury heavy-chested, broad-shouldered robust cut. Murphy describes it thus: 'A classic London cut of coat with high armhole and strong shoulder but with a more pronounced waist and skirt, all balanced on the fulcrum of the house signature one-button fastening.' The one-button is notoriously difficult to balance – the cutter's answer to a perfect pirouette en pointe – hence Huntsman's pride in it.

The roots of Huntsman's business go back to 1809, when the firm was described as a 'Gaiter and Breeches Maker'. From 1819, the company traded from No. 126 New Bond Street, where under the management of Henry Huntsman it earned a first Royal Warrant as Leather Breeches Maker to the Prince of Wales (later Edward VII), followed by that of Queen Victoria's second son Prince Alfred, Duke of Saxe-Coburg-Gotha, in 1876, and Queen Victoria herself in 1888. As experts in equestrian tailoring – the foundation for the modern suit jacket – Huntsman led the field in regal and aristocratic riding and country attire. A 1900 advertisement in the company archive depicts: 'Huntsman's Patent Breeches. Without seam inside

As Prince of Wales, the Duke of Windsor was a keen steeplechaser and polo player, and rode to hounds. His Huntsman orders in the early 1920s included drab cavalry twill breeches, white flannel polo breeches and several pink whipcord morning coats embellished with individually cast crested hunt buttons.

Above: Henry Thomas
Alken study of an English
country house hunting party
(c. 1810), titled *Tally-ho*.

Opposite, left: Huntsman's
famous house check cloth
has been woven for over
eighty years by the Islay
woollen mill in Scotland,
Britain's oldest working
mill, founded in 1550.

Opposite, right: Huntsman
hunting pinks tailored in
the 1950s and preserved in
the house archive.

the knee. Fitting as close as ordinary breeches.
The only firm in the UK who have the patent
right to supply the above shewn knickerbockers
breeches for riding, walking and shooting are
Huntsman & Co.'

Between 1898 and 1919, Huntsman traded from
No. 41 Albemarle Street, and the ledgers of the era
record in faded newsprint a generation of young
men lost in the trenches. The move to No. 11 Savile
Row at the close of the First World War signalled
a change of pace. The birth of the Jazz Age, rather
than the death of Edward VII in 1910, was the real
end of the Edwardian social order. The aristocracy
still divided its time between townhouse and
country seat but, led by the Prince of Wales (later
Edward VIII), added trips to the French Riviera,
tennis parties, cocktails and nightclubs to the social
round. The Prince (known to his circle as David)
introduced his rather fast set to Huntsman. His
1922 order book records monthly accounts sent to
his clerk comptroller at St James's Palace: showing,
in other words, he was that rare regal fellow who

paid his bills promptly. Not only that, in 1921
breeches ordered by his then mistress Thelma,
Viscountess Furness, were credited to
the Prince's account.

Where David led, the smart set followed,
including his brother the Duke of Kent, Lord
Louis Mountbatten, Lord Charles Cavendish
(future husband of Fred Astaire's sister Adele),
courtier and dandy Victor Spencer, Viscount
Churchill, King Alfonso XIII of Spain
(who conferred his Royal Warrant in 1926),
Ivor Novello, Rudolph Valentino, Robert
Montgomery, and press barons Lords Beaverbrook
and Castlerosse, not to mention the Maharajas
of Rajpipla and Cooch Behar. Huntsman's
fame as an equestrian tailor also attracted the
most glamorous, if scandalous, ladies in 1920s
society to its door. Measurement books record
actresses and aristocrats Gertrude Lawrence,
Adele Astaire, Joan Bennett, Edwina, Lady
Mountbatten and Lady Diana Cooper being
measured-up 'astride'.

Huntsman customer the Duke of Teck, brother of Queen Mary, illustrated in a 1902 *Vanity Fair* Spy cartoon astride.

The Huntsman customer ledgers also record the vogue for impoverished and/or indecent aristocrats moving to the colonies. In 1928, the most infamous member of Kenya's Happy Valley set, Idina, Countess of Erroll, is measured-up 'astride'. Considering the reputation of this five-times-divorced promiscuous lady who scandalized society, this is not without irony. Her story, including the unsolved murder of her ex-husband the Earl of Erroll, is told with no little relish by James Fox in his book *White Mischief*. Both the Prince of Wales and Duke of Kent knew the Countess, and visited Nairobi in 1928, where the Duke allegedly formed an unhealthy alliance with Kiki 'the girl with the silver syringe' Preston.

Huntsman entered the 1930s with reputation intact as the tailor to this exotic collection of international royals, maharajas, aristocrats, actors and leading ladies. In 1932, Henry Huntsman's sons conceded the firm to Mr Robert Packer: a

great name on the Row, who, though not a cutter, encouraged what we now know as the Huntsman cut for civilian suiting. 'Its slim, slightly flared look spoke only of Huntsman,' wrote Richard Walker in *The Savile Row Story*. 'Passing strangers on the steps of the Plaza in New York could pause and luxuriate in delicious recognition that they shared a famous tailor. And such an expensive tailor. Pricing was possibly the smartest decision of all – when you are more expensive than anyone else on the Row, you can never be ignored.'

As former managing director Brian Lishak recalled, as a sixteen-year-old apprentice of Mr Packer, 'he had this talent – he loved clothes and he loved quality and he loved people and he put the whole thing together and people adored him'. On a more practical level, Packer broke with Row tradition in Huntsman's workshops by removing the traditional reliance on outworkers and insisting every bespoke stitch was executed

Opposite, clockwise from top left: King Alfonso XIII of Spain, widely considered the best-dressed monarch in Europe, conferred his Royal Warrant on Huntsman in 1926.

A rare photograph of a Hollywood legend willingly posing for a photograph leaving his Savile Row tailor (Huntsman) in 1954. Stewart Granger is first recorded in Huntsman's ledgers from the early 1940s.

Hollywood matinee idol Robert Young and his girlfriend Karen Morley photographed wearing jodhpurs tailored by Huntsman in 1932.

Clark Gable, photographed by Clarence Sinclair Bull wearing Savile Row-tailored jodhpurs in 1932, appears in Huntsman's ledgers as a private client. He also ordered costumes paid for by MGM in 1953 for the film *Mogambo,* co-starring Grace Kelly and Ava Gardner.

The last ruling Maharaja of Jaipur, photographed with his sons outside the Dorchester Hotel in 1946, showing off Huntsman tailoring.

in-house. A Huntsman suit was thus just that: untouched by hands not trained by the craftsmen who were largely the firm's staff for life. In 1945, Packer was made director of Huntsman and oversaw a boom in American trade, not least with Hollywood men (similar to that of Anderson & Sheppard, reigning celluloid tailor in the 1920s and 1930s).

Leading men in the 1940s and 1950s were as square-jawed and heroic as they had been elegant and debonair in the 1920s and 1930s, thus suiting the Huntsman cut. Huntsman was the tailor of choice for Clark Gable, Stewart Granger, Ronald Reagan, Laurence Olivier, Gregory Peck and Dirk Bogarde, not to mention those masculine grandes dames Katharine Hepburn and Marlene Dietrich.

Huntsman had its own leading man in the shape of Colin Hammick, who had joined the firm as a fifteen-year-old apprentice in 1942 and rose to the rank of head cutter in the 1950s. General

manager Peter Smith recalls, 'Mr Hammick was absolute talent; an absolute craftsman. The Huntsman cut as we know it today was very much devised by Mr Hammick and it is fair to say he was its finest model.' Tall, lean and with the posture of a guardsman, Hammick was a great ambassador for the Row, beating Rex Harrison, the Duke of Windsor and Lord Snowdon to the top of the *Tailor & Cutter*'s best-dressed list of 1971. As his *Times* obituary recorded in 2008, 'In the late 1950s Huntsman found itself competing with Carnaby Street – whose Teddy boys, and later Mods and Rockers, were also wearing close-fitting trousers and brocade waistcoats – but it remained confident there would always be a market for uncompromising quality.'

Edward Packer, Robert's son, was convinced that 'sooner or later the young gadabouts will settle down to a more sane level of sartorial elegance', but it was Hammick's generation, such as Henry

Above, left: Huntsman's legendary head cutter Colin Hammick.

Above, right: These gentlemen photographed in Huntsman's workrooms in the early 1960s show that sharp *Mad Men*-style tailoring was not restricted to Manhattan.

Poole & Co. chairman Angus Cundey, who resolved to take the fight to the fashion industry by showing biannual Men's Fashion Council presentations at London's Savoy Hotel. As far back as 1951, a Huntsman promotion reads: 'It's the younger men who are today's fashion leaders. No doubt about that. And oldsters follow where they lead.'

By 1959, Huntsman was regularly shooting stock models to publicize trends in bespoke tailoring such as the slimmer shawl collar, the ivory 'tropical tailcoat', the slim turned-up trouser with a double-breasted pinstripe, or the Flare Line (an extreme A-line coat with subtly flared cuffs). These images invariably featured Savile Row stalwarts such as the Coke (bowler) hat, furled umbrella or pipe to reassure Huntsman customers that the Row was not getting too hip.

All through the 1970s and 1980s, Huntsman produced advertising campaigns and promotions that would make Gucci under the Tom Ford regime look modest and unassuming. Shot in lurid colour with props such as sports cars, Concorde,

stately homes and heavily made-up women, this collection shows Huntsman embracing the flared trouser, kipper tie and Mr Fish-style psychedelic shirts with splayed collars.

In 1981, the *New York Times* reported that Huntsman's sales for the year previous were $2.4 million, 70 per cent of which was export. This is only half the story. With 130 employees, Huntsman was the largest firm on the Row. Overheads – such as workshops, whose rent had increased by 250 per cent – necessitated doubling the price of a Huntsman suit over five years, to reach £800 by 1986. The 1980s – the decade in which Armani and designer ready-to-wear temporarily overwhelmed bespoke tailoring – forced houses such as Huntsman to introduce ready-to-wear. It is to Hammick's credit that he resisted all calls to relocate Huntsman, right up to his retirement in 1994. So, too, did Brian Lishak, who became managing director in 1997.

In 2002, a valiant (and intriguing) attempt by Huntsman to revive interest in bespoke saw a joint venture between the house and former Anderson

Right: Huntsman demonstrated its excellence in tailoring period costume most notably for *Kind Hearts and Coronets* (1949) and Gregory Peck's Edwardian comedy *The Million Pound Note* (1954), which features a famous if fanciful scene shot in an imagined Savile Row tailor's shop recreated on set.

Following pages: Huntsman was relatively unusual on Savile Row in the late 1950s and early 1960s in photographing promotional images of bespoke models shot on location in London and in studios. These pictures have since lain dormant as yellowing transparencies and faded prints in forgotten cupboards and files in Huntsman's basement.

Above: The doorway to Huntsman's showroom at No. 11 Savile Row. To the far right is a painted shield celebrating the house's Royal Warrant as leather breeches maker to the Prince of Wales (later Edward VII) in 1861.

Opposite: In 2009, Huntsman marketing director Poppy Charles commissioned photographer Guy Hills to recreate the spirit of the late 1950s/early 1960s advertising shots modelling bespoke stock made for 'The London Cut' exhibitions.

& Sheppard apprentice, the late Alexander McQueen. The McQueen name added a £1,000 premium to Huntsman's already mammoth prices and – bar an order for a black frock coat encrusted with a jet peacock motif ordered by David Furnish – was unsuccessful. The house even flirted with liquidation in 2004 before a coalition of new investors led by David Coleridge, the present managing director, saved Huntsman and reversed its fortunes. 'When the existing shareholders invited me to take a look at Huntsman, I took the customer list home,' says Coleridge. 'Those 4,000 names of people who had bought from Huntsman over the last five years were the great and good of the country: aristocrats, politicians, celebrities, musicians, captains of industry. I thought, "Crikey, most luxury goods companies would die for this kind of customer base." Huntsman dresses the men who have already achieved.

'Savile Row is like the royal family; a little less remote but not completely demystified. That's the magic. At Huntsman, the talent was there. The customers were loyal but the management was lacking. The bespoke business is led by people. Huntsman had to rebuild the team and get back the culture developed over so many years. Our first ambition was to make the finest suit in London. Our second was to provide the best service in the world. Our third was to make a profit.' Coleridge's mission is well on its way to being accomplished. Huntsman is as reassuringly expensive as it has been in its illustrious past. No. 11 Savile Row would be familiar to the late Mr Hammick, for whom one of the fitting rooms has been named. As Patrick Murphy says, 'It is very important that we respect the traditions at Huntsman, but also that we create new ones for future generations. That's what Savile Row is all about.'

Chapter 2

THE BEAUX ON THE ROW

Men who Led Fashion

T he purpose of the dandy is to be admired. More pertinently, his motive is to be admired by his social superiors, who will open doors to a world enchanted (and not a little intimidated) by the exceptionally dressed. To a man, the greatest Savile Row dandies of the past two centuries have used the language of clothes to communicate with their social superiors and advance. So when Beau Brummell declared, 'If people turn to look at you in the street you are not well dressed, but either too stiff, too tight, or too fashionable,' we can safely assume that the supreme Regency dandy and father of the Savile Row suit was lying. Neither titled nor wealthy, Brummell needed to get noticed in order to advance socially and financially. For this he turned to tailoring.

Though exaggerated, a scene from the 2006 BBC costume drama *This Charming Man* illustrates how shocking Brummell's severe dandy fashions must have been. Two powdered, bewigged grotesques in ancien régime court dress challenge Mr Brummell in the street with the insult, 'Dandy!' to which he responds, 'Fop!' before giving them a sound thrashing. As the Boswell of the Beaux, Captain Gronow, wrote in his *Regency Recollections* of 1865, 'Amongst the curious freaks of fortune there is

none more remarkable in my memory than the sudden appearance, in the highest and best society in London, of a young man whose antecedents warranted a much less conspicuous career. I refer to the famous Beau Brummell. There are comparatively few examples of men obtaining a similarly elevated position simply from their attractive personal appearance and fascinating manners.'

It is one of history's ironies that this man, whose reputation rested entirely on how he dressed rather than what he said or did, should leave the world without a single full-length portrait. Miniatures and caricatures vary widely but one model rings true: a sloe-eyed Beau with his nose in the air and Cupid's bow lips pursed in a half-smile. A face such as this would explain the swiftness of Brummell's rise. By the age of seventeen, the Eton- and Oxford-educated Brummell had joined the 10th Light Dragoons, whose new colonel-in-chief was the Prince of Wales (later the Prince Regent). The regiment had a reputation for the finest uniforms and the coarsest morals. Within the year, a drunken Brummell would stand as chevalier d'honneur at the Prince's disastrous wedding to Caroline of Brunswick in 1795.

A line engraving of George 'Beau' Brummell by John Cook (1844) after an unknown miniaturist, published four years after the Beau's death.

Poster and film stills from the lavish if fanciful 1954 MGM film *Beau Brummell*, starring Stewart Granger tailored by Huntsman.

Lithograph of Alfred, Count
d'Orsay, by Daniel Maclise
from a pen-and-ink drawing
(early 1830s).

Vanity Fair cartoon by Spy
of Montague John Guest
wearing a generously skirted
double-breasted frock coat,
black tie and pearl tiepin,
framed handsomely by a
starched stand collar (1880).

In 1799, he acquired No. 4 Chesterfield Street, which became a clubhouse for Brummell's band of brothers, the 'Dandiacal Body', which included Lord Byron and the Prince of Wales. Fashion historian Dion Clayton Calthrop paints the finest picture of Brummell's morning levee: 'A servant produces a shirt with a 12-inch collar fixed to it, assists the Beau into it, arranges it and stands aside. The collar nearly hides the Beau's face. Now, with his hand protected with a discarded shirt, he folds his collar down to the required height. Now he takes his white stock and folds it carefully round the collar; the stock is a foot high and slightly starched. A supreme moment of artistic decision and the stock and collar take their perfect creases.' As Lord Byron said, 'There was nothing very peculiar about his clothes except an exquisite propriety.'

Though Captain Gronow credited Brummell's wardrobe to 'that superior genius Mr Weston of Old Bond Street', Ian Kelly's masterly 2006 biography of Brummell reveals that Schweitzer & Davidson on Cork Street cut his blue tailcoats, experimenting with new systems of darting, padding and weighting tails to enhance a Neoclassical physique. Jonathan Meyer of Conduit Street, a grand old firm that still trades today as Meyer & Mortimer on Sackville Street, sculpted Brummell's buff breeches and pioneered close-fitting trousers strapped under the riding boot. Mr Weston laced his ivory waistcoats at the lower back to emphasize a heroic chest. Without full-length portraits, we have a surprisingly accurate recreation of Brummell's wardrobe by Huntsman, for the 1954 film *Beau Brummell*.

Alas, as Captain Gronow wrote, 'The reign of the King of fashion, like all other reigns, was not destined to continue forever.' Crippling gambling debts, creditors' bills and the loss of the Regent's favour forced Brummell into exile in Calais in 1816. It would take him another twenty-four years to die of tertiary syphilis in the asylum of Bon Saveur outside Caen. The Beau's Icarus-like fall from fame to infamy echoed that of Beau Nash,

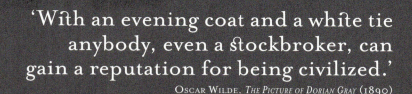

'With an evening coat and a white tie anybody, even a stockbroker, can gain a reputation for being civilized.'

OSCAR WILDE, *THE PICTURE OF DORIAN GRAY* (1890)

From left to right: *Vanity Fair* cartoon of Sir Charles Craddock-Hartopp in 1912, drawn by W. H. Willis, who exaggerates Sir Charles's waisted high-break three-button morning coat and cuffs. In the original print, a lady's shadow has been drawn, suggesting that the rakish Sir Charles has company.

Vanity Fair cartoon of Colonel James Keith Fraser, drawn by Spy in 1880. The Colonel sports a flamboyant black-and-white polka dot oversized bow-tied cravat, waisted frock coat and slim trousers that break immaculately over dainty riding boots.

Vanity Fair Spy cartoon of the Rt Hon. Lord Sandhurst, captioned 'A Soldier's Son' (1889). His Lordship has the optimum figure for late-Victorian Row tailoring and stands inquisitively, showing off the strict line of his pinstripe trousers, and sporting a flamboyant buttonhole.

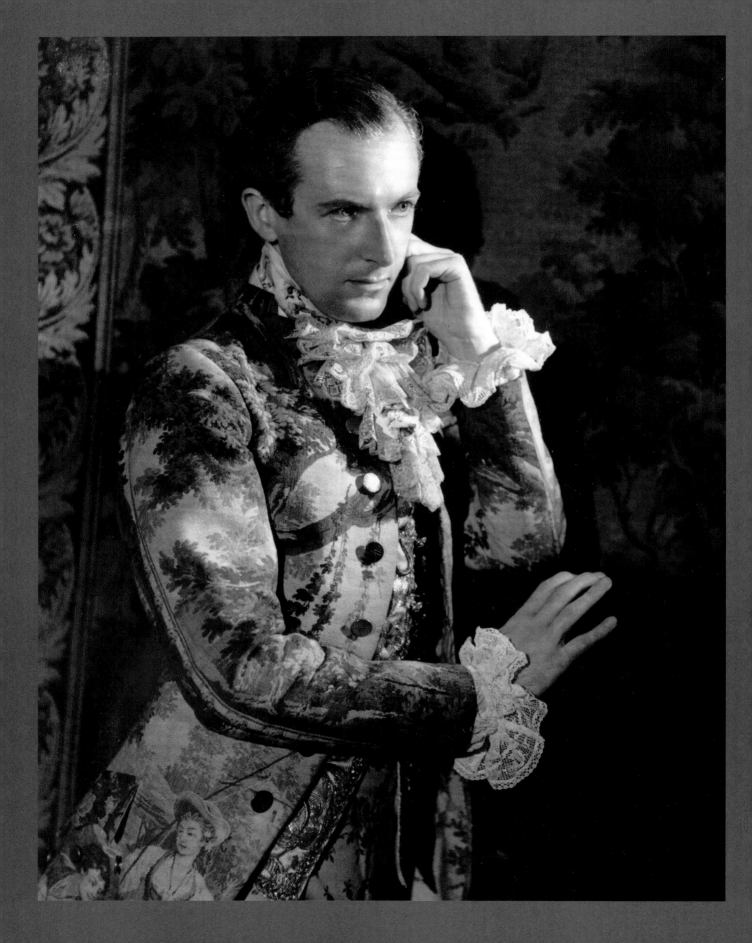

master of ceremonies and leader of Georgian society in Bath who, on his death in 1762, was buried in a pauper's grave. The last of the great dandies after Brummell was the Count d'Orsay. On 5 August 1952, the *Tailor & Cutter* marked the centenary of his death: '100 years ago today the last of the dandies died. His peak years of fame were between 1832 and 1841 but his influence in the world of dress was felt for a considerable time after his death. In a carriage, d'Orsay looked like a gorgeous dragonfly skimming through the air, as though all was dazzling and showy, yet there was a kind of harmony which precluded any idea or accusation of bad taste.'

According to Captain Gronow, d'Orsay was 'the greatest swell of his day. He always drove in faultless white kid gloves with his shirt wristbands turned back over his coat cuffs.' Mrs Carlyle (wife of Thomas Carlyle, the satirist, essayist and historian) called him 'this Phoebus Apollo of Dandyism' and went into raptures over his 'invisible inexpressibles [breeches] that are skin coloured and fitting like a glove'. The Count outlived his era by twenty years. When Queen Victoria came to the throne in 1837, she reversed the social mobility enjoyed by Regency Beaux and did her level best to banish flamboyance from acceptable aristocratic dress.

She did not, however, entirely succeed; for evidence of this we have a collection of cartoons of eminent gentlemen published weekly in society journal *Vanity Fair* between 1868 and 1914. By far the most prolific artist was Leslie Ward, who signed himself 'Spy' and drew over half of the 2,300 cartoons. He left the most detailed record of Victorian dandy dress, which would otherwise have been forgotten. Take Mr Montague John Guest

MP, sketched in 1880. The pen portrait reads: 'He is indeed the very type of the better kind of social darling; for he is handsome, intelligent, very amiable, very kindly and tender hearted, cheerful, and well provided with all the social talents of the more fascinating kin.' Could this apply to any MP sitting in the House today?

Another alumnus of *Vanity Fair* 1880 is Colonel James Keith Fraser. 'Scarcely yet middle-aged, he has seen all that is best in London Society, and taken part in all that is most amusing of social life. His manners are excellent without being exquisite; his voice is sympathetic without being feminine; his soldiering is energetic without being rough; he has a fine sense of the proprieties, a nice sense of honour, and he is as quiet and well-bred a man as may be found in these islands.'

The Spy cartoons ended in 1914 – as did a golden age of formal dress – with the advent of the First World War. The social-climbing Beau would not emerge again until the 1920s, when bright young things such as society photographer Cecil Beaton and aristocrat manqué Stephen Tennant would feminize men's tailoring to such an extent that they could not help but be noticed by the social pages of *Tatler* and *Vogue* magazines. Beaton and his boys – satirized one and all as the louche Miles Malpractice in Evelyn Waugh's 1930 novel *Vile Bodies* – were responsible for 'dandy' coming to mean flamboyant dress rather than Brummelesque restraint.

From the early 1920s, as an undergraduate at Cambridge, Beaton bombarded *Vogue* editor Dorothy Todd with highly stylized portraits of his set, including Boy Lebas, George Rylands and Stephen Tennant, at period costume parties,

Gordon Anthony captures Cecil Beaton in *c.* 1935 posing pensively in 18th-century French court dress. In his diaries, Beaton writes: 'I do so want to make my name – and a full page thing of me as a Marchioness making me look like a Madonna would make the most terrific sensation – and I should hold my head high all the season.'

elaborate picnics and amateur theatricals dressed as Regency fops, courtiers at Versailles or historical grandes dames. His methods may have appalled Brummell but his motives were exactly the same: social climbing. The tragedy for those who later aspired to be dandies in the grand tradition of Brummell and Beaton is that after the Second World War there wasn't much of a society left to climb.

A new ambassador of dandyism appeared on Savile Row in 1946, when debonair couturier and former spy Hardy Amies opened his house at No. 14. His circle included Neil 'Bunny' Roger, surely the most flamboyant of the Row's 20th-century peacocks, who pursued Neo-Edwardian tailoring well into the 1990s and struck an increasingly anachronistic pose. Scion of a plutocratic family, Mr Roger was famed during the Second World War for going into battle with the Rifle Brigade wearing rouge, a chiffon scarf and carrying his subscription to *Vogue*.

Post-war, dandies became increasingly nostalgic. Rather than following the lead of sartorial terrorists such as Brummell, they looked back in languor upon Beaton's *entre deux guerres* idyll. The 1920s and 1930s were a last hurrah for correct male attire, when society chaps knew precisely what to wear and when, be that Fair Isle sweater and flannels for breakfast or evening tails at the opera. 'It is interesting how every generation since goes back to that period in men's dress and reassesses it for the present,' says Timothy Everest. 'Tommy Nutter, for example, was very turned on by the twenties and thirties. His look was rooted in nostalgia but he subverted it, as we do.'

The most romantic evocation of male fashions of the era is the BBC's 1981 adaptation of Waugh's *Brideshead Revisited*, starring Anthony Andrews as effete but adorable aristocrat Lord Sebastian Flyte. 'Sebastian was a hero to all us aesthetes,' says Nick Hart of the bespoke label Spencer Hart. 'I was in love with the Oxford and Cambridge scene of the time: the costume, the acid put-downs, the romanticism, the decadence and the poor boy/rich boy dynamic. I had friends at Oxford and we used to play at picnics and punting, blazers with braiding, white cricket flannels and reciting poetry. It was sheer escapism.' 'Sebastian's clothes are without fail perfect,' says Norton & Sons managing director Patrick Grant. 'He had the right clothes for whatever he was doing, be that punting on the Isis or hosting dinner in his set. He always had an appropriate outfit.'

Only men with the appropriate life to merit numerous appropriate outfits can be considered dandies today. The Beaton of our era is US *Vogue* European-editor-at-large Hamish Bowles, a man who has taken the bright young things of the 1920s as his sartorial and social idols. He has supported Richard James since the house opened in 1992. In 1998, he acquired ten coats from the Sotheby's estate sale of Bunny Roger and slimmed himself into Mr Roger's 28-inch (71-cm) waist to debut his hourglass lilac tweed coat at the international collections that season. Bowles is outstanding, but so too is every man who orders a bespoke suit on Savile Row today. As the number of men who purchase suits declines, the gentleman who wears a bespoke suit will stand out as a peacock surrounded by sartorial sparrows in ready-to-wear. In this respect, all bespoke customers today can be considered dandy.

Opposite, clockwise from top left: The famous Royal Ascot scene from *My Fair Lady* (1954) costumed by Beaton and tailored by Sullivan, Wooley & Co. (later bought by Henry Poole & Co). It was Rex Harrison's suggestion to dress his character Henry Higgins in a woefully inappropriate tweed three-piece that would not have gained entry to the Royal Enclosure.

A still from the 1981 television adaptation of Evelyn Waugh's *Brideshead Revisited* (1945): Lord Sebastian Flyte (Anthony Andrews) and Charles Ryder (Jeremy Irons) languidly dressed in their straw-boatered best.

A scene from 2003 film *Bright Young Things*, based on Evelyn Waugh's 1930 novel *Vile Bodies*, satirizing the glamorous if vacuous smart set. From left to right: Agatha Runcible (Fenella Woolgar), Miles Malpractice (Michael Sheen) and Adam Fenwick-Symes (Stephen Campbell-Moore).

'One day when I was at Davies my tailor's, a very smartly dressed old gentleman, wearing a checked suit, came in. Before I could stop him, my bulldog Punch rushed at him and tore a huge piece out of his trousers.'

PRINCE FELIX YOUSSOUPOF, *LOST SPLENDOUR: THE AMAZING MEMOIRS OF THE MAN WHO KILLED RASPUTIN* (1953)

DAVIES & SON

-- ESTABLISHED 1803

By 1804, Beau Brummell's influence over the haut ton was at its height. He was elected to the two grandest of St James's gentlemen's clubs, White's and Brook's, and the Prince of Wales was practically his puppet. It was in 1804 that Thomas Davies, principal clerk to army agents Greenwood, Cox & Co., inherited his brother's thriving Cork Street tailoring business (founded in 1803) and moved it to a grand townhouse at No. 19 Hanover Street. Greenwood's was a Georgian banking dynasty and Davies's title of clerk belies his importance. It was his remit to coordinate payroll for army officers, organize the provision of uniform and sell commissions. His decision to take a punt on his brother's tailoring firm was entrepreneurial and an astute gamble in the era of the Beaux.

Admiral Lord Nelson was an early customer, and well within Thomas Davies's lifetime the house claimed to dress 'all the crowned heads of Europe', though the Royal Warrants to prove it have not survived. Davies also had the privilege of tailoring for Sir Robert Peel, twice Tory Prime Minister in the 19th century and father of the police force (hence the English slang 'bobby', meaning policeman on the beat). When Davies & Son finally

had to leave Hanover Street in 1979, a bill for the great man dated 1829 was found for the sum of £128. The date tallies with Sir Thomas Lawrence's 1830 portrait of Peel, resplendent in Brummelesque tails.

We have a tailoring sweatshop scandal of 1892 to thank for dating the Princes Eddy and George (sons of the Prince of Wales, later Edward VII) as Davies & Son customers. When the scandal reached the national newspapers, it was reported in *Lloyd's Weekly London Newspaper* that both Princes had patronized the house for over a decade. We know their naval and military uniforms were tailored elsewhere, so can confidently surmise that civilian suiting seen in photographs of the Princes and their mother Queen Alexandra is the work of Davies & Son.

The scandal of the 'Duke of York's trousers' is told in a yellowing newspaper cuttings book made by a Davies tailoress in 1892 as the story unfolded. It broke on 11 September, when *Lloyd's* front page announced: 'The Duke of York's [Prince

Valentin Serov paints Prince Felix Youssoupoff and his pet bulldog Punch at the Moika Palace in St Petersburg in 1903 (above), the time of his first visits to London and his chosen tailor Davies & Son; and the finished painting (opposite). The mischievous Prince once smuggled Punch from Paris to London disguised as a baby and hired a courtesan to play the part of nanny. The Prince would go down in history as the man who murdered Rasputin in 1916.

84   THE BEAUX ON THE ROW

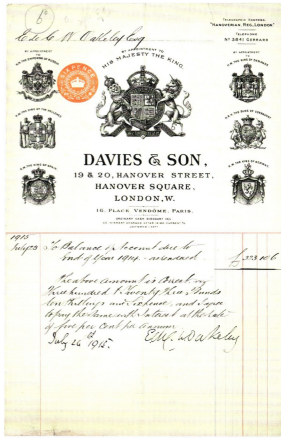

George's] trowsers [sic] made in a fever room'. *The Star* elaborated with: 'Garments for Princes and Peers made at sweating rates in crowded tenements where fever lurks'. In January that year Prince Eddy had died and the press made a connection between his death, the Duke of York's trousers and Davies & Son. The spectre of 'sweating', the name for the trade carried out in disease-ridden tailor's workshops gathered around Soho's Carnaby Street, had risen again.

In 1880, Angelica Patience Fraser, the tailors' Florence Nightingale, had called a conference to protest against the horrific conditions in London's tailoring sweatshops that had led to a resolution signed by houses such as Henry Poole & Co., Meyer & Mortimer and Davies & Son to improve working practices. The matter reached committee level at the House of Lords. But in 1892, a Miss Fanny Hicks told her Trades Union Congress in Glasgow that the Duke of York's trousers were made in a sweatshop, subcontracted by Davies & Son, where fever had broken out.

The scandal was sufficient for the Prince of Wales to call rival tailors Meyer & Mortimer to Marlborough House for an audience. It was further enflamed by *The Star*, who wrote: 'We now know that the tailor who clothes the extremities of members of the blood Royal sends the garments out to the tailoresses just as if they were suits from the windows of the ready-made shops, there to take

Above, left: Near-twin royal cousins Tsar Nicholas II of Russia (left) and King George V, photographed at Cowes in 1910 with their sons, the future Duke of Windsor and Tsarevich Alexei, took great delight in dressing identically. Above, right: A recently discovered Davies & Son letterhead dated 1915 bears the crest of the Tsar as well as the King, strongly suggesting their yachting blazers and flannels are tailored by the house.

their chance of picking up any stray fever germs that may be floating around.' *The Star* was even moved to campaign against sweating in verse:

> *In vain we told the awful truth*
> *Of sickness and starvation,*
> *And pictured fetid fever dens*
> *And crime and degredation [sic].*
> *It passed unheeded, but, forsooth,*
> *Twill perhaps be altered now, Sirs,*
> *Because within a fever den*
> *They've found a Prince's trousers.*

Davies & Son emerged from the scandal with their Royal Warrant for Prince George intact and, from 1910, dressed King George V for his entire reign. *The Savile Row Story* reports: 'Davies created a room for his exclusive use – a sharp departure from the royal rule of having tradesmen call – and fitted it with panels and a tube like a hosepipe, which communicated with the tailors upstairs. It is to be assumed that by this time the fifth-floor shenanigans [where rooms were made available for gentlemen and their lady friends] had abated.' Though in time-honoured tradition, his sons did not remain loyal, Davies & Son was the first house to tailor for the future King Edward VIII, King George VI and the Dukes of Kent and Gloucester.

The last of the Davies family exited the firm in 1935 (a year before the old King George V's death) and it was taken over by its cutters, who continued to run the company until 1996. Hollywood big beasts Clark Gable, Tyrone Power and Douglas Fairbanks Jr patronized the house, as did political heavyweights President Harry Truman and Ambassador Joseph Kennedy (father of John F. Kennedy). The Hanover Street flagship store closed down in 1979, and many ledgers, pattern books, correspondence and accounts were given to the Westminster Library. By this time, 90 per cent of Davies's trade was export and the house lost the status of being 'Built on the clothing requirements of the aristocracy of Europe and Great Britain'. The man who saved Davies & Son was Mr Alan Bennett, who bought the business in 1997 and brought it to No. 38 Savile Row.

Mr Bennett served a formidable apprenticeship working at Huntsman, Kilgour, French & Stanbury, Dege & Skinner, Denman & Goddard and under his own name. Since acquiring Davies & Son, Mr Bennett has made a habit of buying grand old bespoke houses and incorporating them. To date he has bought James & James (who in turn absorbed Scholte), Wells of Mayfair (once bigger than Henry Poole & Co.), royal and military tailor Johns & Pegg, and Bunny Roger's tailor, Watson, Fargerstrom & Hughes. Though unassuming, Mr Bennett is a guardian of Savile Row history and a human archive for memories of legends such as Kilgour's Fred and Louis Stanbury, Huntsman's Colin Hammick, renowned tailor Harry Helman and Dege & Skinner chairman Michael Skinner, not to mention eccentrics such as Tommy Nutter and Bobby Valentine.

Left: A black pen-and-ink silhouette of Davies & Son founder Thomas Davies that hangs in the present shop at No. 38 Savile Row.

Right: The magnificence that was Davies & Son's townhouse at No. 19–20 Hanover Street, a street once as populated with tailors as Savile Row. Much of the listed interior survives, though the building is now a wine bar.

Prototype Dashing Tweeds cape woven with wool worsted and patented reflective yarn Lumatwill™, designed by London College of Fashion student Erin Lewis and tailored by Davies & Son.

Modelled on a 1967 Mr Fish suit in the Victoria & Albert Museum, Davies & Son managing director Alan Bennett cut a suit evoking Savile Row's Tommy Nutter era from a luridly striped Dashing Tweed co-designed by Guy Hills and Kirsty McDougall.

While ostensibly too busy making money to pay much attention to archive, he will casually pull out of a drawer the Duke of Windsor's patterns; while not boasting about it, his knowledge of ceremonial tailoring has brought Madame Tussauds to his door to tailor liveries, uniforms and robes for waxwork kings, generals and admirals. Trained by Colin McNaughton (the maestro of ambassadorial tailoring, who traded at Adeney & Boutroy on Sackville Street until his retirement in 1988), Bennett brought to Davies & Son a reputation as the Row's leading ambassadorial tailor. He still makes heavily embellished court coatees for Britain's remaining colonial high commissioners and, in the late 1990s, sold an ambassadorial coatee to the late Michael Jackson.

As befitting a house that dressed the Duke of Windsor man and boy, Davies & Son is now earning notoriety as the leading tailor for Guy Hills's dandy Dashing Tweeds collection.

Established in 2006 by fashion photographer Hills and weaver Kirsty McDougall, Dashing Tweeds are jazzy, wildly patterned cloths woven with light-reflective fibres and cut in silhouettes with details long lost to conservative Savile Row. 'Dashing Tweeds gravitated towards Davies for several reasons,' says Hills. 'Firstly, Alan Bennett is an excellent cutter with a very wide experience. I am always trying to push the boundaries of sensible menswear and keep my eyes open to all new ideas. Alan will listen to ideas without passing judgment, and help create them.' The bespoke prototypes Bennett has cut for Hills have seen the Autumn/Winter 2009 collection sold in London's edgy Dover Street Market concept store, owned by Comme des Garçons designer Rei Kawakubo, as well as Beams in Tokyo. The madly dandy Dashing Tweeds at Davies & Son is arguably the most directional, optimistic collaboration on Savile Row today.

HARDY AMIES

-- ESTABLISHED 1945

T hough he would doubtless curl a lip at the mere thought, Sir Hardy Amies was the definitive Savile Row dandy of the 20th century. His house at No. 14 is remembered as Queen Elizabeth II's favoured British couturier, but Sir Hardy was as knowledgeable about gentlemen's tailoring as any of his neighbours on the Row. He made forays into licensed men's tailoring in the 1960s that were easily as influential as French futurist Pierre Cardin's. Many of the prototypes for his fashion-forward Hepworths ready-to-wear collections were cut by a bespoke tailor, neighbouring Norton & Sons. At his 2003 memorial, at which his client the (now Dowager) Duchess of Devonshire and Sir Roy Strong spoke, he was remembered as 'vain of his appearance but with the redeeming feature that he was funny with it. Although he revelled in being a Knight of the Realm and was never happier than when a Duchess loomed, that went hand-in-hand with never passing himself off as other than what he said he was: trade.'

Cecil Beaton's favourite epigram suits Sir Hardy: 'I wasn't born with a silver spoon in my mouth. I put it there.' In a particularly catty but perceptive profile written in 1949 and stored in the Hardy Amies archive, Jonathan Brice describes him thus: 'Hardy Amies would have floated to the top no matter what sea of endeavour he had chosen for his life's work. His immediately obvious qualities are those of humourless personal drive and ruthless concentration. These are the essential qualities of success, no matter where you find them.... He was born on the steps of Miss Gray's dressmaking shop in Brook Street where his mother spent the greater part of her business life as a vendeuse....

'When Hardy Amies went to Lachasse in February 1934, he was 22 and had never designed a dress, coat or suit. Six months later he produced his first full collection, and he went right on producing collections up to the beginning of the war. Now I would like to pause for a moment and try to make you realize just what this means. Imagine yourself in a position where everyone around you is more familiar with the media in which you are working than you are yourself. Where everyone regards you as a potential enemy, a nominee of the boss, a possible spy, a certain destroyer of the old engine whatever it may have been. At the age of 22, how would you react to such an atmosphere? Hardy's

Hardy Amies photographed
in his Pont Street apartment
in 1947 in the spirit of
a Hollywood studio portrait.

Left: Hardy Amies (second from left) holds court outside No. 14 Savile Row in 1967 with co-director Michael Bentley and PR man David Harvey (third and fourth from left).

Opposite, clockwise from top left: Hardy Amies employed his personal bespoke tailors to cut blocks for his ready-to-wear men's collections in the 1960s, including Norton & Sons and Huntsman. He brings fashion and fine tailoring together in this dynamic early 1960s ensemble.

Hardy Amies directing a model fitting in the grand salon of No. 14 in 1957. Ken Fleetwood is pictured with his back to the camera.

Model Peter Christian strikes a pose sporting a late 1950s double-breasted Hardy Amies dinner suit. The coat is square in the style popularized by Kilgour, French & Stanbury at the time, and the trousers are narrow with pronounced creases.

Hardy Amies camps it up at No. 14 in 1951 for photographer Chris Ware. Scrawled on the wall is a statement beginning: 'To hell with *Vogue*!'

reaction, paraphrased, was "you can all do what you like as long as you pull your weight in getting the collection made because the collection is going to be made and it is going to be made by me".'

Unintentionally, Mr Brice draws an admirable pen portrait of a man with the steely self-assurance of a latter-day Brummell. He also highlights Amies's self-reliance and backbone, which saw him serve his country in the British Intelligence Service during the Second World War. When he returned to England in 1945, No. 14 Savile Row was a derelict husk of a Regency house that had once been the townhouse of Georgian playwright Richard Brinsley Sheridan. Amies, walking down Savile Row, saw the Blitzed ruin, broke in and resolved to restore it as the couture house of Hardy Amies. Sending out cards to customers that he had served while working from the House of Worth at No. 50 Grosvenor Street (the London atelier of Charles Worth's Parisian couture house), Amies announced: 'He has acquired larger premises at 14 Savile Row. Here, aided by a staff headed by Miss Campbell, Miss Violet, Mddle Odette and Mr Victor, he will be showing a Spring/Summer collection in February 1946.'

The attention of fashion history was firmly on Paris at this point, when the houses of Pierre Balmain and (in 1947) Christian Dior introduced the extravagant, indulgent New Look, echoing the belle époque for a post-war world keening for escapist glamour. Amies was two seasons ahead of Dior, telling the *Tatler* of March 1946 that 'after six years of sterility in fashion, women want graceful, feminine clothes'. The *Daily Telegraph* 'woman reporter' writes of Spring/Summer 1946 at Hardy Amies: 'The new silhouette that emerged from the first day's collection is that of a softly curved figure in contrast to the severe military lines of the war years. Styles that came off the secret list included padded hips, small waists and sloping shoulders' – in other words, the New Look before the New Look.

The house first dressed Princess Elizabeth in 1951 and, though she wore a gown tailored by the Queen Mother's favoured couturier Norman Hartnell at her coronation in 1953, Her Majesty would confer the Royal Warrant on Hardy Amies in 1955. The two houses shared the honour of dressing the sovereign. Though royal appointment brought the house of Hardy Amies attention – and a gaggle

TO H.S. ...VOGUE! (but don't be made to...
WE MUST...CHIFFON DRESS FIRST (AUG '50)
DON'T ORD...UNTIL YOU'VE SEEN ALL THE COLLECTIONS
WHERE W...WEAR IT? (OR EVEN WHO?)
IT IS DA...TO BE TOO SAFE.

Right: Neil 'Bunny' Roger
photographed in a relatively
sober Watson, Fargerstrom
& Hughes suit in 1959. The
house was subsequently
acquired by Davies &
Son's managing director
Alan Bennett.

Opposite, top left: Bill
the commissionaire was
a regular fixture outside
No. 14 and features in many
model shots in the late
1960s such as this.

Top right: In 1968 Hardy
Amies took his show on the
road and showed his take
on the matador cape at an
al fresco fashion happening
in Portugal.

Below, left and right: In
1967 Hardy Amies presented
the first catwalk show set
to music in the Lancaster
Ballroom of the Savoy
Hotel. These stills were
taken in Embankment
Gardens on the Thames
side of the hotel. The house
of Hardy Amies reprised
the Savoy fashion show in
September 2010.

of his beloved duchesses – it also served to curb his creativity. His couture could never be less than dignified. Sir Hardy's successor Jon Moore ponders that the constraints of the Royal Warrant may have led to Amies letting off creative steam in the 1960s with his men's tailoring collections. The *New York Herald Tribune*'s fashion editor Eugenia Sheppard agreed in an October 1965 column: 'In fashion Hardy Amies leads a double life. As a custom order designer he dresses besides the Queen a conservative clientele. In his other phase he produces much further out men's fashion. One fashion that may not be around in 2001 he prophesies is a man's dinner coat. After all the white tie has virtually disappeared in favour of the dinner coat. Signs now indicate that the status of the dinner coat is shaky. In St Moritz, the men are already wearing blazers instead. They're the next step down in informality.'

From 1965 Amies was increasingly prone to Delphic pronouncements about the future of men's style, along with grandiose asides, such as: 'I pity American men. They have no time to think about clothes.' But however outrageous (if intentionally provocative) his dictates, they were nothing compared with the 'out there' men's tailoring he unleashed, in globally touring fashion shows and in film work, such as his costumes for Stanley

Kubrick's 1968 film *2001: A Space Odyssey*. In 1967, the *Liverpool Daily Echo* wrote: 'Amies makes the flower people look drab: lime green, purple, guardsman's red and tangerine are among the shades you will see wandering down Church Street next year if Mr Amies has his way.' Amies's own suits, cut after 1969 at Tommy Nutter, embraced the turn-up flare and lapels as wide as Concorde's wings.

Amies surrounded himself with an equally handsome fleet of gentlemen, such as his right-hand man Ken Fleetwood (a great favourite of the Queen) and PR man David Harvey. But none was more exceptional than Neil 'Bunny' Roger, who designed for his own clients from No. 14. Roger scandalized London society with fetish-themed parties that moved his mother, Lady Roger, to exclaim: 'I wonder how the men managed to walk in those high-heeled shoes all night.' In the 1998 Sotheby's auction catalogue of Bunny's prolific wardrobe, Kerry Taylor writes: 'Bunny Roger had a sinuous figure which many women would envy; with broad shoulders, narrow waist, long legs and he dressed in a manner which served to emphasise this. He used to immodestly quip that his waist measurement was the same as Princess Diana's.

'By day he could be seen adorning the streets of Mayfair and Piccadilly in an impeccably tailored

Above: Models for Hardy Amies Autumn/Winter 1995 collection designed by Ian Garlant, including an audacious wolf's fur greatcoat. After a brief hiatus at Aquascutum, Garlant returned to Amies as creative director between 2002 and 2008.

Opposite: Detail of Spring/Summer 2009 Hardy Amies bespoke grey three-piece morning coat cut to celebrate the renaissance of the great British couture house as a men's tailor.

double-breasted frock coat with velvet collar, side-buttoned ankle boots with faux spats, a co-ordinating curly brimmed Coke (bowler), gloves and a silver-topped cane – perfection from head to toe. By night he really let rip with suits in delicious brocatelles, soft silk velvets and glistening satins. For these more exotic projects he thought costumers such as Bermans to be more appropriate than his Savile Row tailor Watson, Fargerstrom & Hughes, from whom he would order up to fifteen suits a year each costing £2000.'

While Bunny became increasingly eccentric, Amies eased into his role as grand old man of British fashion. By 1992, his worldwide licensing sales peaked in excess of £200 million from over forty licensees. In 1996, he was knighted and design director Jon Moore took over his duties dressing the Queen. When Sir Hardy Amies died in 2003, the house he founded entered an era of uncertainty, with companies such as the Luxury Brands Group and overseas investors passing it around while Amies's creative heir Ian Garlant continued to present couture and ready-to-wear collections amidst the managerial chaos. It is a great pleasure and no small relief to report that

in 2009 the firm passed into the hands of private investors, who have reinstated Jon Moore as design director and invited Amies's friend, interior designer Ann Boyd, to sensitively redecorate the house.

Hardy Amies reopened with a men's bespoke, made-to-measure and ready-to-wear collection very much inspired by his groundbreaking tailoring of the 1960s and 1970s. The couture atelier on the top floor, where the Queen's mannequin still stands padded and pinned with silk satin to mirror her figure, will be preserved as a permanent archive (guarded by Mr Austin Mutti-Mewse) to house over 500 sketches of Her Majesty's gowns, with embroidered fabric swatches still pinned to the boards. The dress collection in the first-floor salon includes donations from past customers such as Raine, Countess Spencer and Princess Michael of Kent, and will be displayed throughout the house. It is a testimony to bespoke tailoring that the new owners of Hardy Amies have chosen to focus on the founder's menswear. But it would be curious if Hardy Amies couture, and possibly Norman Hartnell, which is also owned by the family, did not make a welcome comeback.

MARK POWELL

-- ESTABLISHED 1984

When *The Guardian* newspaper reported on the Row's 'new kids' in 1995, Soho tailor Mark Powell had been in the business for well over a decade. His is perhaps the strongest signature of the late 20th-century Row tailors, and Powell – the daddy of the Gangster Dandy style – is his own finest model. Aged just twenty-four, he opened 'gents' outfitters' Powell & Co. on Soho's Archer Street, selling 1940s and 1950s dead stock suits found in a warehouse in Stoke Newington. But his addiction to men's tailoring goes back to childhood. As Paul Gorman writes in his definitive study of London street style *The Look* (2006), 'Powell's career as a menswear obsessive started when he acquired his first pair of Levi's as a six-year-old in Romford, Essex, and developed as he moved through various youth tribes, from pre-pubescent suedehead to rockabilly via soul boy.' By the very early 1980s he had introduced an in-house bespoke service at 1950s men's tailoring specialist Robot, where he first met and dressed 'a naff bunch of guys' called Duran Duran, as well as The Clash and Jack Nicholson.

The bespoke cut that Mark Powell developed in the 1980s owed a lot to his youth in the East End

of London. 'I got into all that Kray twin vibe,' he says of the notorious gangland bosses Ronnie and Reggie, who controlled Soho's many vice rackets in the 1960s. 'My aunt knew them well. I started looking at the image rather than the reality of Ronnie and Reggie. They were all about Savile Row style. I myself was going to the East End tailors since I was twelve or thirteen.'

But to pigeonhole Mark Powell's cut as *Gangster No. 1* is to underestimate one of the true connoisseurs of men's tailoring. 'The Krays were

Above: Like father, like son: Powell and his son Max suited and booted for a Soho night wearing Mark Powell bespoke (2008).

Opposite: Mark Powell at home in his Soho penthouse above Bar Italia in 2010.

a big influence,' says Powell, who eventually tailored for the brothers (by then jailed for life), 'but I would mix a gangster three-piece pinstripe suit with Edwardian details like stud-collar shirts, pearl tiepins and fob watches. When I opened Powell & Co. in 1984, I started to develop my own style from the fifties and sixties influences. I was out and about in the clubs in Soho and also being photographed for the early style bibles like *The Face* and *i-D* so it all went into the mix.'

Long before Richard James, Timothy Everest and Ozwald Boateng (who modelled for Powell) opened up shop, it was Mark Powell and north London tailor Charlie Allen who pioneered what is now known as the New Establishment. Early adopters of Powell & Co. were Bryan Ferry and David Bowie, two of Savile Row's acknowledged patron saints. The shop yielded to the night when Powell opened the first easy listening club on Soho's Brewer Street and named it Violet's, after the Krays' beloved mum. With the looks of Errol Flynn sans moustache and a wardrobe of George Raft-meets-Regency bespoke suits, Powell was one of Soho's social landmarks.

In 1991, Powell opened his first pure bespoke atelier on D'Arblay Street. 'I'd started getting lots of old clients ringing me and asking me to make suits,' he says, 'so I got back into tailoring as a full-time occupation. By 1991, we had Vic Reeves, Jonathan Ross, George Michael, Naomi Campbell and Bryan Ferry as bespoke customers. It was the middle of a recession but I was doing fantastic. I picked up where Tommy Nutter left off in the eighties. I even got bits of press with me and Tommy in the mid-eighties when I had my first shop. Tommy was a bit of a lad. He was a laugh and very, very cool. He was no different to me, really. He wasn't a trained cutter or tailor. He was a designer and stylist and I had the same philosophy. The craft of tailoring is very important but you need the person who meets the client and works on the style of the suit.'

In 1994, *L'Uomo Vogue* picked up on the revival of Savile Row bespoke tailoring and chose Powell to lead the feature. 'They said when you think of English style you think of David Niven dressed immaculately and very debonair in his Savile Row suits,' says Powell, 'then there's also all that

Above: East End gangster twins Ronnie and Reggie Kray suited and booted for a 1964 audience with Judy Garland and her gay fourth husband Mark Herron.

Opposite; Patrizio Di Renzo backstage portraits of Mark Powell's fashion show at Savile Row restaurant Sartoria, combining bespoke stock models and ready-to-wear. London Fashion Week Autumn/Winter 2002 season.

Following pages: Mark Powell Spring/Summer 2007 fashion show held at nightclub Pangea in London's Piccadilly, shot by Andrea Baldrighi.

street culture that's been happening post-war. Mark Powell is somebody who combines the two ingredients. I use the Row influences but my tailoring has got a street edge to it as well.' At this stage in his career, Powell was taking ten bespoke orders per week, holding court at Fred's, the Groucho Club and Soho House, and working with Isabella Blow on album cover looks for Bryan Ferry. He was the first to develop the waisted, three-button jacket, slim trouser and waistcoat silhouette. He was also experimenting with inverted trouser pleats and gauntlet cuffs.

'A lot of people copied what I did, but not well,' he says. 'It tended to look cheap if it wasn't bespoke.' Rather than spreading the word through advertising campaigns and international runway shows, Powell staged fashion shows at the Café de Paris and Savile Row restaurant Sartoria. By 2000, he had moved the look on to what he describes as 'a twenties/thirties-inspired vibe mixed up with a late sixties/early seventies look that Tom Ford picked up on at Gucci. The other look I did was the double-breasted lapel and wide waistband on Oxford bag trousers. I'm about reinvention rather than nostalgia.'

For the past decade, Mark Powell worked by appointment from eagle's nest rooms atop a Soho townhouse at No. 12 Brewer Street. His office/atelier was like a gangster's walk-in wardrobe and his VIP clients in particular liked the one-on-one bespoke service he offered. Twenty-first-century dandies who have climbed the oak-panelled staircase to Mark Powell Bespoke include Paul Bettany and David Thewliss (whom he dressed for the 2000 film *Gangster No. 1*), Daniel Radcliffe (for whom Powell cut the infamous green velvet frock coat worn to the fourth *Harry Potter* premiere), Naomi Campbell (for whom he cut pinstripe pant suits to wear for her many court appearances) and the actor Rupert Friend. In autumn 2009, Powell set up shop in an even more iconic Soho address on Frith Street above Bar Italia (founded in 1949). At present he is running a pure bespoke business and plans to locate a shopfront in Soho. Would he, like his former apprentice Nick Tentis, think about putting his name above a door on Savile Row? 'My workshops are near Savile Row [Clifford Street],' he says, 'but Soho is where Mark Powell belongs.'

Actor Paul Bettany as 'Young Gangster', tailored by Mark Powell for the 2000 thriller *Gangster No. 1*.

Scarlet cashmere corduroy shawl-collared, one-button cocktail suit with fishtail cuff detail, tailored by Mark Powell for 'The London Cut' exhibition in Florence, 2007.

Chapter 3

SAVILE ROW AT WAR

Tailoring for Heroes

Preceding pages, left: Admiral Lord Nelson, painted in 1797 by Lemuel Francis Abbot. Tailored by Gieves Ltd's founding father Melchizidec 'Old Mel' Meredith, Nelson wears the uniform of a Rear Admiral decorated with the Star and Ribbon of the Bath and the Naval Gold medal. Taken from life, this portrait is arguably the most widely accepted likeness of the Royal Navy's greatest hero.

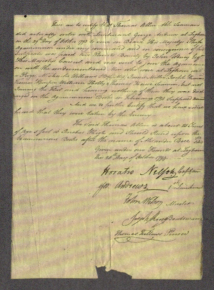

Above, left: Letter dated 28 October 1794 signed by 'Captain Nelson' in the Gieves & Hawkes archive at No. 1 Savile Row.

Above, right: A page from the Hawkes & Co. customer ledger dated 1837 recording the personal orders of Field Marshal the Duke of Wellington.

Opposite: Officer and gentleman Arthur Wellesley, 1st Duke of Wellington, painted by Sir Thomas Lawrence in 1814, several months before the Battle of Waterloo.

M ilitary tailors in late 18th-century London would have been as numerous as branches of McDonald's are today, so it is interesting that the surviving houses can lay claim to almost every hero of the Napoleonic, Crimean, Boer, First and Second World Wars. Savile Row's story is indeed the survival of the fittest. The firm that became Gieves Ltd dressed Admirals Lord Howe, Nelson and Collingwood. Hawkes & Co. customer ledgers dated 1836 record the Duke of Wellington's purchase of military caps such as the plumed bicorn portrayed in William Salter's 1839 portrait. In recent years, Henry Poole & Co. discovered volumes of dated, annotated wax rubbings of military waistcoats and tunics that provide an exact full-size record of heavily embellished uniforms such as those tailored for the Earl of Cardigan, who led the Light Cavalry Brigade in the Crimean War of 1854–55.

Inevitably, the painters and photographers who recorded the Row's naval and military men chose to capture them on parade rather than in action. Thus we have a much stronger record of ceremonial full dress, undress and mess dress than battle dress. The most comprehensive record of Victorian and Edwardian military tailoring is the vast collection of portraits taken by the studios of Bassano (held at the National Portrait Gallery) and Lafayette (now owned by Ede & Ravenscroft).

Though it might appear that the Row would prosper when the nation went into battle, the opposite was in fact true. The prolonged periods of peace in the 19th century were the high-water mark of ceremonial tailoring, which employed its own armies of gold lace makers, furriers and feather curlers. Queen Victoria's status as grandmother of Europe's royal houses guaranteed a steady flow of regal relatives to London throughout the century, bringing the Row's military tailors important Continental trade. In 1862, Kaiser Wilhelm I of Prussia visited London for the marriage of Louis IV, Grand Duke of Hesse, to Princess Alice, daughter of Queen Victoria and mother of the ill-fated last Tsarina of Russia. He conferred his Royal Warrant on Norton & Sons and introduced his uniform-obsessed grandson Wilhelm II to his London tailor. In a classic case of Savile Row making for strange bedfellows, it is entirely possible that the uniform of the 4th Queen's Own Hussars that was tailored for Winston Churchill in 1895 and the Kaiser's 'Death's Head' Hussar's tunic may both have been made by Norton & Sons.

Opposite, clockwise from
top left: Nine Kings pose
united in grief at the death
of King Edward VII ('uncle
of Europe') in 1910 at
Buckingham Palace. Savile
Row tailors held the Royal
Warrants of every monarch
pictured at this precise
moment in history. Back
row, left to right: King
Haakon VII of Norway,
King Ferdinand I of
Bulgaria, King Manuel II of
Portugal, Kaiser Wilhelm II
of Germany, King George I
of Greece and King Albert I
of Belgium. Front row, left
to right: King Alfonso XIII
of Spain, King George V,
and King Frederick VIII
of Denmark.

Winston Churchill in
the uniform of the 4th
Queen's Own Hussars,
aged nineteen, on leaving
the Royal Military College,
Sandhurst (1895).

Over fifty years after his
Sandhurst graduation
portrait, a victorious
Winston Churchill inspects
a guard of honour in Dover
(1946) wearing the uniform
of Warden of the Cinque
Ports, having led Britain
to victory in the Second
World War.

A 1917 portrait of vain,
pugnacious uniform
obsessive Kaiser Wilhelm
II in the uniform of the
aptly named 'Death's
Head' Hussars.

Though many of the names
do not survive, the Lafayette
archive owned by Ede &
Ravenscroft records the finer
details of late 19th-century
military tailoring, such as
this patrol jacket and plumed
astrakan cap worn by an
unidentified captain in the
Royal Irish Rifles regiment.

If one photograph captures the glitter and
gold of the old order before the First World War
shattered the civilized world, it is the 'Nine Kings'
sitting taken at Buckingham Palace on the death
of King Edward VII in 1910. Henry Poole & Co.
held the Royal Warrant for six of the nine, Gieves
Ltd for two and Davies & Son for King George V.
At the close of the First World War the Emperors
of Germany, Russia, Austria and all the German
Grand Duchies had been deposed. British military
tailors would count themselves fortunate that
George V had led the country to victory and
retained a full dress military tradition.

The year of the Russian Revolution, 1917, was a
landmark date for one of the Row's most formidable
military tailors of the 20th century. Welsh &
Jefferies was established on Eton High Street in the
late 19th century but by 1917 the house had moved
to No. 15 Duke Street in the heart of fashionable St
James's. The firm made uniforms for officers of the
Rifle Brigade, the 60th Rifles and the Coldstream
Guards, boasting, 'We have more generals in the
British Army on our books than any other on Savile
Row.' The records of this firm's illustrious past are
entirely lost, though the company survives on Savile
Row and boasts as managing director one of the
finest cutters of his generation, Mr Malcolm Plews.

If Welsh & Jefferies boasted military supremacy,
Gieves Ltd had a special relationship with the
Senior Service. Gieves Ltd tripled in size during
the First World War by virtue of the firm following
the fleet and posting agents in Malta and Gibraltar,

Right: Black fox-fur plumed cap made by Carter & Co., Pall Mall, to be worn with full dress uniform of the 13th Hussars. Tailored by E. Tautz in the 1870s for Lt Colonel Spelling.

Far right: Gordon Highlanders bonnet with black ostrich-feather hood formed on a wire frame with a Highland diced check band. The plume of white vulture feathers is set in a pocket behind the black silk rosette on the side. Last worn in 1932 and now in the Gieves & Hawkes archive.

Opposite: Prince Eddy photographed by the Lafayette Studio in 1889 in Captain's full dress uniform of the 10th (Prince of Wales's Own) Royal Hussars, worn with ADC (aide-de-camp to Queen Victoria) aiguillette. On the Prince's death in 1892, the sculptor Alfred Gilbert chose this image as a model for the Prince's Art Nouveau marble tomb effigy.

as well as all major British seaports. Officers were required to pay for their own uniforms, so the firm introduced a credit system whereby the Navy would dock monthly instalments for uniforms at source. In addition to dress regulations, Gieves saw the war as an opportunity for innovation. Guv'nor 'Mr Jim' Gieve and general manager George Dines collaborated on the patent of the Gieve Life-Saving Waistcoat: a navy worsted waistcoat that concealed an inflatable, vulcanized ring, worn by soldiers and civilians alike (see page 20). The most famous life saved by the Gieves waistcoat was that of the 2nd Baron Montagu of Beaulieu, who was shipwrecked when the passenger liner SS *Persia* was torpedoed by a German U-boat in 1915. His mistress Eleanor Velasco Thornton (model for the Rolls Royce 'Spirit of Ecstasy') did not survive. Two models of the waistcoat plus patent documents do, however, survive in the company archive.

Savile Row was to lose half of its workforce to conscription in the First World War and in response Gieves operated round-the-clock workshop hours

for the duration of the conflict. A letter from Mr Jim to every employee of Gieves Ltd, which hangs in the archive room at No. 1 Savile Row, gives the measure of the loyalty Savile Row felt towards the troops they dressed: 'When war was declared on the fourth day of August you showed the true spirit of co-partnership by doing all or even more than was required of you to assist in dealing with the overwhelming work which was instantly thrown upon us. You know "when service sweats for duty not for need" and you gave of your best with results acknowledged and appreciated by the Admiralty and the whole Navy.'

The traditions of bespoke tailoring emerged relatively unscathed from the First World War. Houses did not go into decline and society as it was pre-war settled back into the daily round of frock coats and black silk top hats by day and evening tails by night. The younger generation, led by the Prince of Wales, rebelled and endeavoured to drink, dance and charleston the memories of mass slaughter away, but formality still ruled and, led by King George V,

'When service sweats for duty not for need.'

1914 LETTER TO GIEVES LTD STAFF FROM MANAGING DIRECTOR JAMES WATSON GIEVE

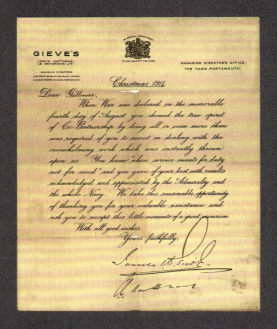

Left: Valedictory letter from Gieves Ltd chairman James Watson Gieve to all members of staff, printed in 1914, commending the company for its efforts at the onset of the First World War.

Opposite, clockwise from top left: Second World War portrait of King George VI in the RAF uniform tailored by Gieves Ltd that he wore to tour the blitzed East End of London. A keen supporter of the RAF since its formation in 1918, the then Duke of York wore RAF uniform in 1939 when he married Elizabeth Bowes-Lyon even though protocol dictated he wear the uniform of the Senior Service.

Edward, Prince of Wales, photographed in 1919 during his royal tour of Canada. The Prince joined the Grenadier Guards on the outbreak of the First World War and, though Secretary of State for War Lord Kitchener denied him active service, he was awarded the Military Cross in 1916.

Hawkes & Co. tailored the khaki uniforms for the 1962 film *Lawrence of Arabia* starring Peter O'Toole as the Arab conflict hero T. E. Lawrence (far left).

dress codes were rigidly upheld. Regulations for the services were sufficiently complex and elaborate for Gieves Ltd to issue a spinning wheel called the Gieves Dress Indicator that simplified the draconian dress codes for naval officers.

If Hitler had mounted a specific campaign to undermine Savile Row bespoke tailoring in 1939, he could not have caused more devastating damage than the Second World War did. The Blitz destroyed fourteen of Gieves' shops and workshops between 1940 and 1942, reducing the No. 21 Old Bond Street flagship to a burnt-out husk and also turning the precious contents of the basement strong room – including all customer ledgers and a collection of Nelson's letters, orders and uniforms – to cinders. Meyer & Mortimer, Jones, Chalk & Dawson, Scholte and J. Dege & Sons were destroyed, though with true Dunkirk spirit Scholte's secretary, Miss Sellack, propped her typewriter on some debris in the street and continued to tap out orders. Dege & Skinner chairman Michael Skinner recalls, 'When J. Dege & Sons on Conduit Street was bombed, my father arrived at the shop to find a great big hole. The shop had gone! Priceless coronation robes in their sealed tin boxes were floating around in

the exposed River Conduit that flowed beneath. But would you believe every last robe survived. Come the 1953 coronation, we realized we'd only misplaced one coronet.'

But the true enemy of Savile Row trade was the government-ordered make-do-and-mend initiative, along with clothes rationing, which demanded that a British 'Utility Suit' be made in grey chalk stripe cloth with low wool content, no waistcoat, no detail and recycled buttons. Privation at home to help the war effort effectively killed the bespoke civilian trade, while uniforms were made to similarly austere patterns. Though ready-mades were familiar to Savile Row before the Second World War, the demob suit made off-the-peg almost mandatory. Firms such as Gieves Ltd continued to serve the Royal Navy as a valet would his gentleman. A cartoon by Russell Brockbank titled 'Business as Usual' shows the Man from Gieves on the shores of Dunkirk: it is a fellow in suit, striped pants and bowler standing centre stage in the war zone. But despite Gieves' sales increasing from £404,000 in 1938 to £739,000 in 1945, the gains were temporary, and the military tailoring world would never be the same again.

DEGE & SKINNER

-- ESTABLISHED J. DEGE & SONS IN 1865

Military and equestrian tailors Dege & Skinner are heroic in their staunch defence of bespoke uniforms tailored to the highest specifications. As chairman Michael Skinner says, 'The blunt truth is that there will always be wars, but the weapons get more devastating every year, with soldiers getting blown to bits rather than fighting face-to-face. Uniforms were traditionally a way of identification in the battlefield. Now they are largely ceremonial, but Dege & Skinner continues to make them, and will continue to do so.' His son and managing director William adds: 'A military tailor can, I am sure, cut a civilian suit. The same cannot be said for a cutter of lounge suits. Military tailoring provides employment for a vast number of skills and businesses such as the makers of embroideries, caps, feather trims, boots, swords and regimental buttons.'

Dege & Skinner's refusal to lower standards is particularly valiant in the modern age, when the Ministry of Defence fires increasingly swift rounds of regiment amalgamation, and rookie tailors undercut prices and then machine-make uniforms for Trooping the Colour. The tone at Dege & Skinner is set by the chairman, who

Mess kit tunic designed and made by Dege & Skinner for King Hamad of Bahrain (2006).

declares: 'The young men and women who serve their regiment and country are a pleasure to dress. The merging of regiments is very sad but I suppose this is another example of the survival of the fittest.' 'When tailoring for the military, you are dealing with people who give orders and take orders,' says William Skinner. 'If they want a uniform made properly and on time and to regulation standards then you expect them to give you short shrift if you don't perform. Non-military folk may find this attitude abrasive but we understand the mindset of the serving officers who give orders.'

An 1885 *Vanity Fair* Spy cartoon of Sir George Compton Archibald Arthur, aged twenty-five, wearing the uniform of the 2nd Life Guards. 'The Mite' fought in the Boer War, was personal private secretary to Lord Kitchener in the First World War and was a prolific biographer of, amongst others, Kitchener, Field Marshal Douglas Haig and King George V.

A young Michael Skinner, present chairman of Dege & Skinner (right), with Huntsman chairman Robert Packer (centre).

Tradition and consistency are held in high esteem by the armed forces and Dege & Skinner has both in spades. The Dege and Skinner families' personal and professional lives have intertwined since 1880. The story began in 1865 when German immigrant Jacob Dege first opened his tailor's shop at No. 13 Conduit Street. At the same time, Skinner's family was tailoring at No. 57 Jermyn Street. Jacob's youngest son Arthur had met William Skinner at Merchant Taylors' School in 1880 and the two friends set up shop as Arthur Dege & Skinner at the turn of the 20th century. The death of Arthur's elder brothers precipitated his return to the family firm in 1910 and the name Dege & Skinner would not appear above a West End tailor's shop for another ninety years.

William Skinner died in 1912 following a riding accident in Richmond Park, and Jacob Dege took William Jr (known as Tim) under his wing. Tim was the present chairman's father. Anti-German sentiment during the First World War forced Jacob Dege to resign in 1917 and in due course Tim Skinner rose to become managing director. It was he who grew the business, purchasing royal robe maker Wilkinson & Son in 1939, opening dedicated tailoring shops at Aldershot and Catterick Camp in 1941 and buying Dege outright in 1947. The company had survived a direct hit on the Conduit Street shop in 1941, and undertook three moves

between Clifford Street and Conduit Street in the next ten years. In 1953, Michael Skinner enters the business. 'I was eighteen when Queen Elizabeth II was crowned and was given two weeks' deferment from National Service to help my father, John Dege and the team,' he says. 'Ede & Ravenscroft and Wilkinson & Son held the Royal Warrants as robe makers and it was my job to robe the peers.'

'You cannot have a finer induction to ceremonial tailoring,' says William Skinner. 'My father not only had to organize the peers' robes and coronets but exercise military precision to dress the peers of the realm on the day, and also know how to address the assembled dukes, earls and barons.' In 1967, Dege bought military tailors Rogers, John Jones and this trebled the firm's size overnight. Rogers were predominantly cavalry and guards tailors and dated from 1774. John Jones, dating back to 1827, made his fortune selling clothing and military equipment in the Crimean War, his great money-spinner being the introduction of mess tins. On his death in 1882, Jones left his collection of Sèvres porcelain to the Victoria & Albert Museum and in 1962 it was valued at £13 million. 'This Rogers, John Jones link introduced us to many new regiments,' says Michael Skinner, 'some of whom have proved invaluable, like the two former cavalry officers who introduced us to the Sultan of Oman.'

Opposite, from top left: Queen Elizabeth II takes the salute at Buckingham Palace in the uniform of the Coldstream Guards, tailored by Bernard Weatherill, the great breeches maker now owned by Kilgour (Trooping the Colour, 1963).

Sultan Qaboos of Oman takes the military salute in Muscat, 2005, marking the Gulf sultanate's 35th National Day in a uniform designed and tailored by Dege & Skinner.

Prince William under review by his grandmother the Queen during the Sovereign's Parade at the Royal Military Academy, Sandhurst in 2006.

The Queen at the inspection of the Yeoman of the Guard (Beefeaters) photographed at Buckingham Palace, 1974. The Yeoman of the Guard uniforms are tailored by Dege & Skinner.

As a military man and keen equestrian, Michael Skinner was responsible for forging even stronger links between Dege & Skinner and the services. In a career that has seen him hold the Queen's Royal Warrant since 1984 (prior to transferring it to William in 2009), and dress many officers of the British Army, Skinner has been keen to nurture good relationships with officer cadets at Sandhurst military academy. 'Our philosophy is this,' he says: 'we clothe young officers at Sandhurst for a very small profit, but almost invariably, when they leave the army and enter the City they remember the name Dege & Skinner when considering their first bespoke civilian suit. If they remain in the Services they stay with us for life.'

The dress of the British Army most familiar in the media is combat dress. But service dress and mess dress, the formal uniforms particular to each regiment, are upheld with great pride by the British services. It is these uniforms that Dege & Skinner excel in tailoring, and which remain the preserve of the bespoke craft. 'The pomp and circumstance of military tailoring may be chipped away in times of conflict,' says William Skinner, 'but it epitomizes the pride our servicemen have in belonging to a regiment that serves Queen and Country.

Amalgamation of regiments may remove the idiosyncrasies of mess dress but it also calls on the trusted tailor to design a new uniform for a new regiment. Traditionally, regiments would always retain two tailors in case of one falling foul. The stronger amalgamated regiment would inevitably make "their" tailor the dominant force. But we at Dege & Skinner are finding that quality will out.'

In 2006, the Queen's Royal Lancers' mess dress was displayed in 'The London Cut' exhibition at Palazzo Pitti in Florence. The kit was cut on a muscular, snake-hipped mannequin that the Savile Row tailors christened Sebastian (after *Brideshead Revisited*'s Sebastian Flyte). The mess dress tunic, vest, overalls and cap that Dege & Skinner tailored for the dummy fitted like a second skin and served as a reminder that bespoke military tailoring has the precision, dash and pomp that have made the British Army so formidable since the Duke of Wellington's day in 1815. The amount of work that goes into military tailoring is not cost-effective when taking into consideration the intensity of craft and labour. But that is not the point for Dege & Skinner. Others may undercut and plane off corners in production, but true military tailoring is as much a tribute to the men and women who serve as it is to commercial enterprise.

Dege & Skinner's honesty and integrity have been its salvation. A ready-made uniform no better than fancy dress would not have invited the attention of foreign monarchs such as Sultan Qaboos of Oman or King Hamad of Bahrain, who came to the house for ceremonial military uniforms. 'There is a history and pedigree to British military uniforms,' says William Skinner. 'For the military, tradition is held very strongly and regulation mandatory. As fewer Savile Row tailors serve the military, it becomes more important that standards are set and quality of work is maintained. The craft is very much alive and well on Savile Row but cost-cutting is becoming increasingly aggressive. We at Dege & Skinner believe that loyalty, pride in one's appearance and honouring one's regiment will always assure that ceremonial military tailoring will thrive and survive.'

Left: Detail of Queen's Royal Lancers' mess dress made for 'The London Cut' exhibition, Florence, and photographed by Jason Pietra for *Qvest* magazine in 2007.

Opposite: Detail of orange silk 'Phitwell' lining of a three-piece check cashmere shooting suit shot for *Qvest* by Jason Pietra in 2007. The 'Phitwell' lining is sprung to allow the coat to sit on the shoulder as the gun takes aim.

'A man from Gieves, the naval outfitters, came to measure me for my uniform, the trying on of which my father personally supervised. I was proud of the blue, round jacket with its brass buttons and cadet's white collar tab and of my naval cap, and paraded in them before my sister and brothers.'

A King's Story: The Memoirs of HRH the Duke of Windsor (1951)

GIEVES & HAWKES

-- Established 1785 & 1771 respectively

Gieves & Hawkes are the undisputed titans of naval and military tailoring respectively. The name and the No. 1 Savile Row address resonate with a grandeur that suggests centuries of history. But though each house is well over 200 years old, Hawkes (established in 1771) and Gieves (in 1785) were autonomous until 1974, when an IRA bomb obliterated Gieves's No. 27 Old Bond Street flagship at the same time as the firm was negotiating a takeover of Hawkes & Co., and its magnificent shop at No. 1 Savile Row, from where the united houses now trade. Together, Gieves Ltd and Hawkes & Co. notch up 464 years of tailoring uniforms for heroes and kings. The founding father of Gieves, Melchizidec 'Old Mel' Meredith, set up shop in Portsmouth in 1785 and tailored for Vice-Admirals Lord Nelson, Collingwood and Howe, and Flag Captain Hardy.

Thomas Hawkes established Hawkes & Co. in 1771 as a military cap maker, earning the Royal Warrants of King George III, Queen Charlotte and their son, the future Prince Regent. Though Hawkes died in 1809, the house went on to craft caps for the Duke of Wellington and his regiment, which were worn at the Battle of Waterloo in 1815.

The story of the Gieve family's special relationship with the Royal Navy begins during the Crimean War (1854–55) when the fleet was mobilized for the first time in forty years. In 1852, Mr James Gieve joined the Portsmouth firm owned by Joseph Galt, who had previously bought out Old Mel's son. By 1854, British troops were fighting in the Crimea and Galt & Gieve fitted out an amenity ship (a floating tailor's shop-cum-supply ship) and sailed it to Sebastopol to service the fleet. It is also around this date that Galt & Gieve patented the Naval Officer's Sea Chest that became a mainstay of the fleet for more than a century.

In 1887, Gieve & Co. was incorporated. It retained Edward, Prince of Wales's (later King Edward VII) Royal Warrant as naval outfitters for his sons, Princes Eddy and George, who were naval cadets. By 1900, 52 per cent of the world's shipping was owned by Great Britain and Gieve & Co. was tailor by appointment to the Royal Navy. Between 1903 and 1921, 98 per cent of cadets at the Royal Naval College, Osborne, were kitted out by Gieves. What set Gieves' naval uniforms apart was the quality of indigo-dyed merino woollens – dyed

Above: Edward, Prince of Wales (later the Duke of Windsor), wearing the naval cadet's tunic tailored by Gieves Ltd for his entry into Osborne Naval College in 1907.

Opposite: Prince George, Duke of York, photographed at the Viceregal Lodge, Dublin, by the Lafayette Studio in 1897. The Prince wears the uniform of a British naval captain tailored by Gieves Ltd.

Clockwise from top left:
Lord Louis Mountbatten
photographed in the full dress
uniform of an Admiral of the
Fleet. The photograph is signed
to Gieves Ltd, who tailored for
the Earl until his assassination
by the IRA in 1979.

Queen Elizabeth II wearing
the Gieves Ltd boat cloak
commissioned by the
Admiralty to celebrate her 1953
coronation, pictured here in
the mid-1950s. Her Majesty
has subsequently been painted
and photographed wearing
the Gieves boat cloak by Cecil
Beaton, Pietro Annigoni and
Annie Leibovitz.

From left to right: Royal
brothers the Duke of
Gloucester, the Prince of Wales,
the Duke of York and cousin
Lord Louis Mountbatten depart
for a royal tour of Australia in
1920. The naval uniforms are
tailored by Gieves Ltd.

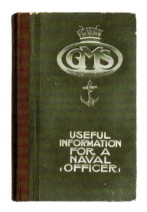

'Useful Information for a Naval Officer' published by Gieves, Matthews & Seagrove Ltd in 1911. This hardcover catalogue shows the breadth of product sold, using a comprehensive telegraphic code for the Royal Navy's orders. The firm would dispatch to serving officers everything from a shirt stud to a sea chest.

in the wool to ensure exact evenness and match of colour – produced by Strachan & Co. of Stroud, and the ingenuity of Joseph Starkey Ltd gold lace and gold wire embroideries.

The company's service to the Navy has spawned many stories, none more charming than that of the 'postal collar'. In 1908, an officer on board HMS *Hawke* wrote: 'please send two dozen collars to this pattern exactly' on the back of a discarded starch collar, addressed it and posted the collar to Gieves's flagship in Portsmouth. The collar hangs framed in the company archive. Alongside such eccentricities were innovations. In 1911, the firm published 'Useful Information for a Naval Officer': in essence a mail order catalogue with telegraphic codes for every conceivable piece of kit. The same year, James Gieve was granted the Royal Warrant of 'Sailor King' George V and his four sons, Princes Edward, Albert, George and Henry, as Royal Naval Outfitter.

The sheer volume of custom in the early 20th century was phenomenal: how else could the firm operate on a credit system that allowed customers to leave accounts unsettled for years? How else could Mr Jim write off the outstanding debts of all Gieves men killed in action at the end of the First World War? In 1920, Gieves moved into a palatial building at No. 21 Old Bond Street that had once been occupied by the celebrated art dealer Joseph Duveen. On the death of Mr Jim in 1927, the reins passed to his eldest son, Rodney Watson Gieve, who steered the firm through the Great Depression. By 1933, sales had sunk below £300,000. But the firm had deep pockets. David Gieve estimates that in 1938 officers of the Royal Navy owed Gieves Ltd £500,000: enough, he said, to have paid for quite a respectable warship. Ironically, it was during the peacetime between the First and Second World Wars that naval uniform reached unprecedented heights of complexity and grandeur, as seen in

Left: Early Victorian tinted etching depicting Queen Victoria with Prince Albert, who is wearing the Colonel-in-Chief's uniform of Prince Albert's Own 11th Hussars. On the chair to the Prince's right is the fur cap made for the regiment in 1840 by Hawkes & Co.

Below: An 1845 Hawkes & Co. card advertising the firm as 'Helmet, Army Cap & Accoutrement Makers to Her Majesty Queen Victoria, HRH the Prince Albert and HRH the Duke of Cambridge'.

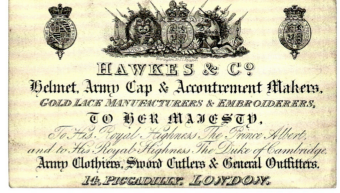

Admiral's full dress uniforms tailored for the Kings of England, Denmark, Norway, Sweden, Greece, Romania and Yugoslavia by the firm.

The Second World War saw sales increase, from £404,000 in 1939 to £739,000 in 1945. It also saw the beginning of the end of the unlimited credit system. David Gieve recalls the tactics employed by tailoring manager Hubert Quirk: 'Mr Quirk had a sort of respectful effrontery with customers on occasion, which could be quite breathtaking to the onlooker but which was nearly always successful. "Surely, my Lord, you do not expect Mr Gieve to accept an order for yet another uniform before you have paid for the greatcoat which you have been wearing these past two winters!"'

The advent of off-the-peg suits was resisted with spirit reminiscent of the Blitz. In the 1950s, when Gieves made the decision to stock ready-mades, the manager of No. 27 Old Bond Street told buyer Mr Wright: 'There's a wardrobe just outside my office, Wright. Put them [ready-mades] in there and give me the key, so that every time you want to sell one of your damned ready-made suits you have to come to me to get it. You will soon get tired of that and send the customers along to the tailoring department where they belong.' The coronation of Queen Elizabeth II in 1953 heralded a revival of ceremonial tailoring that allowed the Row to show its expertise. Gieves tailored a boat cloak for Her Majesty commissioned by the Admiralty that she has since famously worn for formal portraits taken by Cecil Beaton and (most recently) Annie Leibovitz for *Vanity Fair*.

It is telling that in David Gieve's history of Gieves & Hawkes, Hawkes & Co. merited no more than a brief appendix. However, the little known about founder Thomas Hawkes suggests he was one of the great entrepreneurs of late Georgian England. On his death in 1809, Hawkes left £20,000 (equivalent to approximately £1,600,000 today) in his will: a king's ransom for a king's hatmaker. His fortune was made on discovering the secret of 'jacking' leather to make it hard enough to withstand the cut of a sword blade.

Opposite: Prince Albert painted at Windsor Castle in the mid-19th century by John Lucas. The magnificent bicorn hat trimmed with white and red-dyed swan's feathers is made by Hawkes & Co. As in the image above, an officer of the Prince Consort's regiment attends with his horse Nimrod.

Hawkes patented the shako – a tall shellac headdress adopted by the British and Continental armies – one of which survives in the company archive. Arguably the most extraordinary find in the archive were copies of letters sent by Hawkes & Co. between 1837 and 1856 to the great and the good of early Victorian England, naming Prince Albert, the Duke of Buckingham, the Duke of Cambridge, King Leopold of the Belgians, Baron de Stockmar, Earl de Grey and the Earl of Cardigan (of the Charge of the Light Brigade fame): names that would have been lost to the house without its discovery.

The letter to Prince Albert solicits appointment as Cap Maker to HRH as Colonel-in-Chief of the 11th Hussars; it was a successful approach, as confirmed by an 1845 calling card bearing the crests of Queen Victoria, Prince Albert and the Duke of Cambridge. The address, No. 14 Piccadilly, was the firm's home from 1823 to 1912, when Hawkes & Co. acquired No. 1 Savile Row from the Royal Geographical Society. A further discovery was made in the strong room in the basement of No. 1: a Hawkes & Co. Dress Regulation Ledger (1860–90) recording '11th Prince Albert's Own Hussars' with a cutting of gold lace pinned to the page.

It was during the Crimean War that Henry White acquired Hawkes & Co. from the heirs of the founder. It was he who scored a comparable success to the shako, when a stranger came into No. 14 Piccadilly with a helmet made of cork held together with a rubber solution. White clinched a deal,

improved the design and put it on the market as the Hawkes Helmet or solar topee. The Hawkes Helmet was a great success with the British Army and was first worn in the Abyssinian Campaign of 1897 under Lord Napier. Waterproof as well as sun-proof, the troops found it most useful for watering their horses when their buckets were lost or unobtainable. In explorer Henry M. Stanley's 1890 book *How I Found Livingstone*, the author writes: 'The first words I heard in Ugogo were from a Wagogo elder, of sturdy form, who in an indolent way tended the flocks, but showed a marked interest in the stranger clad in white flannels, with a Hawkes' patent cork solar topee on his head…'.

We have Henry White's grandson's unpublished memoirs (sadly unsigned) to thank for the last century of Hawkes' history, including the rise of head cutter George Ballingall, who joined the firm in 1899, moved the company from Piccadilly to No. 1 Savile Row (paying £38,000 for it in 1912), introduced display windows in the shop and in 1929 sold the first 'immediate wear' suits that compensated for the decline in dress uniform sales. Hawkes maintained traditions such as dressing the Honourable Corps of Gentlemen at Arms, who guard Her Majesty at major state functions including the Opening of Parliament, but by 1974 it was a house in decline. The aforementioned IRA bomb prompted the merger and establishment of Gieves & Hawkes at No. 1 Savile Row in 1985.

Below, left: Gieves Ltd at No. 27 Old Bond Street in 1947. The house was destroyed by an IRA bomb in 1974.

Below, right: A 1940s photograph of Hawkes & Co. at No. 1 Savile Row.

Above; Panoramic photographs of the archive room at No. 1 Savile Row in 2009.

Following pages: Gieves & Hawkes Autumn/Winter 2009 campaign. From left to right: velvet smoking jacket with quilted lapels, midnight-blue dinner suit with black satin peak lapels and black bespoke evening coat with frogging detail inspired by a 19th-century Royal Artillery tunic in the Gieves & Hawkes archive.

For the past decade, managing director (now vice-chairman) Mark Henderson has steered the ship and also chaired the Savile Row Bespoke Association. 'I think a lot needed changing, and it has changed,' he says. 'The pride in bespoke is there. When I arrived at Gieves, the majority of our business was ready-to-wear. In the bespoke rooms, the people loved their craft and they had a very private relationship with the customers. The company didn't really play a part in the bespoke world and the tailors felt neglected. We had to reconnect them to Gieves & Hawkes.'

Thanks largely to Mr Henderson, there exists today a synergy between the design department and the bespoke rooms. Head of design Frederik Willems says, 'Although we are trying to design collections that are relevant for the gentlemen of today, the beauty, craftsmanship and detail of historical garments in the archive inspire the collections season after season.' Head cutter Kathryn Sargent adds, 'The collaborative process between bespoke and design is very much alive. The design team look to bespoke as there are no limitations, and we look to be challenged by design.' In January 2009, No. 1 Savile Row received a royal seal of approval with a visit from the Prince of Wales and the Duchess of Cornwall. The focus of the visit was the bespoke workrooms and the archive room that serves as permanent tribute to the life's work of the late Mr Robert James Watson Gieve, last of the family to work for the firm, and the formidable history of Gieves & Hawkes.

'It's all about the best of British materials treated in a way that allows the craft to speak for itself. We're all about simple elegance here.'
PATRICK GRANT, MANAGING DIRECTOR OF NORTON & SONS

NORTON & SONS

-- ESTABLISHED 1821

Henry Poole & Co. chairman Angus Cundey keeps a book in his office labelled 'Enemy Debts', into which a Poole's clerk diligently transferred all German, Austrian and Italian customer accounts on the outbreak of the Second World War. Norton & Sons, a house founded by Walter Charles Norton on the Strand in 1821, had a particularly strong link with Germany, dating back to 1862 when Kaiser Wilhelm I conferred his Royal Warrant on the house. Present owner Patrick Grant is particularly pleased to have Baron Manfred von Richthofen (the First World War flying ace known as the Red Baron) on his books. If Nortons' men can be classified, they share a collective glamour associated with endeavour as explorers, adventurers, soldiers and bounders.

As with all historic tailors, Norton & Sons incorporates once-majestic houses such as Hammond & Co., who dressed Europe's royalty, and the military/sporting specialists E. Tautz & Sons. Norton & Sons moved to Conduit Street in the 1850s, and in 1859 founder's son George James Norton was awarded the Freedom of the City of London for his services to 'rugged, robust' tailoring. Customers included explorers Henry

M. Stanley and the Marquis de Vogüé, but the finest photographic record of Norton & Sons' style depicts the dashing Lord Carnarvon in the Valley of Kings in the early 1920s, captured in the heat of the day sporting what look like 20-ounce tweed three-piece suits, stiff-collar shirts and silk bow ties. With a strong tradition in tailoring to colonial Africa, India and the near East, Norton & Sons developed an expertise in lightweight touring and safari tailoring, even if Carnarvon did not subscribe.

The Second World War brought US Ambassador to the Allied Governments, Anthony Drexel-Biddle Jr, once named 'the world's best-dressed man', to Norton & Sons in 1944. Post-war, Hollywood males followed, such as Alfred Hitchcock, Cary Grant, Bing Crosby, David Niven and Gary Cooper. By 1970, Norton & Sons had been sold to Hardy Amies-trained John Granger, who would increase the firm's trips to the US to six visits per year, adding smaller, richer pockets of income such as the Hamptons and Boca Raton as well as the major cities. *The Savile Row Story* describes Nortons' shop at No. 16 Savile Row (acquired in 1981) as 'exuding the cute cosiness of a yuppy clothing boutique in the Hamptons'. One of the

Norton & Sons owner and managing director Patrick Grant in 2010.

Christian B. Barker, former editor of *The Rake*, ponders suiting cloth with Patrick Grant.

Opposite, from top left: Kaiser Wilhelm II of Germany photographed at Sandringham House in 1902 on a visit to his uncle, King Edward VII. Though the Kaiser was, like his grandfather, a Nortons customer, the house may be reluctant to claim this pretentious hunting get-up.

Norton & Sons man German flying ace Baron Manfred von Richthofen (the Red Baron), with his hound Moritz.

Ever the gentleman even in the colonies: British Egyptologist Lord Carnarvon photographed while excavating the tomb of Pharaoh Tutankhamun in 1923.

US Ambassador Anthony Drexel-Biddle Jr photographed in London in 1944.

best customers was neighbouring couturier Hardy Amies, who in one order purchased eighteen suits, three jackets, seven trousers, two overcoats and a Marcella dress vest.

The Granger era at Norton & Sons ended in 2005, when John Granger's sons sold the business to thirty-five-year-old Savile Row newcomer Patrick Grant. With the exception of Anderson & Sheppard, no other change of ownership has reconnected a firm as cleverly with its past. Grant responded to an advertisement in the *Financial Times* reading: 'Savile Row tailors for sale'. 'I was at Oxford writing a thesis about repositioning old brands in the spirit of Burberry and had studied Dege & Skinner and Kilgour as two extremes: one who remained traditional and the other wishing to be relevant, luxurious and modern. I was interested in determining whether a Savile Row house could "do a Burberry".'

What Grant achieved at Nortons is little short of pitch-perfect. First the shop (once the Regency home of Sir Benjamin Collins Brodie, physician to George IV, William IV and Queen Victoria) was stripped back with brisk simplicity: little but good antique furniture, lustrous wooden floorboards, whitewashed walls with the occasional antelope head. He retained Nicholas Granger's emphasis on field sports tailoring and added his own passion for his native Scots tweeds: a neat echo of Lord

Carnarvon. Like a Howard Carter of Harris, Grant explored the weavers' huts secreted on the Hebridean Isles in search of the finest tweed. 'People connect to Harris tweed,' he says. 'They understand the history and the provenance of the cloth. There is something about it that creates in people's minds something quite special and romantic.' So evangelical is Grant about Harris tweed that the BBC followed his adventures on the Isles for a 2010 documentary.

Nortons retained head cutter John Kent, who holds the Royal Warrant for the Duke of Edinburgh, until his retirement in 2008, then took over his book. 'Our focus is on fine bespoke tailoring,' says Grant, 'be that for work, weekend or field. There are few on this street that are still exclusively bespoke tailors. Until you've been to Savile Row, I think it's difficult to appreciate how much better clothes can be. Some people just don't know how well-fitting garments can be. Everything that bears our name is handmade in Britain. The essence of this firm is a passion for beautiful tailoring by the best craftsmen in the world. It's all about the best British materials treated in a way that allows the craft to speak for itself.'

Grant is his own best advertisement and has gone some way to breaking the style press monopoly held until 2009 by Richard James and Kilgour under Carlo Brandelli. Grant's profile in British fashion is helped by bespoke collaborations with young designers such as Giles Deacon, Richard Nicoll and Christopher Kane. Savile Row stole House of Holland's Autumn/Winter 2008 show with a purple Argyll Dashing Tweed by Guy Hills and Kirsty McDougall that was cut by Norton & Sons.

Taking a leaf out of Alan Bennett's book, Grant decided to launch a tailored ready-to-wear collection under the name of extinct company E. Tautz & Sons for Autumn/Winter 2009. Founded in 1867 as a breeches maker, Tautz (pronounced 'Torts') gave Grant a new history – and an amusing leaping fox logo – to inspire design. A twenty-one-year-old Winston Churchill ordered his first twill overalls from E. Tautz & Sons in 1895 and went on to order such luxuries as white cashmere racing

breeches and a chocolate satin racing jacket with pink sleeves.

The Tautz philosophy is thus: 'We champion the notion of dressing properly and of men taking pride in what they wear.' The debut collection, sold into Harrods, Matches and Beams, borrows heavily from the language of bespoke but adds preppy touches including hand-knitted Shetland V-necks and luxuries such as glossy leather totes designed by Katie Hillier. Norton & Sons remains pure bespoke, with the cutting room led by David Ward and the on-site workshops filling up again with in-house tailors, trouser makers and trimmers. The firm Grant described in 2007 has not wavered in its course: 'Neat, simple and elegant, we are proud to make beautiful, robust clothes for the dashing Englishman at large.'

Opposite: Still life of a ready-to-wear model for the Spring/Summer 2010 E. Tautz collection: a fashion-led, sartorial collection inspired by an extinct sporting and military tailoring firm incorporated into Norton & Sons.

Left: In 2009, Patrick Grant's position astride tailoring and fashion was recognized when he was invited to judge the style element of the biannual Golden Shears competition. It was won by Poole's apprentice Rory Duffy's ensemble (left), with the Silver Shears awarded to Anderson & Sheppard's Paul Nicodemi, who chose to tailor Dashing Tweeds (right).

Right: Agyness Deyn models a Dashing Tweeds tartan commissioned by House of Holland and tailored by Norton & Sons for Autumn/Winter 2008.

Chapter 4

SAVILE ROW IN HOLLYWOOD
Aristocrats of the Silver Screen

Preceding pages, left: The sublime Fred Astaire, in a
relatively rare studio portrait of him dancing in black
tie (c. 1938). The earliest record of Astaire on the
Row is in Anderson & Sheppard's 1923 ledger.

It is one of Hollywood's many ironies
that the world's biggest box-office idols are sent
more tuxedos in any one awards season than Fred
Astaire owned in a lifetime, and yet Astaire remains
an untouchable leader of male fashion, while the
only man in LA today who seems to possess a tie,
let alone dress with formality or flair off-screen,
is George Clooney. Millions of dollars change
hands to license Tom Ford International to replace
Brioni as Mr Bond's *Quantum of Solace* tailor, whereas
even the greatest costume designers for the silver
screen would concede Mr Astaire's wardrobe to the
discretion of his Savile Row tailors Anderson &
Sheppard and Kilgour, French & Stanbury.

The business transactions that underpin
dressing Hollywood men today are beyond
comparison with the half-century between 1920
and 1970, when Savile Row sculpted the sartorial
identities of leading men with little recognition
and no desire for it. Studio designers Travis
Banton, Orry-Kelly, Edith Head, Irene and
Travilla controlled every bugle bead that leading
ladies wore and their names were writ as large as the
director's in the opening credits. Banton curled and
lacquered every cock feather that adorned Marlene
Dietrich in her early 1930s opus of von Sternberg

films. Dietrich's leading men Gary Cooper, Cary
Grant, Charles Boyer and Robert Donat were
all tailored on Savile Row, but tailors never got
a mention as the credits rolled.

Tempting as it is to claim the scalp of every
tuxedo-clad Hollywood silver screen idol for Savile
Row, on-screen provenance is hard to prove or
disprove. Firstly, as Errol Flynn wrote in his 1959
autobiography *My Wicked, Wicked Ways*, he 'discovered
that the wardrobe people are the biggest thieves
of all. They walk off with a gown, suit, a prop, any
piece from the wardrobe, and make the star the
goat.' Secondly, as debonair, moustachioed Adonis-
in-worsted Adolphe Menjou admitted in his 1948
autobiography *It Took Nine Tailors*, his London cutters
Scholte, Anderson & Sheppard, Lesley & Roberts
and Henry Poole & Co. were supplemented by
LA tailor Eddie Schmidt (a genius at copying the
London Cut) as well as European houses Caraceni,
Caraterroi and Knize. Stars were as promiscuous
with their tailors as they were alleged to be in their
private lives. But as the *Tailor & Cutter*'s Christmas 1931
edition proves, Hollywood tailoring was career-
defining and scrutinized with near-obsessive detail:

'Whereas the feminine star must spend
£3000 a year on her clothes, a man can get by on

Above, from left to right:
Gary Cooper, Robert
Montgomery, Clark Gable,
Jack Buchanan and Ronald
Colman painted for a
Park Drive cigarette card
collection dated 1935. With
the exception of Huntsman
hero Gable, each of these
matinee idols was a customer
of Anderson & Sheppard.

Opposite: Studio portrait of
Gary Cooper photographed
by Clarence Sinclair Bull in
1934 wearing a peaked lapel
single-breasted houndstooth
suit. Cooper had been
introduced to Anderson
& Sheppard in 1932.

The impossibly beautiful
Douglas Fairbanks Jr
photographed in 1930
by Elmer Fryer at the
very start of his career.
His actor father Douglas
Fairbanks had introduced
Junior to his London tailor,
Anderson & Sheppard.

The private and public
images of stars such as Clark
Gable (photographed here
in the early 1940s) are
indistinguishable. Only
the tie gives away that this
is not a still from his 1939
film *Gone with the Wind*. First
recorded at Huntsman
in 1943, Gable was also
tailored by Lesley & Roberts
and Stovel & Mason.

Right: Rex Harrison strikes a pose in the 1944 film *Notorious Gentleman* in a linen suit tailored by Sullivan, Wooley & Co. The company was subsequently bought by Henry Poole & Co., who continued to tailor for the actor into his seventh decade.

Opposite, clockwise from top left: Rotund Norton & Sons customer, film director Alfred Hitchcock, photographed outside the Plaza Hotel in New York in 1969.

Joan Crawford attends a 1932 white tie Hollywood premiere flanked by (from left to right) William Haines, husband Douglas Fairbanks Jr and Ivor Novello, all tailored by Anderson & Sheppard.

Rudolph Valentino photographed at home in Hollywood with his German shepherd, Prince, in 1925. He is recorded in Huntsman's ledgers in 1923 and Anderson & Sheppard's in 1924, a year before his untimely death in 1925.

Gary Cooper and Marlene Dietrich on the set of *Desire* in 1937. In 1936 Dietrich first signed her name in Anderson & Sheppard's guest book, having been recommended by Douglas Fairbanks Jr. Though her tails were by Berlin tailor Knize, Anderson & Sheppard tailored her off-screen flannels, tweeds and blazers.

a fourth of this. Robert Montgomery (Anderson & Sheppard) says clothes cost him annually about $2500 (£630). Ben Lyon, another Hollywood best dresser, estimates that he has invested $12,000 (about £3000) on wearing apparel since 1927. His wardrobe contains 45 suits. According to Bob Montgomery, he needs one riding suit, two golf outfits, two dinner suits (one single-breasted and one double), ten business suits, three overcoats, three robes, one cutaway and one full dress outfit. Then, of course, flannels for summer, sweaters, gloves, hats and three or four-dozen shirts.'

In 1931, William Haines compounded his reputation as No. 1 box-office fashion plate with *A Tailor Made Man*. MGM built an entire tailor's workshop on the soundstage, then 'employed a committee of tailors [who] took Haines in hand. They taught him how to press a suit, how to wield a clearing sponge. They instructed him in repairs and explained the mysteries of buttonhole making,' moving Haines to declare in the *Tailor & Cutter*, 'The qualifications of nine men go into one tailor if he's to be a success.' The MGM publicity read: '*A Tailor Made Man* is a rattling story with a good

idea behind it – that social and business success depend on choice clothes. Dress will not make up for brains and character but it gives an ambitious young fellow a chance to show his mettle; for a good appearance is an effective letter of introduction.' Hollywood scripts of the era were nothing if not didactic.

The leading Hollywood houses on the Row bar none were Kilgour, French & Stanbury, Huntsman and Anderson & Sheppard, although Lesley & Roberts was a favourite with Clark Gable and Norton & Sons somehow contrived to upholster the huge frame of Alfred Hitchcock. From 1950, Huntsman built a list of Hollywood greats including Stewart Granger, Tyrone Power, Bing Crosby, Laurence Olivier and Mr Gable. But both Anderson & Sheppard and Kilgour earned their early supremacy as Hollywood tailors because they – in sharp contrast to Hawes & Curtis and Henry Poole & Co. – welcomed performers when it was not considered the form to dress what were essentially men in trade. Henry Poole & Co. made the odd exception for stage performers such as Victorian actor/manager Sir Henry Irving and

royal mistress Lillie Langtry, but their books are markedly bare of 20th-century actors.

As monarchies toppled following the First World War, it was Hollywood idols who became the international ambassadors of male elegance. The sole royal left to rival the glamour of the silver screen idols was Edward VIII, who may have fulfilled his promise as the world's most influential Savile Row man had he not given up the throne in 1937 for the love of Mrs Simpson. Somewhat poignantly, the wit and ease that he brought to the Row when Prince of Wales was more fitting for the screen than a throne. Instead, the Row learnt to worship Fred Astaire, Gary Cooper and Cary Grant, who all slavishly copied tailoring fashion set by the ex-King.

When Fred, partnered by sister Adele Astaire, was dancing George Gershwin's *Stop Flirting* in London in 1924, he was visited backstage by the Prince of Wales. 'HRH was unquestionably the best-dressed young man in the world,' recalls Astaire in Richard Walker's *The Savile Row Story*. 'I was missing none of it. I noted particularly the white waistcoat

lapels – his own special type. The waistcoat did not show below the dress-coat front. I liked that.' Like it he may, but the Prince's tailor Hawes & Curtis would not serve him. Anderson & Sheppard would, however; and, as Astaire recalled, 'It was difficult not to order one of every cloth that was shown to me, especially the vicuñas.' His white tie tailored ten years later by Kilgour, French & Stanbury for the 1935 film *Top Hat* is viewed by some as the apogee of Savile Row style.

One could argue, however, that it is the Astaire of the rehearsal room and informal studio still who embodies Hollywood's contribution to Savile Row. The look is pure Anderson & Sheppard: soft Prince of Wales coat, grey flannel pants, pure ivory silk shirt and cream doe-skin shoes. It is the silk twilly scarf tied around his neck, the stripe foulard scarf knotted around the waist in homage to Fairbanks and the soft trilby hat ordered from James Lock & Co. that make the heart lift like a soufflé. Notice when Astaire dances that his soft-shouldered suits glide as effortlessly as he does. Astaire suits and separates are well-mannered, unassuming and as

A candid photograph of Cary Grant in London en route to tailors Kilgour, French & Stanbury in 1946. Could there be any more fitting evidence to prove the case for Grant as one of Savile Row's greatest heroes?

The Kilgour, French & Stanbury prototype suit tailored for Cary Grant in Alfred Hitchcock's 1946 film *North by Northwest* could have won a Best Supporting Actor Oscar as one of the few film costumes worn throughout an entire picture by the leading man.

'The qualifications of nine men go into one tailor if he's to be a success.'

WILLIAM HAINES IN THE *TAILOR & CUTTER*, ON HIS ROLE IN *A TAILOR MADE MAN* (1931)

pliable as Cyd Charisse. It's a look that is dressy, breezy, carefree but so carefully considered and put together as to be a lesson in how to affect unaffected elegance. As *Cloth & Clothes* said of Rex Harrison in 1959, 'The ideally dressed Englishman has the casual elegance in dress which may look accidental and unrehearsed but is in fact carefully planned.'

The much-maligned studio system dictated that its stars dress 'in character' off-screen, and so fashion leaders like Jack Buchanan, Douglas Fairbanks and Adolphe Menjou gave Savile Row suits an East Coast ease and grace not seen on St James's Street. In his definitive book *Cary Grant: A Celebration of Style*, Richard Torregrossa writes a love letter to the dark grey Kilgour two-piece that Grant wears throughout Hitchcock's *North by Northwest*. Grant's character is famously abducted, drugged, chased by a crop-dusting biplane and hung from Mount Rushmore, and the Kilgour more than rolls with the punches. It is the hero of the picture: indomitable, unruffled and fit for purpose. As Torregrossa says, Grant loved clothes and they loved him. This, above all else, is the secret formula for true glamour in tailoring: the ability to refine and reduce one's style like a gourmet sauce until it is the purest distillation of personal taste.

Huntsman gives a masterclass in tailoring for social advancement in the 1949 Ealing comedy *Kind Hearts and Coronets*. As leading man Dennis Price rises from shop boy to duke, Huntsman furnishes his character with an increasingly dapper wardrobe of yachting blazers, country knickerbockers, City frock coats, evening tails and a magnificent frogged velvet smoking jacket with quilted satin shawl-collar. Douglas Hayward's wardrobe for Steve McQueen in *The Thomas Crown Affair* (1968) masquerades as traditional, sober Savile Row three-piece suits denoting wealth, respectability and class. It is only

on closer inspection that the subtlest of details – a theatrical Edwardian waistcoat with an audaciously low break or anachronistic antique gold fob watch when a vintage Rolex would do – give Crown away as a gentleman thief as debonair as Raffles.

The tipping point at which personal style became product placement had not yet occurred in the 1960s, although Hollywood's tailors had by then learnt a trick or two from the Row. *American Gigolo* (1980) was the watershed moment for men's fashion in film, when the designer dollar replaced Savile Row: the arch-seducer in the movie was not Richard Gere, but Giorgio Armani's wardrobe. Thus stars such as Brad Pitt, George Clooney, Tom Cruise and Christian Bale became 'brand ambassadors', and Armani has dressed them consistently (and beautifully) ever since. Similarly, Armani's mentor Nino Cerruti understood the value of film endorsement, reaching millions more men with his 'greed is good' pinstripe suits for *Wall Street* (1987) than a runway show ever could.

Yet despite the death of the studio system and the birth of product placement, Savile Row retains its special relationship with Hollywood. Anderson & Sheppard customer Ralph Fiennes insists on the house tailoring bespoke costumes for appropriate roles such as *The English Patient* (1996) and *The Avengers* (1998). Michael Caine, who wore Hayward in *Alfie* (1966) and *The Italian Job* (1969), and Terence Stamp, who was dressed by Hayward for *Modesty Blaise* (1966), still insist on Hayward on screen, while superstars Tom Cruise, Daniel Day-Lewis and Brad Pitt wear Richard James, Ozwald Boateng and Timothy Everest respectively. So, despite sponsorship and endorsement dollars, it is gratifying to know that many contemporary stars still seek the authentic connection with old-school Hollywood idols that Savile Row has at its fingertips.

While Faye Dunaway's Theodora van Runkle mini-skirt suits and highly stylized millinery defined late 1960s fashion, Douglas Hayward's suits for Steve McQueen in *The Thomas Crown Affair* (1968) continue to inspire and inform disciples of great tailoring today. The sophistication of the cloths and colour palette is breathtaking.

Left, clockwise for top left: George Clooney, the Cary Grant *de nos jours*, presents the Best Supporting Actress Award at the 2007 Oscar ceremony wearing black tie tailored by Giorgio Armani.

Giorgio Armani's wardrobe for Richard Gere in the 1980 film *American Gigolo* seduced a new generation of men with sublime Italian tailoring.

Arguably the best feature of the 1998 film remake of *The Avengers* was the strict Savile Row tailoring executed by Anderson & Sheppard for Ralph Fiennes's character John Steed, pictured with Uma Thurman as Mrs Peel.

Opposite: Michael Caine poses for the *Vogue* cameras at the Plaza in New York in 1966 to publicize the film *Alfie*, for which he was tailored by his friend Douglas Hayward.

ANDERSON & SHEPPARD

-- ESTABLISHED 1906

Anderson & Sheppard is unique on the Row for keeping daybooks that cite name, date, references and residences in the handwriting of each new customer. The ledgers (chronicling 1924 to the present day) are a tradition almost as old as the firm itself, founded in 1906 by Scholte striker Per Anderson. The story they tell is a complex game of 'six degrees of separation' connecting a chain of Hollywood actors, producers, directors, writers and occasional lovers who dominated the movie business in its golden age between 1920 and 1939.

'Dressed by Anderson & Sheppard, a star still projected the essentially carefree Hollywood mood,' says the firm's co-chairman, Miss Anda Rowland. 'Only customer happiness can account for the glittering roster of American greats in the ledgers. What endeared the house to them? It is not too far from the United States but far enough from the stiffness of English etiquette. It's not too far from casual but very far from unconsidered. The easy comfort of Per Anderson's cut was perhaps the closest Savile Row would ever want to approach the American lounge suit.'

Great names familiar in the annals of male style – icons such as Rudolph Valentino, Fred Astaire, Noël Coward and Cole Porter – were known to Anderson & Sheppard as customers in the 1920s, but lesser-known, if not forgotten, stars previously hidden in the ledgers tell the house's true Hollywood story. In 1924, Jack Buchanan endorsed former silent screen star Lew Codie, husband of drug-addled Mack Sennett star Mabel Norman. His first order (and the name of who endorsed Buchanan) is now lost in one of the missing first five Anderson & Sheppard daybooks.

Buchanan is largely known for a final musical role in the 1957 Fred Astaire/Cyd Charisse vehicle *The Bandwagon*. But the affable, elegant Scotsman may prove to be the missing link between Anderson & Sheppard, Broadway and Hollywood. The West End hit *André Charlot's A-Z Revue*, co-starring Buchanan and Gertrude Lawrence, famously featured a song penned by Ivor Novello called 'And Her Mother Came Too'. This revue transferred to Broadway in 1924 and, not coincidentally, it was Anderson & Sheppard who tailored for Novello, Lawrence and Buchanan.

The view of Old Burlington Street from Anderson & Sheppard's shopfront.

Buchanan's move stateside coincided with the birth of the 'talkies' in 1927 when his Anderson & Sheppard soft-shouldered, elegantly draped suits were as welcome as his vowel sounds. Long before Astaire wore his first tailcoat in his debut movie (*Dancing Lady* in 1933), Buchanan's name was synonymous with elegant evening attire. He was first in a line of English leading men who brought Anderson & Sheppard style to the silver screen, including Ronald Colman, Noël Coward, Herbert Marshall, Robert Donat and Cary Grant. One can add Anglophile honorary Brits Astaire and Gary Cooper (who was educated in England).

Arguably the earliest American Hollywood star to support Savile Row was Douglas Fairbanks. Like Buchanan, his first order at Anderson & Sheppard is pre-1923. Astaire admitted that he learned how to knot his tie around a pair of languid flannel trousers from Fairbanks. An early encounter with Fairbanks on board SS *Olympia* led Cary Grant to 'doggedly strive to keep tanned to emulate his healthful appearance'. Rudolph Valentino signed with the Fairbanks-founded independent studio United Artists in 1924, the same year he first visited Anderson & Sheppard. Is it possible that

Fairbanks recommended his newly signed star to his own tailor?

The Anderson & Sheppard cut is one of the most distinctive on Savile Row. As Clifton Webb described it, 'The shoulders are wider and have less padding, an attempt is made to create a recognizable waistline, there's a better fit around the hips and the sleeves are slimmer.' It is the ease with which we identify Fred Astaire's rehearsal attire or Marlene Dietrich's masculine pleated slacks that demonstrates what Anderson & Sheppard brought to Hollywood.

The Anderson & Sheppard connections are as complex as a spider's web with Astaire, Coward and Webb at the centre. Each is listed as recommending well over twenty men to the house, leading one to wonder if they worked on commission. But smaller cliques speak from the pages of the daybooks that say more about the private lives of Hollywood in the 1920s and 1930s. In 1922, William Haines was the No. 1 box-office draw. He was also at the centre of a movie 'lavender list' that included Webb and director George Cukor. By 1934, Haines's career was over after Louis B. Mayer had given him the ultimatum to marry or lose his contract with MGM.

Anderson & Sheppard's 1932 ledger opened at the page signed by Gary Cooper. He was recommended by his then-lover Countess Dorothy di Frasso, on whose account his suits were signed.

Hollywood leading man Clifton Webb was one of Anderson & Sheppard's most prolific customers, first recorded in 1924, here photographed dancing with Irene Castle in 1933.

Right: Black velvet Anderson & Sheppard smoking jacket embroidered by Hand & Lock for 'The London Cut' exhibition, Tokyo, in 2008.

Left, clockwise from top left: Fred Astaire and co-star Eleanor Powell rehearsed over eighty-seven hours for a single routine in the film *Broadway Melody of 1940*. Note how immaculately Astaire is attired in Anderson & Sheppard flannel pants for what was essentially an off-screen moment.

Handsome, homosexual Hollywood leading man William Haines, photographed by Ruth Harriet Louise in 1932 before MGM ended his career.

Two of the best-dressed men in Hollywood, Robert Montgomery and Ramon Navarro, photographed in 1927.

Gary Cooper and President Roosevelt's elegantly tailored son Elliott compare sartorial notes outside Cooper's dressing room in 1933, on the set of the film *One Sunday Afternoon*. The picture was taken a year after Cooper's first visit to Anderson & Sheppard.

Haines chose to leave the studio and, in the same year, recommended his lover Jimmy Shields (who committed suicide within a year of Haines's death) to Anderson & Sheppard.

A similar scenario played out in 1924, when the Ballets Russes performed in London and the love triangle plus one of impresario Sergei Diaghilev, star Serge Lifar, choreographer Georges Balanchine and librettist Boris Kochno were all listed in the Anderson & Sheppard daybooks. It is amusing to play musical beds with the ledgers. The Countess di Frasso, that notorious Hollywood mantrap, recommended her lover Gary Cooper to the house, having pursued him through Africa like an errant big cat; a star Cecil Beaton also claimed to have bedded, along with fellow customer Peter Watson. Prince George, Duke of Kent, is a name that appears in 1920s folklore as the lover of Noël Coward. What united all these great men of the cloth was not the pursuit of love, but style.

Anderson & Sheppard's Hollywood males were not conservative. They had a licence to exercise a little more flamboyance than the aristocrats and industrialists who made up the bulk of Savile Row's bespoke sales. The world watched, and the details were consumed by a voracious male style press. Matinee idol Robert Montgomery was famed for never carrying a wallet for fear of ruining the drape of his coats. Jack Buchanan had a collection of 300 pocket squares and displayed the hands of an origami artist in folding them. Fred Astaire borrowed the white carnation buttonholes worn by the Prince of Wales and Prince George but insisted on wearing them full-blown. Sharing a tailor, and the recommendation protocol it entailed, was like a VIP pass to *Vanity Fair*'s Oscars party today. It meant you had arrived. Each famous name listed in the daybooks is cross-referred and ticked. 'Knows Noël Coward' was clearly a code for 'check before cutting cloth'.

We may expect that 'the talent' had the wherewithal to locate a particularly creative tailor but the Anderson & Sheppard ledgers relate that the power players in the industry – the studio heads, producers and directors – also anointed the house as Hollywood's cutter of choice. Victor Fleming,

director of *Gone with the Wind* and *The Wizard of Oz*, is recorded in 1934, as is Sam Spiegel, producer of *Lawrence of Arabia*. Joe Schenck, founder of 20th Century Fox and lover of Marilyn Monroe, is there, as is Arthur Freed, the genius who produced *Meet Me in St Louis*, *An American in Paris*, *Singin' in the Rain* and *Gigi*.

Today, Anderson & Sheppard reside in an elegant townhouse equidistant between Savile Row and Bond Street. Their infamous secrecy about customer identity has tempered a little as the paparazzi catch Kate Moss, Manolo Blahnik or Ralph Fiennes leaving the sanctuary. But confidentiality and discretion are still bywords for Anderson & Sheppard's service. The greatest fashion designers of our age – from Calvin Klein, Moschino and Ralph Lauren to Tommy Hilfiger and Tom Ford – choose to observe a masterclass in cutting by asking head cutter Mr Hitchcock to tailor them a suit. So, too, do ladies and gentlemen who would rather be known for their unfathomable chic than for a designer label.

Variously christened 'the limp look' and 'the drape', Anderson & Sheppard's softly tailored bespoke silhouette was passed directly to firm founder Per Anderson by legendary Dutchman F. P. Scholte. In his 1949 obituary, the *Tailor & Cutter* called Scholte 'the man who invented drape', concluding that 'he made one of the greatest changes in men's fashion that has ever been introduced when he began using drape at the end of the last century'. Mr Hitchcock is the present master of the firm's unique drape; coats are cut to be as comfortable as a cardigan.

'Ours is a certain effortless style,' he says. 'We use very little padding and that makes the jacket very comfortable to wear. We are the only tailor on the Row who sets the shoulder by hand rather than by machine. This means that we can cut a very small armhole but still give the jacket a full sleeve by easing the fullness in by hand. The drape of the jacket gives the illusion of slimness on the waist and I always come out a bit wider than the rest with the hips. Hollywood flocked to Anderson & Sheppard for a very good reason. The Anderson & Sheppard cut is very similar to Brooks Brothers before Marks & Spencer got their hands on it. Every young man in America had been to Brooks Brothers and grew up with the softer coat that we're known for. Americans are more used to our style than Huntsman or Henry Poole & Co.'

'The fundamental values that lie beneath what we do – skill, authenticity, durability and strong human involvement – place the well-financed mass-luxury culture of the past two decades in sharp relief,' says Anda Rowland. 'Our books contain the names of some of today's most creative talents, and this has been the case since 1906. Old and new customers are coming in and requesting very specific designs and styles, which only bespoke tailors can deliver. We are on Savile Row for the long term and for a fundamental reason: a sincere love of beautifully tailored and made men's clothing.' Quietly and with as little fuss as possible, Anderson & Sheppard bind the Hollywood connection ever tighter. But like the matinee idols immortalized forever on the silver screen, this bespoke titan of Savile Row will continue to dazzle future generations with who they dressed and – fundamentally – how they dressed.

HAYWARD

-- Established 1967

Expectations were spectacularly low for working-class boys like Douglas Hayward who were born in London in the 1930s. When his mother died, Hayward discovered every pound note he had given her hidden in ice-cream boxes under her bed. The letter that accompanied the banknotes read: 'The money is to get Doug out of prison when they finally get him.'

Mrs Hayward simply could not believe that a humble tailor could earn the money, fame and circle of friends Doug had amassed honestly. And yet five hundred of London's brightest and best – including lifelong friends Michael Caine, Roger Moore and Terence Stamp – gathered at Mayfair's Farm Street Church in May 2008 to celebrate the life of a man who was as well connected as he was loved. For over forty years, Hayward had ruled Mount Street as Hollywood's head cutter, both on screen and off.

Names who came to No. 95 Mount Street for a suit and left with a friend for life include Richard Burton, Peter Sellers, Steve McQueen, Robert Mitchum, David Hemmings, Tony Richardson, James Coburn (who called him 'the Rodin of tweed'), Clint Eastwood, Sammy Davis Jr, Peter Cook, Dudley Moore, Roman Polanski, George Hamilton, Peter Lawford, Omar Sharif, Warren Beatty, Albert Finney, Rod Steiger and Kirk Douglas. The grandees of stage and screen came too: Noël Coward, Laurence Olivier, John Gielgud, Dirk Bogarde and Paul Scofield.

Hayward arrived on Mount Street in 1967. By 1968, the *LA Times* called him 'the hottest thing in English tailoring since Mary Quant'. In 1969, Douglas Hayward dressed what many consider to be his masterpiece: *The Italian Job*. In a bravura display of simplicity, Hayward cut suits for Michael Caine's smooth criminal Charlie Croker that defined an era. Hayward and his 'Girl Friday' Audie Charles styled Caine in spry navy single-breasted suits with audacious tone-on-tone white shirts and ties, steel grey suits with generous notch lapels and tightly knotted ice-blue tie and ecru Italian-weight suits with black leather driving gloves.

Hayward's Mount Street headquarters is streets away from Savile Row and his cut is equally distinctive. As Caine says in the 2008 BBC documentary *British Style Genius*, 'You'd see middle-aged dandies in Mayfair who had their suits made on Savile Row with that pinched waist that was

Clive Arrowsmith captures the mood at No. 95 Mount Street in 2005 as Michael Caine and Douglas Hayward share a laugh at one of the last of many first fittings.

almost like a woman's suit. Doug was completely
against that. You couldn't get anything too
flamboyant here. You put on a Hayward suit and
lost ten or twelve pounds instantly.' Hayward
did make a flamboyant white suit for Caine to
wear in *Dirty Rotten Scoundrels* (1988) but refused
screen credit because it didn't reflect his taste. A
photograph of scoundrels Caine and Steve Martin
now hangs in the lavatory at No. 95.

'I think you could tell a Hayward suit when you
looked at a man from the side,' says Audie Charles,
who worked with Hayward for over forty years
and whose eye dictated the accessories collection
that the house is justifiably famous for. 'There
were no obvious details that said "Hayward". In
fact, Doug would have been appalled if the suit got
more attention than the man wearing it. But there
was just something about the way the jacket was
suppressed and the trousers draped that made
a Hayward suit special.'

For the Bond films, Hayward was credited with
bringing traditional British tailoring back to movies
like *For Your Eyes Only*, *The Spy Who Loved Me*, *Octopussy* and
A View to a Kill. Watch Roger Moore in action today
wearing Hayward's interpretation of the traditional
navy chalk-stripe suit, and not one stitch has dated.
'Bond should always look immaculate,' says Moore,
who admitted on the documentary *British Style Genius*
that he stole all of the now-iconic safari suits that
Hayward made for the tropical locations. In *The Spy
Who Loved Me*, Bond's suits worn in scenes around
the Sphinx and the souks of Cairo are fatally

Above: Douglas Hayward
leaving his Clifford Street
club Burke's, which was
co-owned by Lord Lichfield,
in 1969.

Opposite: Douglas Hayward
photographed in the
entrance of No. 95 Mount
Street the year it opened
(1967).

sharp. A summer-weight cappuccino-toned blazer is cut with strap and buckle detail on the cuffs and clever box pleating across the back. The cut of Bond's cream trouser is magnificent, as displayed in a kickboxing scuffle with a fat, bald henchman on the rooftops of Cairo.

The 1969 film *The Thomas Crown Affair* vies with *The Great Gatsby* and *American Gigolo* for the title of greatest male fashion movie of all time. Hayward's tailoring for leading man Steve McQueen is extraordinary in its classicism. Crown favours three-piece suits with his waistcoats cut in the Edwardian low-break eight-button double-breasted style. His watch is a gold fob and his shirt collars pinched by 18-carat tie bars. Nothing is overstated, stylized or dandy. Every element is correct, but put

together in a style as smooth as a torch song crooned by Sinatra (another Hayward client).

In the days before Mount Street became the headquarters for Mayfair's Rat Pack, Doug would drive to clients' hotels and offices in a battered old Mini (shades of *The Italian Job*?), where he claimed to have perfected his technique of measuring-up the client in his own habitat. 'People pose when they look at themselves in the mirror. Chest out, head back, chin in,' he said. 'But how different they are when they are just being themselves. In their own homes in their underpants they can't pose or act pompously so I'm able to study them and get the right line for their suits. Once I spent three hours with a notebook at the Savoy watching Robert Mitchum's every gesture – the way he sat, the

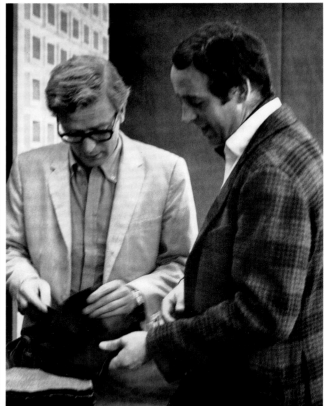

Right: Actor Terence Stamp with model Celia Hammond at the premiere of his 1967 film *Far from the Madding Crowd*. Of Hayward he said, 'I will never go to another tailor. Just tell him how you want to feel and Doug dresses the mood.'

Opposite, clockwise from top left: House icon Michael Caine with wife Shakira and Douglas Hayward in the late 1970s.

Michael Caine around the time of *The Italian Job* (1969) choosing cloth with Hayward, who was credited by *Men in Vogue* (1967) as 'not the over publicized trend setter but rather a trend breaker'.

Michael Caine stars as Charlie Croker in the 1969 caper movie *The Italian Job*. As Caine told Channel 4, 'What happens when you're an actor, you do the hair the way it's supposed to be and put the clothes on and look in the mirror and know exactly who you are. For *The Italian Job* I put Doug's suits on and knew exactly who Charlie Croker was.'

The unmistakable profile of actor Sammy Davis Jr photographed at a fitting with Hayward in the late 1960s.

way he moved, the way he talked.' It is a tribute to Hayward's wit that Mitchum enjoyed his company sufficiently to allow such intensive study.

When he opened the Mount Street shop, Hayward promised: 'No stags' heads coming through the walls and no pictures of the Queen Mum. It's relaxed and nice and easy. Besides, I get a lot of birds in.' Birds included Bianca Jagger, who first met Mick hanging out on Mount Street when she lived next door, Jean Shrimpton, Candice Bergen and Lee Radziwill. The shop was an instant success. In 1967, *The Telegraph* chose Hayward as the mascot for 'the most spectacular rise of the tradesman. Ten years ago, a man would no more have invited his tailor to a party than ask the dustman to dinner. None of Douglas Hayward's customers would think of having a party without inviting him. He was calling them by their Christian names when they were still calling him Mr Hayward.'

The social heights Douglas Hayward scaled would have been unthinkable in the 1950s. In 1969,

he and friend Patrick, Lord Lichfield, opened a dining club called Burke's on Clifford Street, where everyone from Tommy Nutter and Cilla Black to Princess Margaret and Lord Snowdon elbowed to be seen. His Mayfair Orphans Club met at Burke's or Michael Caine's restaurant Langan's, and numbered Terry O'Neill, Johnny Gold, Vidal Sassoon, Roger Moore and Ian McShane as members. His Mount Street Football Club and Marching Society would organize stellar charity matches, boozy lunches and tickets to Arsenal games, at which Steve McQueen or Elizabeth Taylor may be a surprise guest. Caine's characterization of Alfie was said to be modelled on Hayward and he inspired John Le Carré's spy novel and film *The Tailor of Panama*.

Hayward's confidence and ease in the beau monde came easily because many of his celebrity customers had travelled the same route that he did: working-class boys made good. He left school at fifteen and tried to get an apprenticeship on Savile Row. 'One man told me: "Our customers pay a lot of money for their suits and they don't want to be subjected to a cockney accent when they're being fitted,"' Hayward recalled. 'Well, I couldn't get a job in Burton's in Oxford Circus so I ended up in Shepherd's Bush where they all talk like that.'

After national service with the Royal Navy, Hayward cut his teeth with Hammersmith-based Dimi Major. It was during the early 1960s that he first met Michael Caine. 'The first thing I did when I earned a bit of money was get a really decent suit,' says Caine. 'I was recommended to go to Major Hayward. Major Hayward? I was expecting a crusty old army officer. Anyway, Doug came to measure me and we became very, very close friends; one of my closest based probably on the fact that he's one of the people that's most like me. We had the same sense of humour, the same upbringing, he even had a mother who looked like mine.'

Hayward left Major in 1966 and set up a shoebox basement in Pall Mall, where the phone didn't ring for the first three weeks. When it did, it was old mates Michael Caine and Terence Stamp, who called Doug to the Dorchester to measure up Richard Burton. There he met Bryan Forbes, who ordered ten suits. Then Peter Sellers placed an order for twenty-five. As Audie Charles says, 'Suddenly he was just off.'

Hayward was famed for his straight talk, a characteristic that appealed to famous men who were more used to yes men. 'I often talk someone out of having a suit rather than make them one that will look rotten,' he said. 'I had a tussle with Sammy Davis Jr. He has a strong personality and I knew I

would have a hard time with him. Finally at a party I said I would make him one but that I wouldn't let him see the suit until it was finished. As it turned out he liked it. He then brought Jerry Lewis in. I hate his wardrobe. It represents what has been bad about American clothes. Any rate, Jerry Lewis never ordered anything from me. Good. The suit would have had my name on it, not his.'

The death of such a giant of the tailoring world in 2008 inevitably left large shoes to fill, and intervention from family unfamiliar with the world of bespoke put the firm into administration in June 2009. It is a tribute to the buzz around bespoke tailoring (not to mention Doug's client list and Audie's charm) that the official receivers reported unprecedented interest in the business. Great names such as Henry Poole & Co., Ralph Lauren and Joseph had already considered buying it when Doug was still alive.

Whilst in administration, the house was visited by Ralph Lauren, who was in town for Wimbledon and called in at the shop unannounced. Coincidentally, so too was one of Hayward's prospective suitors. Is there a finer endorsement for the loyalty and class of Hayward's clientele than seeing Audie Charles sharing tea and sympathy with the wealthiest fashion tycoon on the planet? The white knights who acquired Hayward in August 2009 were New York-based hedge funders who retained the firm's family unit, brought in the expertise of two ex-Kilgour cutters (Ritchie Charlton and Campbell Carey) and silenced outsider shareholders who could have dismantled Doug's legacy and seen his name disappear.

Though Roger Moore's final appearance as James Bond in 1984's *A View To A Kill* was his least favourite, Douglas Hayward did not let him down with this ivory dinner jacket with very smart pale horn buttons. His co-star, the incomparable Grace Jones, wears Azzedine Alaïa on location at the Château de Chantilly.

KILGOUR

-- ESTABLISHED 1882

In 1965, society photographer-costumer-diarist Cecil Beaton fired a broadside at Savile Row, whose tailors (Anderson & Sheppard, Sullivan, Williams & Co. and Watson, Fargerstrom & Hughes) had dressed him for decades. 'It is ridiculous that they go on turning out clothes that make men look like characters from P. G. Wodehouse. I'm terribly bored with their styling – so behind the times. They really should pay attention to the young mods … the barriers are down and everything goes. Savile Row has got to reorganize itself and, to coin a banal phrase, get with it.' Mr Beaton decamped to Pierre Cardin for a season before returning to Huntsman and becoming an elderly poster boy for the Neo-Edwardian movement. As biographer Hugo Vickers relates in his magnificent 1985 biography, a somewhat bewildered Beaton would be stopped on the King's Road by flick-knife-wielding Teds asking if he was 'ready to rumble'.

The spirit of Beaton's Savile Row critique was voiced thirty years later by Carlo Brandelli, the man who in 1998 would take the reins of one of the Row's biggest beasts: Kilgour, French & Stanbury. 'You've got to see with fresh eyes if you want to do

interesting work,' he says. 'The issue with Savile Row over the last few years is that people are doing exactly what they did one hundred years ago with no new thought. You need to push things forward a

bit. I understand their caution. Savile Row kept everything close to its chest. But in order to move forward you've got to teach that knowledge and a lot of people don't want to do that.'

The interesting point about Brandelli's tenure at Kilgour is that, instead of standing on the shoulders of this giant company that can trace its roots back to 1882, he chose to stand alone. To judge how brave his navigation away from the past proved to be, one must look at the history at his fingertips. The house rose to fame when A. H. Kilgour and T. F. French united to form Kilgour & French in 1923. The addition of Hungarian immigrant brothers Fred and Louis Stanbury in 1925 completed a name that was to dominate Savile Row for the best part of the 20th century. In addition to Hollywood royalty (Fred Astaire,

Above: Bespoke label inside one of Fred Stanbury's suits dated 19 February 1969, held in the EMAP archive at the London College of Fashion.

Opposite: Fashion photographer Nick Knight collaborated with Kilgour creative director Carlo Brandelli and art director Peter Saville on a collection of house icon images between 2004 and 2008. This coat silhouette modelled by Peter Saville is Autumn/Winter 2005.

Edward G. Robinson, Louis B. Mayer, Rex Harrison and Robert Mitchum), Kilgour attracted a list of world power brokers such as JFK's father Ambassador Joseph Kennedy, Adnan Khashoggi and King Faisal of Egypt.

In 1963, a sixteen-year-old Edward Sexton began his apprenticeship with Kilgour, French & Stanbury. 'It was a wonderful, wonderful business,' he says. 'They didn't advertise. Never. It was all networking and introductions back to them.' The Stanbury brothers had what can only be described as star quality. 'In those days I had a very heavy cockney accent,' says Sexton, 'and Mr Stanbury said to me one day, "Edward, they come to you for beautiful clothing, not elocution lessons," and that always stayed with me.'

Davies & Son managing director Alan Bennett recalls: 'Fred was the technician and Louis was the showman. When you went into Kilgour you didn't go wearing your old tailor's clothes. You put on your best suit. I remember going in to see Louis wearing a suit I'd recently made for myself. He looked me up and down and said, "That's a nice bit of work." Then he took his chalk and marked a buttonhole on my lapel. "When you go back to work, better put a buttonhole on that. It'll look grand." Louis was really the salesman. He was the front-of-house man, while Fred was the cutter.' Roy Chittleborough, co-founder of Chittleborough

& Morgan, was an apprentice at Kilgour in the late 1950s. 'Kilgour was magnificent in those days,' he says. 'We had four cutters, four strikers, two trouser cutters and gargantuan workshops exclusively for the firm in Soho. The business was phenomenal. We were making 300 suits a week.'

Kilgour's most enduring icons of the 20th century are Fred Astaire's tailcoat from the 1935 film *Top Hat* and the indestructible grey suit Cary Grant wears throughout Hitchcock's *North by Northwest* in 1959 (see pages 146–47). The former is to men's style what Audrey Hepburn's little black Givenchy dress is to ladies' in *Breakfast at Tiffany's* (1961). The latter has caused more debate amongst the online sartorial forums than Grant's relationship with fellow actor/roommate Randolph Scott. The premier edition of *The Rake* magazine in December 2008 offers the most plausible solution to the conundrum of LA tailor Quintino's label appearing on Grant's Kilgour suit in the film, eloquently put by editorial director Wei Koh: 'For a fleeting instant, [Grant] displays a label bearing the script that appears to read Quintino. One logical conclusion is that Quintino made the suits [many were needed] for the film, but that these were possibly based on an original suit created by Kilgour for Grant.'

The early years of Brandelli's Kilgour were defined by a relationship with the actor Jude Law,

Fred Astaire leads a chorus of white-tie-clad gentlemen in his 1935 film *Top Hat*, tailored by Kilgour, French & Stanbury.

Carlo Brandelli photographed by Nick Knight in 2008. Of his time at Kilgour, Brandelli says: 'It's good to have history but you have to focus on the modern day. I didn't have a choice. I felt the weight on my shoulders and wasn't around in Astaire's or Cary Grant's day, so couldn't connect with it. I had to write a new chapter for Kilgour.'

whom he first dressed for the premiere of *The Talented Mr Ripley* in 1999. 'Actors are like sponges,' Brandelli says. 'They take on a character by some kind of osmosis. In the same respect, Jude was receptive when I suggested we dress him like a modern Cary Grant. At the time I wasn't thinking about the old Kilgour connection. It wasn't about the clothing or what Cary Grant wore. It was about his demeanour rather than his style.'

To his credit, Brandelli did not dress Law as Cary Grant. Instead, he dressed the actor in a style that Brandelli had honed from his own vision of radically chic monotones, almost Neoclassical in their simplicity, and softly sculpted in a line more reminiscent of Italian tailoring than Savile Row. What Savile Row failed to see in Brandelli's interpretation of bespoke tailoring was a reverence born when, as a teenager in Paris, he would buy vintage suits in the 7th Arrondissement. 'Over the years, I studied the workmanship of Huntsman, Kilgour, Anderson & Sheppard and Gieves & Hawkes,' he says. 'I remember wearing a vintage Gieves suit into No. 1 Savile Row when I was a teenager to see if they'd recognize their own hand. One of the senior salesmen came up to me and said, "Is that your father's suit, sonny?" I told him it wasn't and it told me an awful lot about the attitude of Savile Row tailors.'

Like Richard James before him, Brandelli rose to the challenge laid down by the old guard and set about teaching the Row a thing or two about

'relevance'. 'They don't see me working with the small cloth mills in and around Huddersfield, striving to develop new fabrics for Kilgour. I can see parallels between some of the mills and some of the old tailors. The trouble with some of the mills in the UK is that they won't develop anything new for you. They do what they've done for a hundred years and are tricky to work with. Then some will work with you. It's an old-fashioned way of working. You have to build up trust but once you've got it they will produce fabulous things for you. It's a very artisan way of working.'

What Brandelli achieved was to take Kilgour (he dropped the French & Stanbury) into a fashion arena. Tastemakers such as Nick Knight, Peter Saville, Rankin, Sean Ellis, Pete Tong, Roland Mouret, Bobby Gillespie and David LaChapelle felt moved to visit the bespoke workrooms of Kilgour and found the work being produced sympathetic to their lives. Of Kilgour's heritage, Brandelli says, 'Everyone was trying too hard to recreate and not trying hard enough to create something new. The energy should be directed at moving forward not living in the past. I have no idea what the Row thinks of me: not favourable, I would imagine. But I genuinely tried to create something new.'

But the history of the house was more sympathetic to Brandelli than he ever knew. In a story from the *Men's Wear* journal of 1952, managing director Fred Stanbury was recorded speaking to the Men's Fashion Council, of which he was

chairman: 'In a strident speech, Mr Stanbury condemned the cult of praising things just because they happened to be old. Not all that is old is good and this was particularly true of suits.'

Brandelli brought contemporary men to Savile Row who would otherwise have ignored bespoke tailoring. He commissioned Sean Ellis and Nick Knight to produce advertising campaigns to run in the major glossies that were as clean and contemporary as anything produced by Gucci or Prada, including a clever homage to David Hockney's *A Bigger Splash* (see page 26). The first issue of *Men's Vogue* waxed lyrical about Kilgour's 'lean, structured shoulders and the subtle uplift of the chest', quoting Brandelli as saying, 'If you don't have an athletic figure we'll give you one.' Of all the Savile Row tailors, he has been the one to find a point of view that young, modern men want to follow.

The apotheosis of Kilgour under Carlo Brandelli was the dressing of Daniel Craig for the film *Layer Cake* (2004). 'The scene demanded that Daniel Craig's character looked like the quintessential English gentleman even though his character was a gangster. So I said, "Let's dress him like Bond."' This is precisely what Brandelli did, and by 2008 Daniel Craig was Bond in his *Casino Royale* debut.

In Spring 2009, Brandelli announced his resignation from Kilgour almost a year to the day after British-owned Dubai-based company JMH Group bought the business. JMH announced the intention to put the focus firmly back on bespoke and the eight-strong team of cutters in the workshops. No. 8 Savile Row has been subtly restyled to look like a tailor's shop rather than a high fashion boutique, with bales of cloth displayed on dark wood shelves and reassuringly dapper chaps on the shop floor. Kilgour has also made it known on the Row that they will once again enjoy a relationship with their bespoke neighbours.

Kilgour has ambitions to be a global brand exporting bespoke tailoring to target markets such as the Middle East, Asia and the United States. The plan is to open embassies worldwide and send Savile Row-trained master tailors out to these territories to train up local talent. The Row will remain the focus and the headquarters of the company but the outlook is very much towards international trade.

Above: Kilgour's first icon image modelled by Peter Saville in 2004.

Opposite: Kilgour icon image modelled by Peter Saville for Autumn/Winter 2006.

Following pages: The Brandelli mission to place Kilgour at the heart of contemporary fashion was seemingly accomplished with the house's debut at Paris Fashion Week for the Spring/Summer 2009 season. The collection was restrained, elegant and relevant, but within a year Brandelli had resigned.

SAVILE ROW REVIVAL

The New Establishment

Preceding pages, left:
Mayfair hedge fund
manager and polo player
Andrew Baker models a
houndstooth check bespoke
stock model cut by Richard
Anderson in 2007.

'There is an odd atmosphere these days in Savile Row,' wrote *Esquire*'s Nick Sullivan in 1992. 'Nothing tangible, you understand. But from time to time, people stop to peer with uncertainty, with incomprehension, even with vague horror through the plate glass window of No. 37a. There's a new boy in the Row and he's causing quite a stir. What's more, he's not a tailor. Richard James is too busy to worry about the neighbours.'

To reread reports of the advent of Richard James on Savile Row in the early 1990s, you would think he was selling jeans and jocks like Abercrombie & Fitch, so vehement was the response. James was the first to admit that he came from a fashion background: he worked for the formidable Joan Burstein as menswear buyer for South Molton Street boutique Browns, then crossed the floor to show an own-label collection in Paris alongside fellow bright British exports Paul Smith and Katharine Hamnett. What he was proposing from his tiny Savile Row shop was a ready-to-wear collection supplemented by special bespoke orders made for him by neighbouring traditional Row tailor Anthony J. Hewitt. Photographed leaping down the Row grinning like a Cheshire Cat, James told *Vogue*: 'A jacket's got to have that bit of lilac showing through the back flap. An Englishman must learn to be flamboyant again.'

Fellow tailor Timothy Everest understood the cultural barriers Savile Row faced in the 1990s. As he told me in 2007, 'Traditionally, a gentleman would introduce his son to his tailor as a rite of passage. In the eighties it was the sons who introduced their fathers to fashion labels such as Giorgio Armani, Ralph Lauren, Jean-Paul Gaultier, Yohji Yamamoto and Comme des Garçons,' he says. 'The tailors that you christened the New Establishment had to turn men back on to bespoke tailoring.' In 1991, Everest opened his atelier in a 1760 Huguenot house in London's East End, far from the Row. Everest's house was well placed to serve the young City boys working in the Square Mile. Opening on Savile Row would, he says, 'be like moving back in with my parents'. His early customers 'were a bit apprehensive at first, but when they discover they can get something that fits them perfectly, will last for ages and still costs less than a designer suit, they are sold on bespoke.'

Working from a studio in Notting Hill until his move near the Row in 1995, Ozwald Boateng was cutting eye-popping, super-sharp 1960s-inspired suits with raised waistlines and slimmed-down

'Not so much tailors as designers who can actually ſtitch and sew, Ozwald Boateng, Richard James and Timothy Evereſt are a new breed of Savile Row clothier.'

Vanity Fair, March 1997 'London Swings Again' issue

trousers that elongated and refined the line. Soho tailor Mark Powell proposed the Neo-Edwardian cut with a gangſter swagger, while Timothy Evereſt revived his mentor Tommy Nutter's golden era with an early 1970s look. All the new school tailors undercut old Savile Row's average price of £3,000 for a beſpoke suit considerably, which contributed to a 'them' and 'us' mood on the Row.

The noise generated by the New Eſtablishment and the attention of men's ſtyle titles such as *GQ*, *Esquire* and *Arena Homme +* underſtandably irked the older houses. Andrew Ramroop OBE, owner of Maurice Sedwell at No. 19 Savile Row, had pioneered some of the moſt flamboyant beſpoke tailoring seen on the Row in a life-long career that saw him buy out Mr Sedwell in 1988. 'I remember walking to work in a fine pair of trousers that showed off my 26-inch waiſt and two-tone leather and canvas shoes. Tommy [Nutter] would compliment me if he saw me walking down the Row,' says Ramroop. 'One of my earlieſt passions was to make sure the back of the jacket was as intereſting as the front. I'd put shooting pleats into the back of my jackets and was fond of contraſt-colour pîped seams.'

As head cutter at Maurice Sedwell in the early 1980s, Ramroop had a ſtrong following amongſt then-Prime Miniſter Margaret Thatcher's cabinet. Led by Lady Thatcher's private secretary Mark Lennox-Boyd, six cabinet miniſters (including Michael Heseltine and Kenneth Baker) and twenty MPs were Maurice Sedwell men. 'One of the cabinet miniſters told me that Mrs Thatcher enjoyed her miniſters discussing their tailor,' recalls Ramroop. In sharp contraſt to the New Eſtablishment, Andrew Ramroop did not advertise the more exotic beſpoke commissions outside the circle of his cuſtomers.

But the D'Artagnan of New Eſtablishment tailors, *GQ* ſtyle editor John Morgan, put all of his weight behind the new boys. In January 1995, Morgan coordinated a *Sunday Telegraph* ſtory, 'Speaking up for Beſpoke', that went againſt every inſtinct of Savile Row's famed discretion. Four handsome young chaps proud to name their tailors were interviewed and photographed as poſter boys for contemporary beſpoke. Twenty-eight-year-old banker Guy Mettrick declares: 'I would never go back to ready-to-wear…. Tim [Evereſt] is brilliant at interpreting your ideas. You juſt have to mention an outfit ſported by a ſtar in an old film and within minutes Tim has ruſtled up a drawing that exactly matches your thoughts. He has taken

the stuffiness out of going to the tailor, which
is very important for someone of my age.'

Twenty-seven-year-old foreign exchange dealer
Riccardo Borsi, looking sharp in Mark Powell's
Neo-Edwardian cut, says: 'People are looking for
more than the Armani and Boss suit. Mark has
proved that you don't have to be flash if you work
in the foreign exchange.' Solicitor John Armstrong
adds: 'I was attracted to Ozwald's work because
I like simple, gimmick-free clothes where the
emphasis is on cut and fabric rather than details.'
Richard James is endorsed by Princess Margaret's
son David Linley, who says: 'Richard gives me all
the quality and craftsmanship associated with Savile
Row but he does it with his tongue firmly in his
cheek. The result is clothes that are always amusing
but never too noticeable.' As perhaps the most
piquant tableau of new versus old Row, Linley tells
John Morgan that Richard James measured him up
astride his motorbike.

Morgan could not have written a more ringing
endorsement for the New Establishment. He and
fellow foppish scribes US *Vogue* European editor-
at-large Hamish Bowles, *GQ* bespoke editor Nick
Foulkes and fashion journalist/curator Robin Dutt
were influential supporters and promoters of Savile
Row bespoke tailoring, both old and new school.

Morgan, who famously spent his last years living a
Regency dandy life in an Albany set (an apartment
in London's historic private bachelor quarters)
filled with over sixty bespoke suits, three hundred
handmade shirts and ninety pairs of bespoke
Cleverley shoes, died in 2000, thus robbing Savile
Row of one of its greatest ambassadors. He wrote his
own epitaph to introduce the *Sunday Telegraph*'s Savile
Row story: 'Despite very modest circumstances, I
have always managed to maintain a good address
and a better wardrobe.'

Following *Vanity Fair*'s March 1997 'London
Swings Again' portrait of Boateng, Everest and
James, *W* magazine reported: 'It's been happening
for a couple of years now. Men's fashion has
become more elegant, more tailored, more body
conscious: in a word more English. Suddenly,
from Milan to Paris to New York, Savile Row
is everywhere.'

The foundations laid by the New Establishment
in the 1990s encouraged tailors such as Huntsman
head cutter Richard Anderson to open on the Row
under his own name in 2001, and former Royal
Lancer Tony Lutwyche to buy a tailor's shop on
quitting the army in 2000. Like Norton & Sons'
Patrick Grant, Lutwyche is an entrepreneur tailor.
Beginning his bespoke life as a 'suiter on a scooter'

Opposite: Jude Law tailored by Kilgour and
Gwyneth Paltrow wearing Vivienne Westwood
attend the 2004 London premiere of *Sky
Captain and the World of Tomorrow*.

Above: David and Victoria Beckham
photographed in Manhattan in 2008.
Beckham's three-piece suit is tailored
by Timothy Everest.

visiting a largely City clientele in the Square Mile, Lutwyche became a cult in Soho amongst the show-business and media set who populate the quarter. I recall going to interview him at private club Soho House. The girl on reception asked how to spell his name and a very cool customer standing next to me opened his coat and flashed a Lutwyche Bespoke label.

The entrepreneur tailors front the business, employ the talent and have an eye for opportunity. In 2006, Lutwyche bought Cheshire Clothing, the only tailoring factory in the UK that can boast 100 per cent 'Made in England', and rebranded it Cheshire Bespoke. The factory makes made-to-measure for over 50 per cent of the bespoke houses on Savile Row. Lutwyche is to be applauded for mounting the campaign to protect 'Made in England', but are factory-mades the future for Savile Row? Suffice to say, Cheshire Bespoke produces very fine English tailoring, but the Savile Row Bespoke Association still upholds the rule that only suits made within the golden mile are true to the organization's name and aims.

The glamour that the New Establishment tailors shone on Savile Row encouraged fashion brands such as Evisu, Lanvin and Abercrombie & Fitch to open on the street. In 2006, the 30th anniversary year of bespoke house Anthony J. Hewitt, Evisu moved into its No. 9 Savile Row premises and for two years Hewitt managing director Ravi Tailor continued to cut in rooms at the back of the shop. Hewitt had strong links with fashion; cutters Tailor and James Levett had lent designers Georgina Godley, Paul Smith, Koji Tatsuno and Richard James their bespoke expertise. But Evisu's planned bespoke collaboration with Tailor never materialized, and in 2008 Anthony J. Hewitt decamped to L. G. Wilkinson's magnificent Georgian townhouse on St George Street. By 2009, L. G. Wilkinson had been in the shop for ninety years. Present guv'nor David Wilkinson is building a new model of Savile Row premises and has since invited Denman & Goddard (a house famed for its links with Eton College) and talented ex-Henry Poole cutter Joshua Byrne to trade from the building. Of course, 'sitting' tailors are nothing new. The challenge in having four autonomous companies under one roof is how to share skills, and perhaps tailors, but not customers.

Group portrait shot by Guy Hills for a *Financial Times* 'How to Spend It' feature in September 2007. From left to right: Andrew Musson (Davies & Son), Gordon Alsleben (Huntsman), Malcolm Plews (Welsh & Jefferies), Matthew Farnes, Richard James, John Hitchcock (Anderson & Sheppard), Patrick Grant (Norton & Sons), Ozwald Boateng, Simon Cundey (Henry Poole & Co.), Michael Skinner (Dege & Skinner), Kathryn Sargent (Gieves & Hawkes) and Richard Anderson.

'I want to make men look beautiful. For me the best compliment is when one of my clients goes out and someone says to him, "You look beautiful in that suit." What other compliment do you want?'

Ozwald Boateng

OZWALD BOATENG
-- Established 1995

First impressions of statuesque Anglo-Ghanaian 'bespoke couturier' Ozwald Boateng inspire some of the most florid Fleet Street prose. In 1996, *International Herald Tribune* fashion editor Suzy Menkes was moved to write: 'There was only one collection as far as I could see which combined wearability with terminal brilliance. It came from our very own Ozwald Boateng.' *Independent* writer John Walsh famously described him as 'the coolest man on earth' in a 1998 encounter, adding: 'In the British fashion world, he sticks out like a great African flamingo in a field of discreetly competent thrushes and crows.'

Like Beau Brummell, Ozwald Boateng sensationalized Savile Row bespoke tailoring and focused the world's attention back on the suit. True, the Beau endorsed understatement while Boateng's vision was glorious Technicolor. But both of these Savile Row peacocks ruffled the feathers of rivals because their influence woke the world up to the seductive power of fine tailoring.

Boateng thinks and works on a grand scale, inviting the inevitable booms and busts that this buccaneering attitude usually entails. His mindset is as far removed from traditional Savile Row as

Hollywood is from the House of Lords. Who else would close the Row to host a forty-five-model open-air 'Savile Row Street Party' catwalk show in 2002, or star in an eight-part *House of Boateng* documentary commissioned for Robert Redford's Sundance Channel? Not content to build a fashion empire, his 'Made in Africa' foundation also makes him a player in the political and economic life of that continent.

But his showmanship and self-appointed ambassadorial role tend to obscure Boateng's skill and significance as a tailor. When he arrived on the Row (or, strictly speaking, just off it, at No. 9 Vigo Street) in November 1995, only Richard James had blazed the trail for fashion on Savile Row. Bespoke had not been relevant outside the closed circle of old faithful customers for more than a decade. Working with the tension between fashion design and bespoke craftsmanship, Boateng re-energized (if not revolutionized) the street.

'I call what I do Bespoke Couture because it brings design and craft together,' he says. 'I'm about modernizing tradition. I went to Savile Row to modernize it because I really believed in it. Why would I want to be there if I didn't have total respect

His own greatest model: Ozwald Boateng photographed for *Drama* magazine in 2009.

for the heritage? I am one million per cent correct.
Even the cloth I use is correct. It's just that I've
translated it and made it a little more modern. If
you can just get past the colour and look at the style
of my suits, they are incredibly traditional. There
will always be a tension between a creative person
who doesn't cut and the craftsman. The craftsman
is thinking in mathematical proportions: working
from the measurements. A creative person would
look at the aesthetic balance, what the eye is drawn
to. The creative person would try to alter those
measurements to create a more beautiful suit.'

Boateng nailed his colours to the Savile Row
mast before he had even opened his Vigo Street
shop. The real launch of Bespoke Couture came
in summer 1994, when Boateng presented an
on-schedule runway show at Paris Men's Fashion
Week. Friends such as artist and style icon Duggie
Fields modelled lean, 1960s Modernist suits in
scarlet, Yves Klein blue and Boateng's signature
purple mohair. 'I invested every penny I had and
gambled but I believed in what I was doing. English
menswear deserved recognition,' he says.

What Savile Row failed to grasp when Boateng
first arrived in 1995 was his sense of predestination.
He had first walked the Row in 1987, aged nineteen,
and encountered Tommy Nutter. 'The reason he
came out of his shop was to check out what I was
wearing,' says Boateng. 'It was this three-quarter-
length grey flannel suit; very high closing. The waist
was sculpted, cut like an hourglass. In those days the
shoulder line was wider. I was wearing a white shirt
and a polka-dot tie and highly polished Church's
shoes. That was the look.' Entirely self-taught,
Boateng literally sold suits off his back in these early
years, eventually opening a studio on Portobello
Road in 1991, aged twenty-three. 'I was so goddamn
cheeky then,' he says. 'I could tell you about the
fabric, the buttonhole, the cut. I could tell you
sweet poetry like you'd never heard. You would have
been running to my studio so that I could make
you a suit.' Even when Boateng was just nineteen,
Nutter had seen something of his younger self in
him and invited him into the shop. 'He showed me
the beauty of tailoring and from that point I was
inspired to work in the same way.'

Despite running his bespoke operation from
No. 12a Savile Row since 2002, Boateng's dream
to own a shopfront on the Row only came true in
2007, when he took over the majestic corner site
vacated by Anderson & Sheppard at No. 30. In
2009, Boateng said: 'When I left Tommy Nutter's

Opposite, clockwise from
top left: Paul Bettany
attends London's *GQ* Men
of the Year awards in
2004 tailored by Bespoke
Couture, with wife
Jennifer Connelly.

David Bowie performs
at the 2002 VH1/*Vogue*
Fashion Awards wearing
Bespoke Couture.

Daniel Day-Lewis and wife
Rebecca Miller attend the
2003 Oscars. Day-Lewis's
cocktail suit was re-cut
for 'The London Cut'
exhibition, Florence,
in 2007.

Bespoke Couture bad boy
Billy Zane adjusts Lawrence
Fishburne's bow tie at the
2002 Bespoke Couture
show in New York.

Dame Vivienne Westwood
and Ozwald Boateng
photographed in 2006.

shop, I could see Anderson & Sheppard across the street and I had what can only be described as a light going on. I knew I was going to open a shop on Savile Row.' The sense of predestination stretches even further back. In the archive at No. 30 is a small photograph of Boateng aged five. It is his birthday party and he is wearing a double-breasted 'Bespoke Couture purple' suit tailored by his mother.

Boateng's relationship with prestige customers is alien to Savile Row's code of silence. That said, his style is so identifiable that it doesn't take Suzy Menkes to spot Bespoke Couture at five thousand paces. The impact of his high media profile provoked one tailor to say to *Sunday Times* 'Style' writer Rebecca Lowthorpe: 'He'd be dead in the water without his celebs.' Teasing truth out of the malice, it would be correct to say that the Boateng cut and colour palette are pleasing to men who welcome attention. In 2005, the Victoria & Albert Museum hosted a retrospective fashion show honouring him that justified *Sunday Express* writer Michelle Stanistreet's assertion that 'Ozwald Boateng has done more to revitalize gentlemen's suits than any other fashion designer'.

Fortunately for Boateng, his suits do not disappear once they leave the shop: they are more

than likely to be photographed in Cannes or Hollywood, as worn by Samuel L. Jackson, Keanu Reeves, Jamie Foxx, Daniel Day-Lewis, Will Smith, Mick Jagger, Billy Zane, Jude Law, Russell Crowe, Jensen Button, Paul Bettany or friend and mentor Laurence Fishburne. An oft-repeated critique that can't be denied is that Boateng is his own greatest model, and there are few tailors on the Row (with the exception of Nick Hart and his front-of-house boys Petter and Anthony) who can say the same. Boateng does, however, dispute that his suits are tailored for his physique. 'I've got a way of knocking inches off the waist from the way I cut. I can give you longer legs and a shorter torso, hide your stomach and give you the illusion of a six-pack.'

Confidence in his creativity is not something Boateng is lacking. Wisdom has come after a succession of ill-timed body blows that could (and briefly did) knock him off his perch. In 1997, New Labour came to power and Boateng became a totem for Tony Blair's multicultural Cool Britannia. He told *The Times*, 'The concept of Cool Britannia? I don't know who is responsible for it but if you're talking about optimism, if that's what it really means, being optimistic about the future and saying creativity and British design is good then you've got

to look at what's happening abroad. A lot of foreign companies are taking on British talent.'

By April 1998, under the headline 'Chill East Wind Hits Cool Britannia', the *Sunday Times* reported: 'Cool Britannia may have lost its swagger. Ozwald Boateng, the favoured designer of Blairite ministers and young pop stars, has gone bust.' But what is striking about Boateng's career on and off Savile Row is the fact that when he comes back, he comes back stronger, faster and louder. It is interesting to see how Boateng has tempered his early exuberance by looking at more than a decade of Bespoke Couture on the catwalk. Apart from brief forays onto the Paris runway by Gieves and Kilgour, Boateng is the only Savile Row house to have consistently shown biannual collections in Paris and Milan. His own label was shown from 1996 to 2008 and his collections as creative director of Givenchy Homme from 2004 to 2007.

'[LVMH CEO] Bernard Arnault came to the table with three offers,' says Boateng, who also had interest from the Richemont Group to revive Sulka and Dunhill. 'I was offered Kenzo, Givenchy Homme and Dior Homme. My decision was made by the desire to keep my own label going. I had worked too hard to build my brand.' On his appointment at Givenchy in 2003, the temptation would have been to bring the Bespoke Couture aesthetic to Givenchy Homme, a house that had no references other than the immaculate Monsieur de Givenchy. Looking back at his Givenchy collections, it is impressive to see a softer, more romantic silhouette that relied less on sharp urban suits, shirts and ties and moved towards a Riviera mood of European glamour. At the time, he said, 'It's my time now. For LVMH to say Savile Row is where it's at is a BIG statement.'

The end of Boateng's Givenchy contract came in 2007, when he put into motion the acquisition of his first Savile Row flagship shopfront at No. 30. The store, co-designed with architect David Adjaye, is a cool, dark and handsome temple to Bespoke Couture. A spotlit dark wood catwalk stretches from Savile Row to Old Burlington Street, accessories are displayed like artworks in glass boxes and walls of shirts, ties and suits lit like religious icons are displayed in black lacquered cubes. The bespoke room is a Bond villain's dream, secreted behind mirrored sliding doors. The sprawling basement below is home to Boateng's lair as well as his design and bespoke tailoring operation.

Of the global economic meltdown in 2009, Boateng said, 'Like it or not, the deck is changing. The world is changing. Will there be a place for bespoke tailoring? Absolutely. Will Savile Row survive? You bet it will. I have consistently invested my time, my energy, my creativity and my money in talking up this street. I have banged that drum. I have PR-ed it like you wouldn't believe. Why do I continue to do it? Because Savile Row is worth saving.'

Ozwald Boateng stands outside Buckingham Palace in 2006 having just received the OBE from the Queen.

Ozwald Boateng's flagship store at No. 30 Savile Row.

'There are no average men on Savile Row.
Every man is unique.'
RICHARD ANDERSON

RICHARD ANDERSON

-- ESTABLISHED 2001

I n the foreword to Richard Anderson's 2009 tailoring memoir *Bespoke: Savile Row Ripped and Smoothed*, US *Vogue* editor-at-large André Leon Talley writes: 'One of life's greatest pleasures is to have the opportunity to experience a bespoke suit from a fine English firm such as Richard Anderson's.... To be dressed in a suit cut by Richard gives me empowerment and confidence; I show the world my best side in his exquisite bespoke.'

Talley's is one of the most knowledgeable minds in the fashion industry. For him to endorse Anderson is a powerful statement about this bespoke house founded in 2001. Richard Anderson is not in the same school as designer-tailors Ozwald Boateng and Richard James. Working his way from seventeen-year-old apprentice at Huntsman in 1982 to head cutter, he has the craft of bespoke written into his DNA. When he and co-director Brian Lishak left Huntsman, they took seventy years of combined knowledge to No. 13 Savile Row and became the first new pure bespoke tailoring name on the Row since Edward Sexton in 1981.

Richard Anderson executes what Bryan Ferry – one of the most prolific customers of Row tailoring of his generation – calls 'the traditions of Savile Row with a modern twist'. He rigidly upholds the Huntsman cut taught to him by the maestro Colin Hammick, but is adventurous with less traditional fabrics. It is this openness to new ideas that brings a client list of men with sophisticated tastes such as Sir Ian McKellen, Sebastian Horsley, Benicio del Toro and Simon Cowell to his door.

The hugely entertaining *Bespoke: Savile Row Ripped and Smoothed* tells the story of an apprenticeship at Huntsman that could have taken place in 1882 rather than 1982, with 'young Richard' at the beck and call of great cutting duo Messrs Hammick and Hall, who call to mind Roald Dahl's Aunts Spiker and Sponge from *James and the Giant Peach* (with Anderson as the much-maligned James). But it was these gentlemen who instilled the craft and traditions of Savile Row into Richard Anderson.

Even the grandest customers would be told lugubriously that 'Mr Hall will see you now',

Above: Richard Anderson's mentor, Huntsman head cutter Colin Hammick.

Opposite: Richard Anderson photographed on Savile Row in 2008.

Richard Anderson bespoke stock models. From left to right:
navy pinstripe single-breasted suit, grey double-breasted suit
with pink windowpane check, double-breasted Cheviot tweed
suit, black sequin dinner jacket, one-button Escorial check
sports jacket and house check single-breasted overcoat.

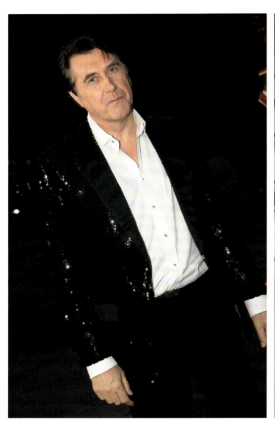

as if they were schoolboys cowering outside the headmaster's office. The chain-smoking perfectionist Mr Hammick was so fastidious that he worked to the sixteenth of an inch. As Anderson writes, 'Show me a lobotomist who can work to the sixteenth of an inch using ten-inch shears.' At 1 p.m. on the dot, the lights would be switched off, the customers asked to leave and the front door locked while the shop took an hour for lunch.

'Colin Hammick was an artist,' says Anderson. 'He was charismatic, a complete character. He could do nothing but cut a coat pattern and smoke. He couldn't drive, couldn't wind his watch, but at a cutting board no one could touch him. It was Mr Hammick who developed the Huntsman cut as we know it and who taught me. What he cut was a combination of the dinner jacket and the riding coat for a lounge suit. The single-button fastening was his way of simplifying the silhouette and keeping the line of the coat unbroken. The coat was slim and fitted like a hacking coat with

armholes cut high to allow movement while keeping the collar and lapels close.'

It is a Savile Row tradition in the cutting rooms that apprentices have to earn the trust of their 'masters'. 'I loved going to work every day and slowly learning the craft,' says Anderson. 'Some people were reluctant to teach you. You had to earn their trust.' The cutter's choice of 'heir' is as finely considered as the line of succession of a royal family. You may not wish to bring a young cutter on too early and, conversely, cannot leave it too late or the secrets learnt will be lost. Anderson was Mr Hall's apprentice in the early 1980s but, under the tutelage of Mr Hammick, he went on to cut 70 per cent of Huntsman's bespoke production by 1995 (the year after Hammick retired).

Looking at photographs of Mr Hammick modelling his own cut for Huntsman, he is Huntsman's greatest advertisement. Compare them to photographs of Anderson modelling his interpretation of the Hammick cut and you can hazard a guess why Mr Hammick chose him. He,

Above, left: Bryan Ferry wearing a bespoke black sequin dinner jacket tailored by Richard Anderson.

Above, right: Richard Anderson bespoke customer André Leon Talley, US *Vogue* editor-at-large, attends Gucci's Spring/Summer 2009 show in Milan with editor-in-chief Anna Wintour.

Richard Anderson drafts a pattern at his cutting board at No. 13 Savile Row.

like the handsome Messers Nutter and Sexton in the 1970s and latterly Ozwald Boateng, effectively sells the suits off his back. A hazard of this approach is the customer never quite looking as good as his tailor in the same suit. 'Our job as cutters is to make anyone look better than they are,' says Anderson. 'That's what we are here for. If we can't achieve that, we are not much better than ready-to-wear.'

In 2001, Richard Anderson opened under his own name with co-director Brian Lishak. Both agreed it should be the head cutter's name above the door. But with over half a century of service to bespoke tailoring, Mr Lishak had sufficient pedigree to reassure traditional customers while Anderson attracted new ones. As a salesman and a raconteur he is second to none, as his reminiscences about Huntsman demonstrate.

'Who were my favourite clients? Katie Hepburn was unique: one of the best. We even made bespoke denim for her. Omar Sharif had very, very good taste. I recall that we made all his tailcoats and his dinner suits for the premiere of *Lawrence of Arabia*.

Stewart Granger was the most loyal Hollywood customer. I'd see him in LA well after he'd turned eighty, although in his prime old Mr Packer had to tell him to mind his language in front of the cutters. Bing Crosby I used to see at his home in San Francisco. Clark Gable was a good customer, as were Rex Harrison, Laurence Olivier and Peter Sellers.'

Though trained in the old school – not least being of an age to have travelled on his early US trips on board the *Queen Mary* – Brian Lishak has a young, exuberant eye for 'jazzy' orders, such as Sebastian Horsley's summer 2009 request for a ruby red velvet three-piece, or Anderson's production of stock models such as a bright tangerine pea coat tailored from snooker table baize. 'The changes, sea and rail to air, propeller plane to jet and so on have been enormous,' he says, 'but what remains constant is the demand for quality, style and individuality: in a nutshell, bespoke tailoring. Savile Row must in my opinion champion forward thinking while remaining relevant to the demands of the bespoke customer.'

'When we first came into Savile Row, ready-to-wear was what we were about and bespoke the icing on the cake. We have changed our point of view.'
RICHARD JAMES

RICHARD JAMES

-- Established 1992

'There is a new character on Savile Row who is proving a worthy successor to Mr Nutter,' wrote Robin Dutt in the *Sunday Times* 'Style' supplement in June 1995. Time has necessitated an amendment to this statement. Tommy Nutter's golden age was brief: between 1969 and 1976, before his relationship with head cutter Edward Sexton broke down irrevocably. Richard James and his co-founder Sean Dixon have quietly and confidently built their business from little more than a shoebox in 1992 to a vast glass-fronted corner site on Savile Row that opened in 2000, followed by an elegant three-storey Clifford Street bespoke townhouse in 2007. Their ready-to-wear collection sells worldwide and is supplemented by shoes, accessories, perfume and leather goods. Richard James Bespoke is one of the slickest operations on the Row.

Dixon and James are a fine example of a business and creative partnership that has timed its growth to perfection, seeing bespoke progress from 'icing on the cake' to outselling the ready-to-wear shop by 2009. 'We did not set out to establish a bespoke business,' says James, 'but some of our clients wanted bespoke so we did it in our way.

But I will say this. Sean and I were respectful of the craft of Savile Row and rapidly got to a stage when 80 per cent of the cloths tailored at Richard James were exclusive to us.' 'We must be one of the most successful bespoke businesses on Savile Row at the moment,' says Dixon, 'and I think that's because we approach it in a more modern way. The guys in our bespoke shop are in their thirties. They know about fashion as well as bespoke. They make you feel comfortable rather than pressurizing or trying to estimate your net worth.'

Richard James Bespoke is one of the most elegant interiors on (or, more accurately, just off) the Row: exposed brickwork behind sunken showcases, lilac walls, mirrored changing rooms and darkly stained floorboards suggest a reassuringly rich but contemporary outlook. James was the first bespoke tailor to advertise in the men's style monthlies and the first to art direct a TV advertisement. In the short film screened for the first (and last) time in London cinemas, a young man is shown dressing himself beautifully in suit, shirt and tie before jumping to his death from the top of a high-rise building. The caption reads: 'Richard James: Clothes for all occasions'.

Richard James photographed by John Spinks. 'The art of tailoring is doing what the customer wants,' says James. 'I think we introduced bespoke to a lot of people and that we have made it more accessible.'

The advertisement was banned but the point that bespoke was dangerous and edgy hit the bullseye. It was to James that the beautiful people of the 1990s came to be suited, such as David Beckham, Paul Bettany, Daniel Craig, Jude Law, Tom Cruise, Guy Ritchie, David Furnish and Hugh Grant.

James was the bridge for fashionable men between Yohji Yamamoto, Comme des Garçons and Jean-Paul Gaultier, and the New Establishment tailors. 'We were helped by the men's style council, such as Hamish Bowles, Mario Testino, Patrick Cox and Rupert Everett,' says James. 'I had an understanding of fashion which was missing in Savile Row because I could empathize with people who had always previously worn designer clothes.' Sean Dixon identifies the gearshift thus: 'In the eighties it was a question of "Who designed your suit?" We knew we'd succeeded when a Richard James suit invited comments such as "You look well," or "You've lost weight," or "You look younger."' Long and lean, the Richard James suit block was an exaggeration of the hourglass

Huntsman cut. In their first year of trading (1992), *Esquire*'s Nick Sullivan wrote that 'even the most fashion-aware customers can find James's signature look rather unnerving at first. Cut close to the chest and flared over the hips with long double vents, the jackets are throwbacks to a murky golden age of British tailoring.'

In 2000, according to James, 'We really went for it. We took the lease on the biggest shop on the Row and installed wraparound windows that showed the world what we were doing inside. It was the opposite of the traditional Savile Row tailor and that's not a criticism. But we didn't have scary animal heads on the wall or old chesterfields.' No. 29 Savile Row's windows became a stomping ground for London's paparazzi eager to shoot Madonna, Gianni Versace, Elton John, Robbie Williams or Pete Doherty through the goldfish-bowl windows.

The Independent's Cole Morton reported: 'It's scissors at dawn in Savile Row,' quoting one traditional tailor from Welsh & Jefferies calling Richard James 'parasites who don't know one end

In Spring/Summer 2000, Richard James design director Toby Lamb and photographer John Spinks commenced a series of award-winning advertising campaigns that redefined Savile Row tailoring for a fashion-literate new generation. From left: Spring/Summer 2006, Autumn/Winter 2006, Spring/Summer 2007, Autumn/Winter 2007.

Autumn/Winter 2005 Richard James advertising campaign.

Hugh Grant tailored in Richard James Bespoke, photographed with Elizabeth Hurley (in Versace Couture) and Prince Charles (Anderson & Sheppard) at the De Beers/Versace 'Diamonds Are Forever' party at Syon House in 1999.

The Richard James Bespoke block is an exaggeration of the hourglass Huntsman cut. Nowhere was its ability to make a man walk taller apparent than when worn by Tom Cruise at the 1997 Oscars (photographed with then-wife Nicole Kidman in Christian Dior Couture).

of a needle from another'. Picking up on James's comment that he made suits for 'It boys', the tailor retorted: 'The traditional tailors of Savile Row are making suits for It men, the ones who pay the It boys' wages. They say Savile Row was dead until they arrived. Well, some of the companies along here have been dying for the last 200 years and will continue to die for the next 200.'

But some of the Savile Row royal family defended James. Comparing him to Tommy Nutter, Kilgour chairman Hugh Holland told *Arena* in June 2002: 'They were the forerunners of the modern tailors of the 1990s. Like [Nutters], many on the Row were narked by them coming in without the traditional skills. But they had an eye for colour, style and PR, things that the Row was in need of. Without them the Row wouldn't be so much in its coffin as having the lid nailed down.' James says Hardy Amies, by then the grand old man of Savile Row, 'was marvellous. I think he liked what we were trying to achieve. I well recall his chauffeur-driven car pulling up outside Richard James and Sir Hardy emerging like Lady Bracknell. He'd cast

a lugubrious eye over the bright pink and acid green jackets in our windows before shaking his head at us in mock disbelief. And then he smiled.'

Richard James set a new blueprint for tailors aspiring to open on Savile Row; one that doubtless inspired Kilgour's Carlo Brandelli and Spencer Hart's founder Nick Hart to unapologetically develop ready-to-wear and made-to-measure while never losing sight of the superiority of bespoke. As James says, 'I'm the first person to stand up and say our ready-mades are really lovely. They are not a necessary evil to prop up bespoke. They are lovely garments.' But of his bespoke he adds, 'The shape is almost more Savile Row than Savile Row. It does everything it's supposed to; it's waisted, it's skirted, the shoulders are natural but the armholes are very high to give you length'. The opening of Richard James Bespoke in 2007 was 'a grand gesture and a labour of love that's saying bespoke has a future and that Richard James is committed to its future'.

'Funny,' he muses, 'in some respects you were right to christen us the New Establishment. We have become terribly respectable, haven't we?'

The interior of Richard James Bespoke at No. 19 Clifford Street (formerly the Henry Poole & Co. livery department).

Richard James celebrates Christmas 2007 on Savile Row in his own inimitable style with a cluster of giant disco balls.

SAVILE ROW IN FASHION

The Row Renaissance

D espite post-war privations, Savile Row's princes, bankers, actors and politicians led male fashion until well into the 1950s, when bright young thing John Stephen invaded Carnaby Street with a string of pop boutiques that made London men's fashion swing. Stores with names like Mod Male, Dandy Fashions and Male W1 proposed gender-bending looks such as the male mini-kilt twenty years before Jean-Paul Gaultier. In the mid-1960s, Portobello boutique I Was Lord Kitchener's Valet sold second-hand military tailoring such as the Hussar's tunic worn by Jimi Hendrix. This fashion sadly destroyed uniforms that today would be considered Savile Row relics.

In 1965, psychedelic, druggy, clubby King's Road 'bisexual boutique' Granny Takes a Trip stole Carnaby Street's cool. Aged fifteen, co-founder John Pearse had apprenticed as a coat maker for Dover Street bespoke tailor Hawes & Curtis. 'We were upstairs in the workroom which was like Fagin's den,' he says. 'Those guys were all kind of Mod-y and young even though we were making for the Duke of Edinburgh or the King of Thailand. It gave me a good grounding for the flamboyance to come.' Flamboyances at Granny Takes a Trip included William Morris tapestry jackets tailored for Ossie Clark and George Harrison, velvet trousers cut indecently tight and mad floral silk blouses. 'Everyone wants to talk to me about Jimi Hendrix and Bob Dylan and Mick Jagger and The Beatles,' says Pearse, who returned to bespoke tailoring in the 1980s, opening a shop on Soho's Meard Street. 'It's all a blur, really.'

By 1967, Savile Row had hit back. As Paul Gorman writes in *The Look*, 'The Menswear Association of Britain – which had previously praised Carnaby Street for having liberated male fashion – now condemned it with one conference delegate urging "We must be guided by high fashion, the sort that makes us look like men not perverted peacocks."' And yet it was 'perverted peacock' Tommy Nutter who brought fashion and bespoke tailoring together on Savile Row in 1969. The six brief years when Nutter and head cutter Edward Sexton rocked the Row are remembered to this day as the street's high fashion high-water mark. Designers as diverse as Tom Ford, Thom Browne, Ralph Lauren and Paul Smith have subtly referred to Nutter's roped shoulder, broad lapel, tight pocketless trouser and sinuous flare in recent collections. Vintage Nutter is almost impossible to find because the great customers Elton John, Mick

'Whereas the traditional Savile Row tailor is still doing well by doing nothing to change his image, Tommy Nutter is doing well by doing something.'

US Men's Wear (1971)

The genius of Nutter was the combination of Tommy's imagination and Edward Sexton's hands: the craft of Savile Row tested by the creativity of young peacock. Two early original Nutter sketches owned by Christopher Tarling.

Rolling Stones lead singer Mick Jagger shows off his assets in a closely cut Tommy Nutter suit on honeymoon with Bianca in Venice in 1971.

and Bianca Jagger, Cilla Black, Peter Brown, Lord Montagu of Beaulieu and Prince Rajpípla will never sell.

'Tommy was a trendsetter and the first bespoke tailor who led fashion,' says Prince Rajpípla. 'He had two different types of client: the entertainers who wanted to be photographed and the fellows like me who wanted the thrills sans frills. It was one thing to have your clothes admired and another entirely to be stared at. I wanted classically cut Savile Row suits with that little extra *je ne sais quoi*.' The Prince's collection includes the classic Nutter ivory three-piece trimmed with grosgrain and a black satin Nehru-collared dinner jacket that 'Tommy sketched as I stood in front of him', with onyx and diamond family buttons. 'The years between 1965 and 1975 were the only decade where men took over from women as the focus of fashion,' says the Prince. 'I recall Tommy showing me a wildly outlandish cloth. I said, "Blue and green should never be seen." Quick as a flash he replied, "Clashing coordinates are the fashion."'

It is a truth universally acknowledged that a bespoke tailor's only limitation is the customer's imagination. Sufficient men of fashion were

'Nuttered-up' and photographed to attract a new young generation to Savile Row. When Nutter left the house that bore his name in 1976, Sexton and fellow cutters Roy Chittleborough and Joe Morgan continued to dazzle at Nutters of Savile Row until they, too, parted company in 1981, and Sexton opened up under his own name. 'The bespoke trade in the eighties considered itself above fashion,' says Richard Anderson co-founder Brian Lishak. 'At Huntsman and Wells of Mayfair we did very well in the eighties but the look was so much more classical, conservative even, than the Nutters era.' Former Kilgour creative director Carlo Brandelli believes a customer is not in a position to break the glass ceiling of conservatism until he has ordered at least ten bespoke suits. Of the 10,000 bespoke suits cut on Savile Row annually, only the low hundreds will be what Anderson & Sheppard head cutter Mr Hitchcock calls a 'brave choice'. The £3,000 average price for bespoke and the time invested (twelve weeks minimum) inevitably make customers err on the side of caution: a classic grey flannel two-piece, a navy chalk stripe or perhaps Prince of Wales check. For most, the investment is too great to be at the mercy of fashion.

Henry Poole & Co. proves that traditional Savile Row can compete with Carnaby Street: models sent by Poole's to San Francisco for British Fashion Week in 1971.

Inspired by the film *Atonement*, for which he tailored the leading men's suits in a Tommy Nutter take on the 1930s, Timothy Everest art directs a 'Bentley Boys' shoot for *The Rake* in 2009.

What the New Establishment tailors of the early 1990s did was to reposition bespoke at the pinnacle of fashion, encouraging devil-may-care customers to greater excesses. The Savile Row suit was not dying but it had settled down into comfortable middle age in some of the more traditional houses. Fit without finesse was what Savile Row soul boy Nick Hart objected to. In 2001, he opened Spencer Hart at No. 36 Savile Row: a dark wood labyrinth with hand-stitched leather floors that had the illicit glamour of a speakeasy. In 2006, he told the *Financial Times* that 'there is a lot of snobbery from people who are sometimes producing very mediocre work. Playing devil's advocate, a perfectly fitted suit in a very expensive cloth in the wrong style, colour, pattern and trimmings is still a horrible garment. It just fits well.'

Equally provocative was Kilgour's creative director Carlo Brandelli who, with the blessing of managing director Hugh Holland, had given the house an extreme makeover in 2003 that refashioned it like a slick, glossy cover of *Wallpaper** magazine. Calling the Row 'worse than draconian', Brandelli used his pole position double-fronted flagships to show off a one-button, semi-structured suit block invariably cut in navy or white. Like Boateng, Everest, James and Hart, it was Kilgour's

ambition to be the first global luxury goods brand to emerge from Savile Row.

Brandelli will be the first to admit that he pushed Savile Row away and was even more aloof than old Anderson & Sheppard. But he had a point of view that was firm to the point of fetishizing the one-button suit, and the company was rumoured to be valued at £12 million when Mr Holland sold it in 2008. Brandelli's exit in 2009 and the return of cloth bales and tape-measures around the necks of elderly shop staff mystify Savile Row, as Kilgour appears to have conceded the race to be a global fashion brand and is contented once more to be a bespoke tailor. The same cannot be said for Ozwald Boateng, Richard James and Spencer Hart, who continue to compete for the largest flagship, the biggest headlines and the men of fashion who are their roving ambassadors, such as David Beckham, Robbie Williams and Tom Cruise.

Maybe the most intriguing new character on Savile Row is Dashing Tweeds founder Guy Hills, who has commissioned over ten bespoke houses to cut a wild personal wardrobe of capes, plus-two shooting suits, Flare Line City three-pieces and yachting blazers: all made using light-reflective, sometimes psychedelic tweeds co-designed and woven by Kirsty McDougall. A mad mix of Bertie

Dashing Tweeds urban cycling suit, tailored by Russell Howarth from light-reflective, Teflon-coated tweed co-designed by Guy Hills and Kirsty McDougall as inspired by London's yellow line road markings.

Dashing Tweeds' 'Centre Point' Bauhaus-inspired design, tailored by Huntsman and modelled for *The Rake* by performer Ian Bruce of The Correspondents in 2009.

Wooster dressed by Bunny Roger's tailor, fashion photographer Hills is challenging cutters to incorporate Edwardian military, safari and court tailoring techniques into contemporary fashion tailoring. 'In terms of colour, Beau Brummell stopped the colourful peacock male in his tracks,' says Hills. 'Tweeds were left as almost the sole domain for colour in clothing, but drabness had set in, and not since the seventies have fabulously coloured tweeds been acceptable. I feel now that men want to wear more exciting clothes in terms of cut, colour and cloth. By leading the way with very colourful bold statements, Dashing Tweeds sets the bar at the highest of dandy levels and allows others to rise up and spread their wings without fearing ridicule.'

Hills is one of a new generation on the Row who were born into a fashion-literate age but have rediscovered Savile Row as the last bastion of true personal expression and creativity in clothes. He leads by example. Similarly, a child's size Prince of Wales check blazer in the window of Anderson & Sheppard made to celebrate *GQ* magazine's 20th anniversary caught the eye of Kate Moss. Working with Mr Hitchcock, Miss Moss ordered a collection of shrunken blazers with three-quarter-length sleeves that she dressed with her collection of vintage buttons. Kate Moss is the most obvious example of the new school of Savile Row customer who has the fashion intelligence and personal creativity necessary to know how to inspire a bespoke tailor.

EDWARD SEXTON

-- ESTABLISHED 1969

Tommy Nutter, the louche, loveable *petit prince* of fashionable bespoke in the 1970s, hangs like a bat in the minds of Savile Row's tailors old and new. 'There isn't a day when I don't think of Tommy,' says Edward Sexton, the man who co-founded Nutters of Savile Row in 1969 and keeps the flame burning fifty years hence. As Sexton tells it, 'Tommy was very handsome, very charismatic, very shy, very boyish, very appealing to everybody of either sex. He was a cool, laid-back guy and Savile Row didn't get it. The bitchy old queens said we wouldn't last six months but what they didn't get was the fact that we were very respectful towards the tradition and workmanship of Savile Row.'

Nutter and Sexton began a revolution on the Row, drawing a charmed circle of late 1960s swingers such as Mick and Bianca, John and Yoko, Justin and Twiggy, Hardy Amies, Lord Montagu of Beaulieu and the Duke of Bedford to a house that drenched bespoke tailoring with sex appeal and contemporary cuts such as spread-eagled peak lapels, roped shoulders, wasp waists and trousers that cut tight into the crotch then cascaded into a flare of unprecedented majesty. Though Sexton's cuts of Dashing Tweeds cloth are effervescent,

no house has since equalled the pyrotechnics ignited by Nutter and Sexton.

Valentine's Day 1969 saw the opening of Nutters of Savile Row at No. 35a. Many consider it the date when Youthquake fashion finally arrived on the Row. Languid, lean and seductive, the Nutter silhouette dreamed up by Tommy and cut by Edward after they met at traditional tailor Donaldson, Williams & Ward rocked Savile Row.

Left: A rare candid photograph of Tommy Nutter and Edward Sexton outside the Sunset Melrose Hotel, Los Angeles, in 1974.

Opposite: Elton John's stage costumes allowed Tommy Nutter's sartorial imagination to soar. Sir Elton remains one of Savile Row's most loyal customers. On a single visit to Richard James, he and the late designer Gianni Versace spent $64,000. This early 1970s portrait was taken by the great Norman Parkinson.

Tommy Nutter
photographed in Nutters
of Savile Row in 1970.

Nutter fell into fashion with time, place and people in perfect alignment. A month before the shop opened, The Beatles had played their last live concert on the rooftop of the Apple building at No. 3 Savile Row. Apple executive Peter Brown was Tommy's lover and primary backer. 'I was running Apple at the time,' says Brown. 'The Beatles knew Tommy and liked him a lot so it wasn't a big stretch to have three of them walk across Abbey Road [for the infamous September 1969 album cover] wearing early Nutter suits. Our best friends were [Mersey Beat pop princess] Cilla Black and her fiancé Bobby Willis. They and our friend [House of Lords principal clerk] James Vallance White wanted Tommy to develop his talent and, let's face it, we were all starting to wear bright colours and nobody on Savile Row would cut a suit in anything other than charcoal grey or navy blue pinstripe.'

As Brown tells it, 'Tommy had an incredible eye. We knew we wanted to wear something different and he instinctively knew what was right

Right; Polaroid portraits of Tommy Nutter, Bianca Jagger and model Ingrid Boulting taken at film director John Schlesinger's party in 1974. Unseen since that year, the Polaroids were published in the re-launch issue of *Pop* magazine in 2009.

Opposite, clockwise from top left: One of the defining photographs of 1969: Cilla Black's wedding at Marylebone Registry Office. She wears a red velvet Granny Takes a Trip mini dress while husband Bobby Willis, Tommy Nutter and his lover/backer Peter Brown are 'Nuttered-up' in sharp navy single-breasted suits with full-blown red rose buttonholes.

Model Twiggy and Justin de Villeneuve photographed in 1973. Twiggy's check trouser suit displays Nutter and Sexton's virtuoso clash of textures and patterns, creating a patchwork of tweeds, braids and stripes that by Savile Row standards were nothing short of anarchic.

The Beatles play their last live gig on the roof of the Apple building at No. 3 Savile Row in 1969: a 'happening' that many of the tailors still remember today. Both Paul McCartney and John Lennon are wearing Tommy Nutter suits.

for the times and for the glamorous set he was dressing. He wasn't a cutter? Well, nor was Coco Chanel but it was her vision that changed the course of fashion history.'

'I never had to think twice about investing in Tommy and Edward,' says Cilla Black. 'It was like a marriage. Tommy had the magic and Edward was the best cutter in town. I thought he was the best cutter in the world for ladies' tailoring. I loved trouser suits and Tommy loved making them for me. I had very long legs and his high-waisted trousers and boyish jackets were perfect. Tommy cut the first white three-piece trouser suit for me for my television show; the one he later made for Bianca and Yoko and Twiggy. I do remember he hated taking the inside measurements of women's legs. The guys he didn't mind so much.'

Sexton describes the early silhouette thus: 'A little more emphasis on the shoulder, a little more expression in the chest area. The suit is of a soft construction distinguished by a high-cut armhole and rope shoulder with a distinctive collar and lapel shape and, finally, my touch of a higher waist creating the taller, slender silhouette.' While remaining utterly respectful to the craft that Sexton had honed at Kilgour, French & Stanbury and then Welsh & Jefferies, the Nutter New Look had romance, youth and edge emphasized by Nutter's reckless combinations of cloth, patterns and trims that echoed the style of Savile Row gods the Duke of Windsor and Fred Astaire.

Nutters shattered class barriers: where else on the Row would you find an earl sharing a changing room with a marine? 'If you were in the inner circle and you had talent, then no door was closed to you,' says Cilla Black. 'Tommy was definitely in the circle. Peter and Tommy used to come on holiday with Bobby and I. When we got married at the Marylebone Registry Office, Peter gave me away and Tommy was Bobby's best man. We didn't question sexuality in those days. Bobby absolutely adored Tommy and Peter.'

Christopher Simon Sykes
shoots Savile Row icon
and Rolling Stones
drummer Charlie Watts,
who is wearing a Tommy
Nutter stripe two-piece
suit on the 1975 Stones
'Tour of the Americas'.

Opposite, clockwise from
top left: A teenage Tommy
Nutter photographed in
the late 1950s.

The photograph that
explains why London
society was wild about
Tommy when he first
arrived on the Row in 1962
as shop boy at Donaldson,
Williams & Ward.

Michael 'Mr' Fish, the
Turnbull & Asser-trained
maestro of the kipper
tie (centre), who was a
contemporary and kindred
spirit of Tommy Nutter, at
a party with Christopher
Tarling (right), who
managed the Nutter
standalone shirt shop
on Savile Row.

A 1970 group portrait of
Tommy Nutter, fashion
designer Bill Gibb and
his business partner Kate
Franklin, inscribed: 'To
Tommy, Happy New Year
love from Kate & Billy'.
The Nutter grosgrain-
trimmed lapels are at
their most extreme.

Tommy Nutter is presented
to Princess Margaret at
a Claridge's Hotel fashion
gala co-hosted by Nutter
and Henry Poole & Co.
(c. 1980).

'There's no doubt that our best customers
for public relations were our gay clientele,' says
Sexton. 'Our suits were at all the private cocktail
parties from New York to Paris to London.
So Tommy had opened that door to an extent.
And could those boys dress. They had presence,
elegance, style and they were fucking handsome.
It was a scene; a real network that was gossipy,
waspish and addictive.' Early photographs of Nutter
belonging to Paul Smith Bespoke head Christopher
Tarling (a lover, friend and colleague of Tommy)
show a beautiful boy with the suggestive stare of
Joe Orton's Mr Sloane. 'Tommy was irresistibly
charming to men and women, which is rather a
talent,' says Tarling. 'He was a good-looking boy
with a naughty sense of humour and the most
incredible glamour. Of course all his clients
wanted to socialize with him. Apart from himself,
his greatest advertisement was Stewart Grimshaw,
owner/patron of Provans (the Wolseley of its
day), who looked magnificent in Tommy's tweed

suits trimmed with pink grosgrain or something
equally extravagant.'

Grimshaw ordered four identical suits with
28-inch (71-cm) waist trousers in black, purple,
coral and grey, all with tone-on-tone grosgrain
binding. 'Stewart has more Nutter suits than
all of us,' says Peter Brown. 'He would have
two pairs of trousers cut with each suit: one to
accommodate his Cuban-heeled shoes.' 'Stewart
poured himself into his suits,' says Nutter cutter
Joe Morgan, who continues to cut with immense
flair at his own house Chittleborough & Morgan.
'We would hollow the coats until they were
practically second skins with the sleeves narrowed
gauntlet-tight.'

The party at Nutters of Savile Row was over
by 1976. While Sexton embarked on his first
US tour to seduce new business in New York,
Tommy Nutter walked out for good. He was
thirty-three. Sexton kept the business (and the
name) with fellow cutters Joe Morgan and Roy

To Tommy Happy New Year & love from Billy Kate + Billy

Far left: Joe Morgan models an original Nutter suit that he cut in the early 1970s while working at the house. As he reflects, 'Tom needed a serious, business-minded person to guide him and put a break on his extravagance. He socialized with the clients, he had the flair, it was his vision but people increasingly adored Edward too, who did very, very well on the American trips.'

Left: Former Nutters cutter Roy Chittleborough, photographed for *The Rake* in 2009.

Opposite: Double-breasted wool and cashmere suit tailored by Chittleborough & Morgan in 2009.

Chittleborough. 'The problems began because Tom was a generous man surrounded by a fast group of people,' says Morgan. 'He'd take hundreds of people out for dinner and then pay the bill. Basically, he wasn't good with money.'

Peter Brown tells another story. 'I had left London to work in the States and suggested to the shareholders that we had done very nicely out of Nutters, had wonderful suits made at substantial discounts and weren't really in need of the money. So I gave my shares back to Tommy. Sadly, Tommy couldn't even count and gave away more than half, at which point Edward decided he could do a better job at running things. When Tommy left, he left his name and his reputation.' 'I regret now that Bobby didn't get involved with Nutters, but he was managing me at the time, so we signed all of our shares over to Tommy,' says Black. 'If Bobby had got involved I think Tommy's name would still be on Savile Row today.'

Sexton will fix you with blue eyes that make Sinatra's look lifeless and say: 'Tommy was a charmer but he wasn't a businessman. The economy was being crucified in 1976 and Savile

Row was dead. We needed to refinance and bring in some new business. That's why I went to America.' With what became known as 'Sexton appeal', Sexton took Manhattan in 1976, despite 'not even knowing at that stage that it was an island', and was later christened 'Savile Row's ambassador to Studio 54'. So cocksure was Sexton by 1987 that he declared – on record – of soigné 1930s-style suits tailored for the American television Barbara Hutton biopic *Poor Little Rich Girl*: 'When the actors put on these clothes, they got an erection.'

Nutter meanwhile had been offered sanctuary at Kilgour, French & Stanbury, where he stayed until in the early 1980s he opened up under his own name on Savile Row in what is now Maurice Sedwell at No. 19. Nutter alumni include Timothy Everest, John Galliano and Rowland Lowe-MacKenzie, the late PR director of Turnbull & Asser. 'At that stage, he'd forgotten more than I'll ever know,' says Everest, who has fond memories of Nutter calling him 'doll'.

'Even in the later years, Tommy still had the touch,' says Brown. 'One of the last suits he cut for me was a regular pinstripe. I wanted single-breasted and he said I couldn't have it so I let

Tommy do what he wanted. A few years later, I was having lunch with Ralph Lauren in New York. I noticed that he kept looking at my lapel. He was transfixed by it. When I finally asked him what he was looking at, Ralph said, "That lapel. It is just brilliant."'

Sexton had a career that was no less volatile, developing a ready-to-wear line for Saks Fifth Avenue in the 1980s and exiting the Row in 1990 to relocate in Knightsbridge. He has since enjoyed a major comeback in British fashion, first mentoring Stella McCartney for her early Chloe collections and, most recently, cutting the prototypes for client Bernie Ecclestone's daughter Petra's fashion tailoring collection, Form. Visiting

his Beauchamp Place studio, you are as likely to see new generation musicians Pete Doherty and James McCartney as old friends Lady Bamford or Lord Montagu of Beaulieu.

For his last hurrah, Nutter cut the cartoonish imperial purple tailcoat for Jack Nicholson's Joker in the 1989 *Batman* film. Stewart Grimshaw and Elton John continued to support him with requests for bespoke suits and stage costumes. But the booze, boys and bad luck eventually engulfed him. He died of an AIDS-related illness in 1992. Poole's chairman Angus Cundey offered the most fitting epitaph: 'Tommy Nutter saved Savile Row, really. This place was dying on its feet and he was a bit of a whirlwind that blew through and put us back on the map.'

Above: The dashing Edward Sexton takes Manhattan on one of his earliest trips to New York in 1973, where he poses on the roof of the Biltmore Hotel for Tommy's brother, David Nutter.

Opposite: The 1985 opening night soirée at Saks Fifth Avenue for Edward Sexton's first ready-to-wear collection in New York.

SPENCER HART

-- ESTABLISHED 2002

In 2002, Spencer Hart arrived on Savile Row with blacked-out windows and a locked glass door smoked like a Mafia don's limousine. Inside, dark wood walls snaked a labyrinthine path to an inner sanctum furnished only with a leather banquette, a full-length mirror and a 1960s Modernist chandelier. Navy, grey and black one-button suits with unfeasibly narrow shawl or notch lapels loomed out of the gloom in pools of pin spotlight. A rail of white Marcella shirts shimmered clinically from a rail. The television screen sunk into a wall played footage of *Sinatra at the Sands* and a pall of cigar smoke added to the ambience of lazy, louche elegance.

'I always knew there was a gap in the market for someone to open a modern but really cool store on Savile Row,' says Nick Hart. 'I wanted people to walk into my store and walk into a different world: a world that could transform them. It was important for me that the shop was a little bit clubby and that our clients would want to spend time just hanging out.' I recall smoking cigarettes and enjoying a decadent mid-afternoon glass of champagne at Spencer Hart in the early years, when anybody from David Bowie or George Michael to Joseph Ettedgui

or Estée Lauder president John Demsey could be behind the concealed dressing-room door. 'Our clients are opinion-makers, entrepreneurs, creatives and people who have created their own world,' says Hart. 'Possibly modernists and often rebels, they are the cool, reckless guys who other guys want to be. Our look is and was pared down, rich, restrained and precise in the way politicians dressed in the sixties and cool actors like Steve McQueen and musicians dressed. We only sold white shirts (which had all but disappeared), very textured dark ties and ultra-sharp heavily canvassed structured tailoring using lots of old forgotten details.'

Hart has form in both fashion and bespoke tailoring. Aged between thirteen and sixteen, Hart worked every holiday for a men's tailor in Berkshire, thus paying his dues in old-school Savile Row fashion. He worked with the creative teams behind Diesel, Joseph, Voyage and Mandarina Duck and was director of menswear at Kenzo, which he built into a 40-million-euro a year business. He was at the coalface of the Savile Row revival in the 1990s, working with Timothy Everest. Hart was creative director of Chester Barrie

Nick Hart photographed for *The Rake* with the author in Claridge's Fumoir bar, both wearing Spencer Hart bespoke cocktail suits (2009).

when, over a lunch on 11 September 2001 with Ozwald Boateng, Hart was encouraged to open under his own (or rather his son Spencer's) name. Remortgaging his house, Hart opened his shop offering bespoke, made-to-measure and ready-made suits, making him a triple threat to the New Establishment tailors.

Nick Hart is one of the great communicators on Savile Row: painfully blunt at times (dismissing the 'new school, some of whom make crap quality but pretend it isn't'), but touching genius in communicating what his Rat Pack of cool guys wants at any given time. He riffs on the bespoke upswing in the 2009 recession in a staccato stream-of-consciousness interview for that year's April *Times Luxx*: 'Savile Row is a reminder of qualities and values that outlast and transcend depressions, recessions, fads and here-today-gone-tomorrow fashion. People are looking for the real deal, for the quality and substance and longevity. It's unflashy with a strong point of view: an edge which is not forced but comes naturally. It is a luxury but somehow not frivolous or flashy. We are certainly witnessing a new group of clients who are looking

for lasting, intrinsic value, not quick fixes that the designer brands promise but never deliver. Men are enjoying the process of ordering and waiting for the product. It's almost a new frugalism.'

It is not coincidental that Spencer Hart achieved a cult status in the music business. Nick Hart is a passionate soul boy. What is surprising is the diversity of artists drawn to the label: The Rolling Stones, Led Zeppelin, Duran Duran's John Taylor, The Red Hot Chili Peppers, The Arctic Monkeys, Franz Ferdinand, Placebo, Massive Attack, Suede's Brett Anderson, Kanye West, Jay-Z and Damon Dash. As Hart says, 'My suits look seriously radical on Damon. They're not the usual hip-hop pinstripe gangster suits with pink ties.'

In 2002, Robbie Williams flew him over to LA and greeted Hart with the words: 'Fuck me, man, I love your clothes.' For Williams's October 2009 comeback album *Reality Killed the Video Star*, Spencer Hart tailored a slick black three-piece suit, shirt and tie look that could only have been cut on Savile Row. Spencer Hart has gained a reputation as the tailor to men who behave badly. On the inside pockets of early suits there was a label reading: 'Spencer Hart

The original dark, labyrinthine concept for No. 36 Savile Row, photographed in 2004. 'We care almost too much about not being vulgar or ostentatious,' Hart said in 2007.

Spencer Hart's narrow colour spectrum (picked up later by Kilgour) and his passion for sophisticated, textured tone-on-tone cloths woven by specialist mills such as Moxon, were in stark contrast to the Technicolor tailoring of James and Boateng. Hart's skinny shawl collars, narrow shoulders and white Marcella shirts are instantly recognizable.

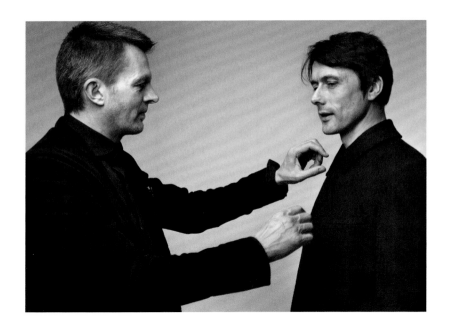

Nick Hart photographed with former Suede lead singer Brett Anderson for Aquascutum's Autumn/Winter 2007 ad campaign, shot by Roger Rich.

sincerely hopes you get laid in this product'. 'I like the idea of old-school naughty men who frequent nightclubs and get into trouble,' he says. 'They are men who come alive at night. It's a black-and-white aesthetic: very hard-edged and cynical. It's Sinatra and Crosby singing a duet in *High Society*. It's the Rat Pack in sharp suits gambling at the dog tracks and behaving like hounds. When I was a kid the cool guys danced. You went clubbing to dance and show off to other guys how well dressed you were.'

The success of Spencer Hart on Savile Row came to the attention of Aquascutum CEO Kim Winser, who in 2006 invited Hart to design a top-end tailoring collection, Aquascutum Limited, to lend the British heritage brand a little of the buzz surrounding bespoke. In 2008, department store Liberty opened a Spencer Hart shop-within-shop to help revitalize the men's fashion floor. The year 2009 saw Nick Hart open up the blacked-out windows of his Savile Row shop and 'aim to be a little more friendly and welcoming'. Of the future for Spencer Hart, he says, 'You'll never stay the coolest or the newest but if you have an obsessive attention to quality then your survival on Savile Row is more secure.'

Though bespoke sales remain strong, Savile Row is not at the forefront of Hart's mind or his business strategy. 'The Row is relevant and useful but it is not the be all and end all for Spencer Hart,'

he says. 'Bespoke is a healthy business but the only way to grow it is to start doing those ghastly trunk shows to America and I don't want to spend the rest of my life pandering to Republicans because, let's face it, that's your customer.... What I want to do is create a very dynamic men's retail environment: some of it high end and some of it affordable and more fun. The space will include a private club element and will sell everything from Japanese bebop CD imports to exquisite silk pyjamas. Not everything will be own-label.'

This gearshift from one of the smallest shops on Savile Row to a fashion flagship in greater Mayfair can only be achieved smoothly with major investment, which Hart appears to have secured. He has not turned his back on bespoke, however. 'Bespoke is totally relevant and we are taking more orders than ever before,' says Hart. 'What we sell day to day to serious people (bankers, lawyers, grooms) are a one-button narrow notch suit, high in the armhole, double vented with approximately 76 cm [30 inches] back length in charcoal grey, dark navy and a lot of variations on pindots. What I think the Spencer Hart flagship should be looking at is dressing that Mayfair guy who wants his shirts made-to-measure, his jackets bespoke, his shoes the very finest Edward Green's and his jeans a cool brand. That's the man we can dress from head to toe at the lifestyle store.'

David Bowie wearing a Spencer Hart bespoke dinner suit accompanies wife Iman (in 3.1 Phillip Lim) to the Metropolitan Museum of Art's annual Costume Institute Ball in 2008.

TIMOTHY EVEREST

-- ESTABLISHED 1991

When Timothy Everest replied to an advertisement reading 'Boy wanted for Savile Row tailor', he was well aware of Tommy Nutter's wicked sense of humour and reputation on the Row. 'Possibly he was a little jaded by the late eighties,' says Everest, 'but actually Tommy was very funny and elegant and charming. He was also very modest. He'd be happier in a rough pub than the Ritz. He was the kind of man who would always order fish pie instead of foie gras. I don't think he ever forgot he was from Neasden.' As sales manager at Nutters, Everest describes a chaotic, camp environment more like the chorus line of a West End revue than a tailor's workshop. 'I suppose the Nutters boys were a bit naughtier than the neighbours,' he says. 'We had [designer John] Galliano in the workrooms doing his Mae West impression. Another guy on the shop floor had peroxide blonde hair that was most unusual on Savile Row at the time. His boyfriends used to pick him up after work in vintage Rolls-Royces or Bentleys.'

In 1991, Everest fell in love with a derelict house on Princelet Street in the Spitalfields quarter of London's East End: formerly the home to generations of Huguenot and Jewish tailors since the 16th century. He explained his decision to leave Savile Row as 'wanting to build my own ladder, not climb up someone else's'. In the early days, Everest employed St Martins fashion student Hussein Chalayan, who went on to be one of the major voices in 1990s British fashion. The most idiosyncratic of the New Establishment tailors, Everest attracted a customer to bespoke who would otherwise shop at Paul Smith, Martin Margiela or Jil Sander.

'There is very little loyalty in made-to-measure, but your bespoke tailor is sacrosanct, like your doctor or barber. The spine of your wardrobe is made by your tailor,' he says. 'The designer is placed high above the consumer, so that if the consumer doesn't understand the clothes, the implication is that he's stupid. But bespoke is about tearing this wall down and having the designer serve your needs, not vice versa. Isn't it a refreshing change to have the person whose name is on the door of the firm serve you?'

Instead of imposing a strong house style like Ozwald Boateng, Everest could be as traditional as Henry Poole & Co. or subversive as Tommy Nutter depending on the customer's dictates. As he told

Timothy Everest dinner suit photographed for *The Rake* in 2009.

Timothy Everest photographed at his Elder Street townhouse in 2009.

The Rake, 'From a craftsmanship perspective, we are much closer to Henry Poole or Anderson & Sheppard, considering the quality of our bespoke garments and how much is manufactured on the premises. The difference is that from a marketing, communications and design perspective, we're more aligned with the likes of Richard James or even Tom Ford.'

In 1996, Everest moved the flagship into an exquisitely restored Georgian townhouse on Elder Street once occupied by Bloomsbury artist Mark Gertler. Painter Richard Clark fitted out the townhouse with distressed leather chesterfield sofas, architectural salvage cast-iron radiators, wooden school benches and vintage standing lamps. Decorating the walls in the hall and ground-floor salon are what at first glance look like Cubist prints but on closer inspection are pure pornography. 'I liked the images first before I knew what they were depicting,' says Everest. 'I thought they were appropriate for a man's bespoke tailoring shop.

You look and admire. Then you look closer and realize they're really rather rude.'

The same principle could be applied to Everest bespoke. His cut is solid and robust (square roped shoulder, high, tight collar and flared skirt) but there is naughtiness in details that *The Rake* applauds, such as 'turn-back cuffs revealing audacious flashes of sugar-pink linings, louche velvet under collars and irreverent contrast piping'. But he is insistent that he is a tailor who designs rather than a designer who tailors. Everest has been the most successful of the new generation of tailors in lending the expertise of a bespoke tailor to mass-market fashion labels. In 2000, he began a three-year collaboration with Daks, tailoring a cocky, young collection of suits titled Daks E1. He has designed for Marks & Spencer's upper-tier Autograph collection and has forged a formidable trade in Japan, opening his 17th shop in 2008. Edging closer to the Row in 2005, he opened a West End atelier in Bruton Place.

Everest's 18th-century Spitalfields bespoke house gets the balance between grandeur, intimacy and East End cool absolutely right. He was adamant that the interior would please younger eyes who may be intimidated or put off by the more traditional face of Savile Row. It is often said that bespoke customers feel like members of a private club and this is precisely what Everest has created on Elder Street. It has been said that No. 32 Elder Street is cooler than neighbouring private members' club Shoreditch House.

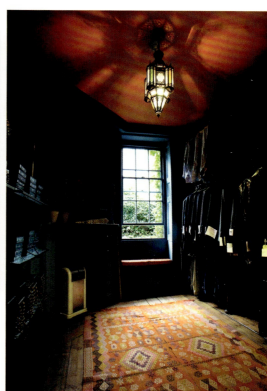

James McAvoy wearing a bespoke dinner suit tailored by Timothy Everest for the 2007 film *Atonement*, photographed on set with Keira Knightley.

Timothy Everest's 2009 *Rake* shoot inspired by his work on *Atonement*: two Everest bespoke black tie models flank an Alberta Ferretti cocktail dress.

Everest, awarded the MBE in 2010 for services to tailoring, has been a model of discretion about his bespoke customers, even though the fashion press did tease out of him the names of high-profile clients such as David Beckham and politicians Gordon Brown and David Cameron. His on-screen credits include tailoring suits for a muscular Tom Cruise in *Mission: Impossible* (1996), who had to turn to bespoke because the Donna Karan off-the-peg pieces he was given were twisting on the shoulder.

Despite his business interests worldwide and collaborations on fashion projects, Timothy Everest has become one of the leading advocates for traditional Savile Row bespoke tailoring. In 2008 he said: 'It is time to champion the cause. The world and his wife run around with bunches [cloth books] pretending they are bespoke tailors and bastardizing the word. We at Timothy Everest have gone back to basics, really; investing in new workrooms, training up sufficient cutters and tailors to do everything in-house and improving the way we sell.' Everest has also endeavoured to reduce the bespoke process to between eight and ten weeks rather than the traditional twelve.

As a columnist for *The Rake*, 'Mr Tim' answers questions from the global bespoke faithful and is positively evangelical about the virtue and integrity of bespoke. 'To a large extent, in recent decades, men's fashion has been hijacked by a very small minority of people who are creating and writing about clothes that the vast majority of men will never wear,' he writes. 'But when you see even the world's most successful designer, Tom Ford, embrace classic elegance, I think it's a pretty big wake-up call. As a whole, I think it's very beneficial to our culture because it's a statement that British tailoring is still the most relevant inspiration today. Ford is a fantastic stylist and brings positive attention to British tailoring through brilliant communication.' Of his own future in bespoke, Everest says, 'You have to think of a tailor for more than just your suit. We are now considering the bespoke wardrobe. I like our customers to feel like they are making the decisions. They are leading the dance. That is the true beauty of bespoke.'

GENTLEMEN'S
REQUISITES

hough Meyer & Mortimer is the last Regency tailor standing known
to have cut for the Beau, at least five St James's Street addresses patronized
by Brummell still trade at the heart of London's gentlemen's club quarter.
Like Savile Row, St James's Street and Jermyn Street have somehow managed
to smuggle their charms past Father Time and continue to be populated by
barbers, bootmakers and shirtmakers one, two and three centuries old. Their
survival is a testimony to the enduring appeal of craftsmanship, quality and
consistency in demand for fine gentlemen's requisites.

Barbers & Perfumers

J. Floris, London's oldest barber, comb maker and
perfumer, was founded by Juan Floris at No. 89
Jermyn Street in the 1730s, where it remains nearly
three hundred years later. Born on the island of
Menorca, Señor Floris brought a Mediterranean
sensibility to his colognes and perfumes, such
as his Limes formula, which is still sold today. A
favourite of Eva Peron, Special 127 was formulated
for the Grand Duke Orloff in 1890, and was
christened 127 because that was the page on which
it appeared in the firm's ledgers, where each
formula is recorded on a single, numbered page.
Also preserved at No. 89 are mahogany cases
crafted to display Floris products at the Great
Exhibition of 1851, which are not dissimilar to
the Hawkes & Co. Great Exhibition case held in
the Gieves & Hawkes archive at No. 1 Savile Row.
Like Hawkes, Floris has an unbroken line of Royal
Warrants from George IV to our present Queen
and Prince of Wales.

Established in 1805, barber, perfumer and
wigmaker by appointment to King George III,
Truefitt & Hill was founded at the height of
Brummell's reign as king of Regency fashion. The
house retains appointment books from the days of
founder William Truefitt and currently resides at
No. 71 St James's Street, holding the Royal Warrant
of the Duke of Edinburgh.

William Penhaligon, by all accounts a rake
of the highest order, opened his first barbershop
on Jermyn Street in 1870 and formulated his
first gentlemen's perfume, Hammam Bouquet,
in 1872. It was named for the famed Jermyn
Street Turkish baths next door to his shop that
were patronized by Mr Brummell. Penhaligon's
is now one of the most beloved English perfume
houses, with branches in Mayfair, Covent
Garden and the City. Mr Penhaligon's diaries
and formulae survive in the house archive and
classics such as the 1902 Blenheim Bouquet
that was made for the Duke of Marlborough
remain bestsellers.

Though Geo. F Trumper retains a shop on
Jermyn Street, it is the original barbershop opened
at No. 9 Curzon Street by George Trumper in 1875
that dukes and gentlemen prefer. The reception is
lined with Royal Warrants and portraits recording
the patronage of King Edward VII, George V
and his sons the Dukes of Windsor, Kent and
Gloucester. On the cutting floor, each barber's
chair is secreted behind velvet-curtained mahogany
booths facing original Victorian marble basins.
Like all of the barbers and perfumers mentioned
above, Trumper still offers wet shaving with
steamed towels, skin foods and historic colognes
such as Spanish Leather, Bay Rum and Rose.

Preceding pages, left:
The shop floor of John Lobb
Ltd at No. 9 St James's
Street, with mahogany
museum cabinet showcasing
treasures such as Queen
Victoria's button-trim boots.

Opposite: Geo. F. Trumper's
Curzon Street emporium.

Hatters

Opened at the turn of the century by Mr Edward Bates, Bates Gentlemen's Hatter at No. 21a Jermyn Street was until recently a charming little shop that had changed little since Queen Victoria's twilight years. Its floor-to-ceiling hatboxes were still lifted down by a wooden hook and a prayer that the shelves would not collapse. The uninitiated were startled to say the least by Binks the top-hatted tabby cat, at large between 1921 and 1926 but subsequently stuffed behind glass in the shopfront. Following the redevelopment of this site in 2010, Bates have relocated temporarily to Hilditch & Key.

Now trading from Swaine Adeney Brigg at No. 54 St James's Street, military and civilian hatter Herbert Johnson has impeccable Royal provenance. Legend has it that as an apprentice Mr Johnson happened to be present when, riding in Hyde Park, the Prince of Wales had his topper blown off by the wind. Johnson offered to repair the hat and delivered it to the future King Edward VII at Marlborough House, whereby the Prince advised him to go into business. This he did with partner Mr Glazier in 1889, and his customers – including Prince Edward's son the Duke of Clarence and Avondale, Kaiser Wilhelm II of Germany, Tsar Nicholas II of Russia and King George I of Greece – suggest that Prince Edward proved a loyal friend to the house. Herbert Johnson is proud to boast that it has made caps for over 90 per cent of regiments in the British armed forces and continues a thriving trade in chauffeur's caps. It was to Herbert Johnson that Steven Spielberg and Harrison Ford turned in 1981 to create the iconic Indiana Jones wide-brim fur felt hat, inspired by a 19th-century model called the 'poet'.

Founded in 1676, James Lock & Co. is the oldest family-owned and run hatter in the world. Lock has resided at No. 6 St James's Street, in the shadow of St James's Palace, since 1765. When history was made, a Lock hat was invariably at hand. Customer Lord Byron lodged a few doors down, upstairs at No. 9 (now Lobb the shoemaker). One of Admiral Lord Nelson's last acts in London before embarking to fight his last Battle of Trafalgar in 1805 was to settle Mr Lock's bill for 'the usual' cocked hat and cockade, fashioned with a green velvet eyeshade to cover the blinded right eye. An unpaid Lock bill dated 1895 was left by the imprisoned aesthete Oscar Wilde; the bill was later paid on the 200th anniversary of Wilde's disgrace by a well-wisher. Lock's conformature (a mechanical device used to measure the head) was employed by Crown Jeweller Garrard to refashion the Imperial State Crown for Queen Elizabeth II's coronation in 1953.

In the history of hatmaking, Lock can claim the Coke (bowler) designed in 1850 for William Coke's gamekeepers; the trilby, named for George du Maurier's Victorian literary heroine; and the fez, created for King Amanullah of Afghanistan's private detectives, who needed both protection from the occasional cosh plus an absence of brim to allow them to genuflect in prayer. Lock's decision not to extend credit to the Prince of Wales may go some way towards explaining the Prince's patronage of Herbert Johnson. No matter; his grandson, the future Duke of Windsor, proved to be one of Lock's most loyal fashion leaders. Even today, parts of the shop would be recognizable even to Sir Walter Raleigh, never mind Beau Brummell. Lock is achingly picturesque and works its charms equally on young marquises wanting grandfather's black silk topper reconditioned for Royal Ascot, movie stars such as Johnny Depp and fashion stylists like Patricia Fields, who gave a Lock hatbox top billing in the second *Sex and the City* movie.

James Lock & Co. renovated vintage silk plush top hat and faux carved ivory evening cane photographed with Huntsman bespoke white tie.

Shirtmakers

Traditionally, Savile Row did not tailor shirts. As the shirtmakers will tell you, a tailor can rip-down and remake after a fitting, but if a bespoke shirt is incorrect, the maker has to go back to his board and cut again. There is no margin for error. So though Dege & Skinner, Norton & Sons and Huntsman offer a bespoke shirt service, the giants of the trade still reside on Jermyn Street. Hilditch & Key arrived in 1899 and won the patronage of the dandy Prince of Wales. In 1925, the company was sufficiently established to open an outpost on the Rue de Rivoli in Paris, where it survived the Second World War and continues to trade. Unique amongst the bespoke shirtmakers, Hilditch & Key has earned a reputation cutting for female fashion icons such as Marlene Dietrich, Paloma Picasso and Claudia Schiffer. Though Hilditch & Key's eye is more towards refining ready-made shirts to a level of excellence that they compete favourably with bespoke, the house continues to serve great dandies such as Chanel creative director Karl Lagerfeld as bespoke shirtmakers.

Budd Ltd at the top of Piccadilly Arcade is a favoured shirtmaker recommended by Savile Row tailors. Traditional to the point of stubbornness, the house will refuse to accommodate the slim fit but it is hard to argue with tailors John Butcher and Martin Levitt, who have clocked up a century in the trade between them. Though the firm was founded in 1910, their owners Webster's have tailored shirts since 1847. On Jermyn Street since 1999, bespoke shirtmaker Emma Willis is already the darling of the gentlemen's club set and dresses as many dukes as she does bright young things. Her choice of cloths – Egyptian and Sea Island cottons or finest silks – walks the fine line between classical elegance and relevance to contemporary luxury.

Once-great names such as Hawes & Curtis – tailor to the Duke of Windsor, Lord Louis Mountbatten and the late Duke of Kent – still trade on Jermyn Street but have conceded bespoke status. Arguably the last of the great Jermyn Street shirtmakers still standing is Turnbull & Asser, who opened on Church Place in 1885 and moved to their present Jermyn Street premises in 1903, where their proficiency in gentlemen's requisites and outdoor wear earned them the patronage of King Edward VII and Queen Alexandra. Turnbull came into its own as shirtmaker to Jazz Age idols such as the Duke of Windsor (when Prince of Wales) and author F. Scott Fitzgerald, whose literary hero Jay Gatsby ordered shirts so exquisite that they reduced his amour Daisy to tears. Whereas other shirtmakers relied on tradition alone, Turnbull & Asser was always smart enough to swing with the fashions of the era for 1950s smoothies Cary Grant, David Niven and Frank Sinatra, and 1960s hipsters Brian Epstein, David Hemmings and Michael Caine, who were drawn to the house by the designs of the legendary Michael 'Mr' Fish.

Perhaps Turnbull & Asser's greatest coup in the late 20th century was being chosen to tailor shirts for every James Bond, from Sean Connery in 1962 to Daniel Craig in 2008. As a main vein to the hearts of modern men the world over, the 007 franchise is arguably more effective than any number of men's style magazine advertisements. But where the house remains a cut above fellow heritage houses is in its dedication to bespoke tailoring. Customers wishing for hand-crafted shirts bypass Jermyn Street and turn the corner to where the house retains its Churchill Rooms bespoke space. It is to here that disciples of the craft turn for masterpieces cut by master tailors.

Turnbull & Asser's
Jermyn Street flagship.

Shoemakers

In much the same spirit as the Duke of Windsor ordered his coats on Savile Row and his trousers in America, there is an increasing trend amongst British bespoke customers to wear a French Berluti shoe polished with the 'caviar finish' patina of a Van Gogh night sky rather than finish the suit with a more traditional English last. Whereas men may still err on the side of conservatism in their suits, they are more inclined to follow the fashion for more streamlined, Italianante shoes, such as those made by Lodger on Clifford Street. But this does not detract from the desire for traditional English shoes made in Northampton by houses such as Edward Green, Trickers or Grenson.

The British bespoke shoemakers are enjoying a renaissance no less profound than Savile Row tailoring. If you wish for a testimonial to the integrity of bespoke shoemaking look no further than January 2009, when Prince Charles and the Duchess of Cornwall paid an official visit to John Lobb on St James's Street. The Prince was wearing bespoke shoes crafted by the house forty years previously. In 1832, founder John Lobb set up shop on Regent Street before moving into Byron's lodgings at No. 9 St James's Street, where he made boots for Queen Victoria and then that most profligate patron of all things bespoke, her son King Edward VII.

Lobb can match Savile Row name for prestigious name, having crafted bespoke shoes for King George V, F. Scott Fitzgerald, Cole Porter, the Duke of Windsor, Katharine Hepburn, Laurence Olivier, Norman Hartnell, Tyrone Power, Fred Astaire, Georges Balanchine, Duff Cooper and Cecil Beaton. Maybe the most poignant last preserved in the basement archive belongs to the late Diana, Princess of Wales, whose name is recorded first as Lady Diana Spencer, then as HRH the Princess of Wales and finally as Diana, Princess of Wales, when she lost the HRH following her divorce. The shop has been christened 'the most beautiful in the world' by *Esquire* magazine, and who can argue, on seeing bespoke craftsmen fashioning lasts on the shop floor, or the basement library of lasts stacked from floor to ceiling?

Though the John Lobb name was acquired and dissipated by Hermès, connoisseurs of bespoke shoes are gratified to know that the St James's Street shop is still owned by descendants of the original Mr Lobb, and that present chairman John Hunter Lobb's sons assure a smooth succession in future generations.

G. J. Cleverley & Co. in the Royal Arcade is a relative newcomer, named for founder George, who commenced trading under his own name in 1958. And yet Cleverley shoes and Savile Row suits have become as inextricably linked as Dubonnet and gin. George's apprenticeship with Clifford Street bespoke shoemaker Tuczek earned the house the right to claim customers such as Rudolph Valentino, Gloria Swanson and Gary Cooper. Cleverley also retains a winning hand of contemporary leaders of fashion such as Charlie Watts, Bryan Ferry, Terence Stamp and David Beckham, who famously mistook a Victorian boot for the new season's model.

G. J. Cleverley's signature bespoke black calf elasticated brogued shoe with blind lacing.

Umbrella, Whip & Stickmakers

Though only politician sex scandals suggest that there is any future in whip-making, there is still a demand for handcrafted whips as made by Swaine Adeney Brigg at No. 54 St James's Street since the company was founded in 1750. James Swaine was privileged to make hunting whips for King George III as well as his sons King George IV and King William IV, and the Dukes of York, Cumberland and Cambridge. The house was one of the few to be patronized by Queen Victoria, who shunned most of the companies preferred by her wicked Hanoverian uncles. Umbrella, whip and stickmaker Brigg, established in 1836, was incorporated into Swaine Adeney in 1943. They had the dubious honour of making umbrellas doctored by the KGB to serve as weapons of political assassination as well as the more soigné distinction of providing the malacca-handled umbrellas for the character Steed in 1960s TV drama *The Avengers*. Today Swaine Adeney Brigg retains the Queen's Royal Warrant as whip and glove maker as well as the Prince of Wales's Warrant as supplier of umbrellas. Since incorporating hatmaker Herbert Johnson, the house has become a quadruple threat, crafting the finest bespoke leather goods, whips, umbrellas and hats.

The maestro of traditional umbrellas is James Smith & Sons, which is incongruously placed on New Oxford Street. The firm was founded in 1830 and lived happily just off Savile Row before a Second World War bomb forced it to relocate to its present premises. Though stranded in a no man's land of gentlemen's requisites, James Smith & Sons has one of the finest Victorian exteriors and interiors to survive untouched in London. The basement workshops still operate, while the ground floor selling space is a dream for tourists wishing to relive an era when Prime Minister Gladstone, Bonar Law and Lord Curzon ordered silver-topped walking sticks and silk canopy umbrellas. Today the lion's share of canopies for umbrellas are synthetic but this is for practicality rather than cost-cutting. You will still find walnut or malacca-handled umbrellas for sale, along with sticks topped with carved wooden hare's heads or silver duck bills that take one back to a more elegant age when no Mayfair buck was fully dressed without a jaunty walking stick.

James Smith & Sons umbrella with scorched maple handle and shaft set with a stag horn.

ANATOMY OF A SUIT

Accordion pleats

Though pleats are not currently popular for City suits, Savile Row will traditionally pleat flannels with two inverted pleats on either side of the trouser waistband.

Balance

This refers to the relationship between the front and back of a garment, though Richard Anderson puts it more eloquently 'The ideal harmony among two or more sections of a garment and its wearer's configuration.'

Blind fly

Though zips are entirely acceptable now on Savile Row, the button fly remains traditional, and is particularly elegant when 'blind' stitched down between each button rather than left open.

Break

The coat break is the point above the top button where the lapel forks into the V-shape. The trouser break is the point at which the hem touches the shoe or boot and ever so slightly puddles the cloth above.

Buttonhole

A bespoke buttonhole is always hand-sewn on the right lapel of a Savile Row coat using a pearl stitch above the breast pocket. A loop is stitched into the reverse side to secure a boutonnière.

Button stand

The distance from the finished edge of a garment to the centre of a button. Of late the tailors have endorsed a single button fastening for single-breasted suits. The one-button is notoriously difficult to balance, hence Savile Row's pride in it. If a suit is cut with two or three buttons, the lowest is always left unfastened.

Canvas

A cloth made from cotton, flax, hemp or jute and used for providing strength and firmness inside the coat.

Chest piece

Layers of natural canvas and felt hand-stitched inside the chest of the coat to give it shape and strength.

Coat

Savile Row insists on calling the suit jacket a coat and the waistcoat a vest.

Cuffs

A Savile Row suit coat cuff will allow the show of 1½ to 2 inches (4 to 5 cm) of shirt cuff. This allows for a flash of cufflink in the mandatory French cuffed shirt.

Drape

Drape refers to the way a cloth flows and falls around a gentleman's figure. The fluidity of drape varies with cloth, cut and canvassing beneath.

Handkerchief

Savile Row chaps pride themselves on the fold of their top pocket handkerchiefs, never chosen to match a tie or bow tie. Popular formations include the cloud of silk, the three-point linen peaks or a slim horizontal line of white cotton.

Jigger button

The inside left double-breasted coat button to secure the underneath forepart in position.

Lapel

The peaked lapel (pictured overleaf) is the most formal Savile Row style, appropriate for double-breasted coats, morning and evening tails. A notch lapel is sewn to the collar at an angle that resembles a step. The notch is the form for single-breasted coats and sports jackets. A small notch is charmingly called a fish mouth.

Shoulder line

The most distinctive Savile Row shoulder line is roped. The sleeve is attached high on the armhole of the coat and stands proud in an elegant incline. House styles vary: Anderson & Sheppard favour a natural line following the curve of the shoulder while Huntsman's, for example, is more angled to present a strong horizontal line.

Preceding pages, left: Timothy Everest bespoke black tie photographed for *The Rake* in 2009.

Right, above: Working cuff buttons.

Right, below: Masterclass from Huntsman's cutters in matching the house check cloth for an audacious tweed shooting suit.

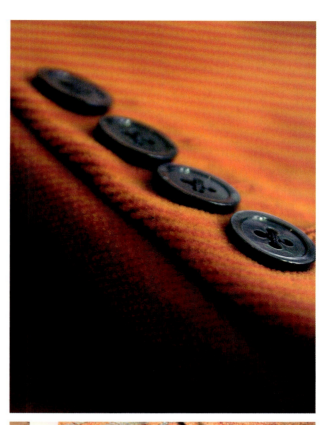

Skirt

A Savile Row bespoke suit is usually cut with a slight flare from the waist that is christened the 'skirt'. The silhouette of the skirt is enhanced by back vents; tail flaps at the back of the coat are either double (one vent cut at either side of the skirt) or single (cut at the centre back seam). Vents have their history in equestrian tailoring and continue to be cut to enhance movement and comfort.

Sleeve heads

Strips of cotton wadding or lambswool fleece hand-stitched around the tops of the sleeves to create a smooth line and to support the roll at the sleeve top.

Trouser curtain

The strip of soft, durable cloth extending below the trouser waistband to keep the waist area from stretching and hold pleats in place.

Trouser pockets

Purists such as Edward Sexton may cut trousers without pockets except for a small fob pocket underneath the waistband seam for coins, cards or nightclub condiments. This is an exception. However, few Row tailors approve of hip pockets in a pair of bespoke trousers.

Turn-ups

Making a strong comeback on Savile Row, the cuffs at the bottom of trouser legs (usually under 2 inches or 5 cm in depth) are known as PTUs (permanent turn-ups).

Undercollar

The part of the coat collar one sees when one lifts the collar up. Tailors such as Ozwald Boateng and Timothy Everest have made the brightly coloured undercollar a signature.

Waistband

Unless expressly requested, Savile Row trousers are not cut with belt loops; the wisdom being that bespoke trousers should be cut to sit effortlessly without the support of a belt spoiling the drape. Trousers are trimmed with side buckles or buttons to adjust the fit. When cut to accommodate braces buttons, the back of the trouser waistband is cut in a higher V-shaped opening christened the 'fishtail'.

Welt pocket

Outside pockets on a suit coat finished with a horizontal band of tone-on-tone cloth. A pocket flap may be cut and concealed inside the welt pocket for variety of wear. A Savile Row suit coat pocket may be angled (a Cross pocket) to add interest, and augmented with a ticket pocket within the right outside breast pocket on a coat.

Working cuff buttons

A bespoke suit will invariably be fastened at the cuff with four working buttons; the button closest to the cuff is usually worn unfastened. Buttons stitched directly to the sleeve surface on ready-to-wear suits are dismissed as 'blind'.

The peaked lapel and pearl stitch buttonhole, crafted by hand at Chittleborough and Morgan.

MAKING A SUIT

Preceding pages, left:
Kilgour icon image shot by
Nick Knight for Autumn/
Winter 2007.

Choosing cloth

Having introduced yourself to the
bespoke house of your choice, discuss
with the cutter or his salesman the
nature of the suit you have bespoken.
You will then begin the painstaking if
pleasurable process of choosing cloth
from books or bunches of swatches:
in the case of Henry Poole & Co.,
over six thousand. Elements of
style and trim (buttons, linings)
are also decided.

Measuring-up

The cutter will then take the
customer's measurements, calling out
the figures to an attendant salesman.
Measuring systems based on the
ideal proportions of Greek statues
formulated in the early 19th century
are still used today, even though each
house has its secret measurements.
Codes are also used to discreetly
convey weak spots such as sloping
shoulders or overdeveloped seats that
must be accommodated.

Drafting the pattern

The cutter now drafts a paper pattern
– cutting it with shorter shears than he
will use to cut cloth – that will be the
blueprint for all future suit patterns
cut for you by the house. If your
weight fluctuates, the pattern will
be let out or taken in as necessary.

Pages 262–65: The story of the bespoke suit's average fifty-two hours of hand work told in twelve images from the workshops of Norton & Sons (1, 2), Henry Poole & Co. (3, 5, 6, 7, 10), Anderson & Sheppard (4, 11) and Richard Anderson (8, 9, 12).

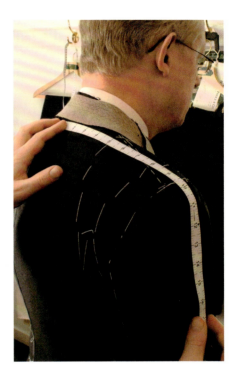

Striking

Your selected cloth is laid out and smoothed on the cutter's board, and the pattern is laid on top for the tailor to chalk the silhouette of the individual pieces. Extra cloth is left at certain inlay seams to allow alteration due to future weight fluctuation. If a cloth is checked, striped or textured in a particular direction, the cutter must match each piece to form an illusion of seamlessness when the suit is assembled.

Baste stitching

The individual pattern pieces are tied into what's known as a 'bundle' and given to a particular tailor who will canvas (pad and shape) the suit by hand, loosely assembling the coat and trousers with visible external white baste stitches in preparation for the first fitting. The more traditional houses like to assign a particular tailor to a customer for the duration of their relationship with the house.

First fitting

The suit is usually ready for a first fitting within a month of the initial order. In the spirit of a sculptor producing a maquette, the loosely basted garment is produced to allow the cutter to measure again and chalk-up marks while the customer is wearing the suit, which will refine and sculpt the cloth closer to the body.

Rip down and reassemble

The cutter will rip down the baste before the individual pattern pieces are trimmed by the cutter and then given back to the tailors (usually a coat maker and trouser maker), who will prepare a more intricately constructed garment in preparation for future fittings.

Tailoring

The chalk marks on the re-cut suit guide the tailors when they begin the process of putting the coat and trousers together in a closer approximation of the finished article. The interior layers of the coat are anchored with hand stitching to shape the shoulder and chest while the linings, buttons and details (pleats, turn-ups, pocket binding) are stitched into place for the second fitting.

Second/third fitting

Savile Row will recommend three fittings for the first suit tailored by the house. The second fitting should be getting closer to the fit and comfort desired of a bespoke suit. The cutter will consider precision point details such as the break over the shoe, the seat of the trouser, the cuff point and the drape. The cutter is now working to pinches of cloth that may need to be taken out to create the perfect portrait in cloth.

Hand-finishing

Once the cutter and customer are satisfied with the second or third fitting, the suit is returned to the tailor/tailoress to hand-finish inside and out. S/he will finish the buttonholes and lining silk to the standard demanded by the house and the customer. The Savile Row hallmark, a label printed with the date of commission and the customer's name, is stitched where it should be: in the inside right pocket of the lining.

Steam and press

The final fitting complete, the suit is handed to those masters of the steam and press to prepare the garment for delivery. Old timers on the Row still press a suit under a damp rag of cloth. Experts in the art deploy the steam iron like a maestro playing a Stradivarius. It is the preferred method of protecting and prolonging the life of a bespoke suit. Dry cleaning should only be inflicted on an annual basis.

Collection

Rather in the spirit of a West End opening night, the final fitting when a customer puts on his finished bespoke suit is a moment of great import. This is the time when the cutter will see his craft literally come to life. It has not been unknown for the workrooms to be called down to witness a masterpiece completed. The customer can now join a private club of alumni such as Nelson, Wellington and Napoleon III.

Following pages: A Dege & Skinner cutter strikes a pattern in the Savile Row cutting room.

SAVILE ROW CLOTH DIRECTORY

Barathea
A soft-finished worsted cloth woven in a broken twill weave effect. In khaki, it makes up well for officers' uniforms. The same weave in silk is used to face dress coats.

Birdseye
Woven cloth with an all-over pattern of tiny pinhead motifs reminiscent of a bird's eye.

Bleached calico
A common cotton cloth that has been passed through a bleaching process. Used for pattern sample-making or inserted for internal supports such as behind pockets.

Bombazine
A fine cloth in open twill with worsted weft on a silk warp, popularized in aristocratic circles as the cloth for 'duster coats' worn when carriage driving.

Botany
Merino wool from near Botany Bay.

Box cloth (or Devon)
A heavy woollen cloth like Melton, used for military overcoats.

Broadcloth
A fine woollen cloth. The custom is to have coat and waistcoat cut from broadcloth with the trousers made in doeskin.

Brocade
A fabric with decorative woven figures or patterns, usually floral, made on a Jacquard loom and popular for fancy waistcoats in the Regency style.

Buckram
A coarse cloth made of linen and stiffended with size or glue, used mainly by tailors as stiffening for military tunic stand collars.

Cambric
A fine muslin cloth used for handkerchiefs and fine underclothing. Also used in some tailors' trimmings.

Camel hair
Fabric with a hairy surface made entirely or partly of camel hair. In cheaper goods, cowhide is used.

Chamois
A trimming material used for pocketing, lining women's riding breeches and for interlining coats.

Corduroy
Anglicized French phrase *corde du Roi*, so called because it was made exclusively for use by the huntsmen of the French kings.

Covert coating
A medium-weight cloth of woollen or worsted yarns that wears well and is used for hunting clothes. The term is taken from the thicket or covert in which the pursued game took refuge during a hunt.

Dandy canvas
A rather heavy make of flax material used to interline coats.

Elongated twill
A class of twills in which the angle is greater than 45 degrees.

Flannel
A soft, woollen fabric of an open texture with a fine nap. Generally woven plain but may be twilled.

Florentine
A kind of twilled silk used in making fancy waistcoats and for covering cloth buttons.

Gabardine
A firm, durable fabric with a diagonal rib and twill weave. From a Spanish word meaning protection against the elements.

Glen Urquhart check
A compound colouring effect, the simplest example of which is two dark and two light threads woven for a number of repeats.

Grosgrain
A firm, stiff, closely woven corded or grained fabric popular for dinner jacket facings and covered buttons.

Herringbone
A pattern very popular in tweeds and worsted cloths, showing sharply zigzagging lines.

Holland

A linen cloth of fine texture, either bleached or unbleached, with a glazed or dull faced finish.

Hopsack

A weave comprising small squares.

Houndstooth/dogtooth check

A medium-sized broken check often used in tweeds. Nicknamed 'spongebag' by certain public schoolboys.

Hunting pink

Vivid scarlet that Melton cloths are dyed when cut for riding to hound. Said to be named after tailor Mr Samuel Pink.

Jacquard

A woven silk, the invention of Joseph Maria Jacquard, of intricate design, most often used for ties or evening coats.

Lawn

A light, thin cotton material usually sized and highly polished that takes its name from the city of Lyon.

Livery cloth

Fabrics of various characters such as buckskin, dress refine, Bedford cord, corduroy, velvet or box cloth used for making uniforms for coachmen and chauffeurs.

Madras

A soft cotton cloth used in shirting.

Marcella

White dimpled cotton shirting cloth used for dress shirts and waistcoats.

Melton

A heavily milled woollen cloth in which the fibres have been made to stand straight up, then the surface cut bare. Named for the town of Melton Mowbray.

Mohair

The fine, soft, silky hair of the Angora goat, now extensively raised in South America.

Moire

Watered or clouded effect on silk, usually by an engraved roller named from the French for 'weave'.

Navy twilled fabric

A heavy wool flannel commonly dyed indigo blue and used in making tunics worn by sailors.

Overcheck

A check introduced over and above a ground check.

Pinstripe

Classic English suit fabric distinguished by thin stripe in contrasting colour to the base. Chalkstripe is a blurred pinstripe while shadow pinstripe is tone on tone. A rain pinstripe is a line of small dots.

Pique

A fabric having a raised surface of cords or welts from selvedge to selvedge.

Seersucker

A lightweight fabric with crinkled stripes that may be laundered without ironing.

Silesia

A coarse linen cloth woven on a wide setting, used for lining.

Vicuña

Long silky hair of the South American vicuña, from which the Rolls Royce of overcoats was cut in the 1920s and 1930s; extremely rare and now very costly.

THE LANGUAGE OF SAVILE ROW

Basics

Bespoke
A hand-crafted suit, preferably ordered (bespoken) on or around Savile Row to the customer's precise specifications. Bespoke is cut by an individual for an individual and made by highly skilled individual craftsmen. The pattern is cut specifically for the customer, and the finished garment will take a minimum of fifty-two hours' work and at least two further fittings.

Cutter
The 'front-of-house' craftsman who measures-up, cuts a pattern and fits the basted garment onto the customer. He is the architect rather than the builder and dictates the pace of the house cutting room.

Guv'nor
The proprietor of a bespoke tailoring house on Savile Row.

Made-to-measure/personally tailored
A made-to-measure suit is cut from a standard pattern and machine-made but amended to fit an individual frame more closely.

Master tailor
In the strictest sense, a master tailor is the director or owner of a tailoring firm who is also a skilled tailor and/or cutter.

Striker
A term for an undercutter or assistant/apprentice to the cutter.

Tailor
The hands that actually make the garment. Tailors are increasingly self-employed outworkers since the demise of the house-owned factories, but the grander houses on the Row still employ (and train) their own coat and trouser makers.

Tools

Baby
Stuffed cloth pad on which the tailor works his cloth.

Banger
Piece of wood with a handle used to draw out steam and smooth cloth during ironing.

Board
Tailor's workbench.

Bodkin
A pointed instrument for piercing holes in cloth and ripping down basted garments.

Darky
Sleeve board.

Dolly
Roll of wet material used as a sponge to dampen cloth when steaming.

Goose iron
Hand iron heated over a naked flame. The weight of the hand irons of old prevented women from gaining employment as pressers.

Mangle/iron tailor
Sewing machine.

Notions
Buttons, hooks and zips required to finish a garment.

Shears
Heavy industrial cutter's scissors; separate pairs used to cut patterns and cloth.

Thimble
Ornate metal thumb-protector worn by the tailors.

Trimmings
The accessories required for making and ornamenting a suit: canvas, buttons, linings, silk.

Tailoring

Back stitch
Known as the tailor's stitch, a hand stitch in which the needle is backed up and stabbed at the end of the previous stitch.

Baste
Garment roughly assembled for the first fitting with visible white stitches that can be rapidly undone.

Beaded
A raised or lapped side seam on trousers.

Block
Paper template of a basic garment pattern shape from which an individual customer's pattern can be cut.

Bound edge
A seam whose fabric edges are bound by thread or lining to prevent fraying.

Bundle
Individual pattern pieces of cloth rolled into a 'bundle' by the cutters in preparation for the tailors.

Draft
Sketch or measured plan of a garment.

Flash basting
Usually refers to the superfluous basting stitches put into the outside of a garment at the trying-on stage with the object of impressing the customer.

Fusing
Use of chemicals and heat to weld the interlining to outer fabric. Bespoke tailors who stitch the canvas into the coat frown upon the practice.

Gorge
Where the collar is attached to the coat.

Inlays
An extra width of fabric left beyond what is required for the seams so that if any mistake has been made the suit can be let out.

Interlining
Material positioned between the lining and the outer fabric to provide shape or warmth.

London shrunk
Describes a cloth-shrinking process. The object is to shrink the cloth to the maximum amount possible so there is no uncontrolled shrinkage in the garment while it is being worked.

Rip down
The deconstruction of a basted coat after the first fitting.

Rock of eye
A master tailor's instinct for cutting as opposed to the technical rules of a mathematical cutting system.

Seat allowance
A quantity, generally from 2 to 3 inches (5 to 7 cm) for trousers, allowed for the expression of the seat when the wearer is seated.

Seat angle
The amount of ease given to the underside of the trousers.

Skye
The armhole or 'arm's eye'.

Shawl collar
A continuously curving lapel traditionally cut on smoking jackets popularised in recent years for City suits by Spencer Hart.

Slang

Balloon
A tailor's week without work or pay.

Basting up a snarl
Starting an argument; not uncommon in the workshop, rare on the cutting floor and a criminal offence on the shop floor.

Bicycled
Slang for work done on a sewing machine that should in a bespoke suit be done by hand.

Bodger
Crude work of an inexperienced or shoddy cutter or tailor.

Boot
19th-century British tradesman's slang for money. A generous tailoring master would give his journeymen 'tall boot'.

Breech
Military tailor's term for the seat.

Bunce
A trade perk such as tickets to the races from a grateful customer.

Bushelman
A journeyman who alters or repairs.

Cabbage
Leftover material that was formerly sold to a scrap man by the ounce.

Cat's face
A small shop opened by a cutter starting out on his own; rarely on ground-floor premises and often at home.

Chuck a dummy
To faint. Comparable to a mannequin falling over.

Clapham Junction
A draft with numerous alterations or additions. Clapham Junction is a London train station where many lines meet.

Codger
A tailor who does up old suits.

Cork
Alternative word for Guv'nor.

Crib
Large scrap of cloth left over from a job; enough to make a pair of trousers.

Crushed beetle
Badly made buttonhole.

Cutting turf
Tailor's term for working in a particularly unskilled and clumsy manner, such as making more body movement than the job warrants to disguise ineptitude.

Damp rag
A journeyman tailor's expression for a depressing person.

Dead … 'a dead horse'
A job that has been paid for in advance.

Doctor
Alterations tailor.

Drag … 'in the drag'
Working behind time.

Drummer
Trouser maker.

Hip stay
The wife.

Jeff
A cutter/tailor who makes the garment from pattern to finish.

Kicking
Looking for another job.

Kicking your heels
No work to do.

Kill
A spoilt job that has to be abandoned.

Kipper
A female tailor.

Lad of wax
Term for a tailor who makes clothes so perfectly that they appear to be modelled in wax.

Make your coffin
Tailor's term for overcharging for a garment.

Mouse in the straw
Slang term for an unsociable tailor.

Mungo
Cloth cuttings collected to be sold to the ragman.

On the back seam
An elegant euphemism for 'on one's arse'. Also to lie down on your board for a short siesta.

On the cod
Gone drinking. A time-honoured and popular pastime on Savile Row.

Pig
An unclaimed garment.

Pig sale
A sale of uncollected garments by the bespoke house.

Pigged
A lapel that curls after some wear.

Pinked … 'in a pinked job'
Making with extreme care for an especially critical or important customer.

Pork
A misfit rejected by a customer.

PT
Doing private work in spare time such as lunch hours or weekends.

Rub o' your thumb
Tailor's slang meaning to pass on luck or knowledge.

Schmutter
A Jewish expression for a piece of poor cloth or a poor garment (a bit of schmutter).

Skiffle
A job needed doing in a hurry.

Skipping it
Making the stitches too big to save time or energy.

Small seams
Warning call when someone being discussed enters the workroom.

Snob
A tailor whose work is unskilled and lacks finishing, as in 'he's snobbed the job', meaning he turned out a poorly made garment.

Soft sew
An easily worked cloth.

Tab
Fussy, difficult customer.

Trotter
Fetcher and carrier or messenger between cutter and tailors.

Tweed merchant
Tailor who does easy work.

Tipping the cat
Travelling around and working in private houses or offices.

CONTACTS

Bespoke Tailors

Anthony J. Hewitt
11 St George Street, W1
Tel: +44 207 495 7171
www.aj-hewitt.co.uk

Anderson & Sheppard
32 Old Burlington Street, W1
Tel: +44 207 245 0594
www.anderson-sheppard.co.uk

Byrne & Burge
1st Floor, 11 St George Street, W1
Tel: +44 207 493 9858
www.byrnesofmayfair.com

Chittleborough & Morgan
12 Savile Row, W1
Tel: +44 207 437 6850
www.chittleboroughandmorgan.co.uk

Davies & Son
38 Savile Row, W1
Tel: +44 207 434 3016
www.daviesandsonsavilerow.com

Dege & Skinner
10 Savile Row, W1
Tel: +44 207 287 2941
www.dege-skinner.co.uk

Denman & Goddard
11 St George Street, W1
Tel: +44 207 629 8668
www.denman-goddard.co.uk

Ede & Ravenscroft
8 Burlington Gardens, W1
Tel: +44 207 734 5450
www.edeandravenscroft.co.uk

Edward Sexton
26 Beauchamp Place, SW3
Tel: +44 207 838 0007
www.edwardsexton.co.uk

Gieves & Hawkes
1 Savile Row, W1
Tel: +44 207 434 2001
www.gievesandhawkes.com

Hardy Amies
14 Savile Row, W1
Tel: +44 207 734 2436
www.hardyamies.com

Hayward
95 Mount Street, W1
Tel: +44 207 499 5574
www.douglashayward.co.uk

Henry Poole & Co.
15 Savile Row, W1
Tel: +44 207 734 5985
www.henrypoole.com

Huntsman
11 Savile Row, W1
Tel: +44 207 734 7441
www.h-huntsman.com

John Pearse
6 Meard Street, W1
Tel: +44 207 434 0730
www.johnpearse.co.uk

Kilgour
8 Savile Row, W1
Tel: +44 203 283 8941
www.kilgour.eu

Lutwyche Bespoke
83 Berwick Street, W1
Tel: +44 207 292 0640
www.lutwyche.co.uk

Mark Powell
Apartment 2, 22 Frith Street, W1
Tel: +44 207 287 5498
www.markpowellbespoke.co.uk

Maurice Sedwell
19 Savile Row, W1
Tel: +44 207 734 0824
www.savilerowtailor.com

Meyer & Mortimer
6 Sackville Street, W1
Tel: +44 207 734 0656
www.meyerandmortimer.co.uk

Norton & Sons
16 Savile Row, W1
Tel: +44 207 437 0829
www.nortonandsons.co.uk

Ozwald Boateng
30 Savile Row, W1
Tel: +44 207 437 0620
www.ozwaldboateng.com

Richard Anderson
13 Savile Row, W1
Tel: +44 207 734 0001
www.richardandersonltd.com

Richard James
29 Savile Row, W1
Tel: +44 207 434 0171

Gentlemen's Requisites

Richard James Bespoke
19 Clifford Street, W1
Tel: +44 207 287 9645
www.richardjames.co.uk

Spencer Hart
62–64 Brook Street, W1
Tel: +44 207 494 0000
www.spencerhart.com

Timothy Everest
32 Elder Street, E1
Tel: +44 207 377 5770
www.timothyeverest.co.uk

Tom Baker
4 D'Arblay Street, W1
Tel: +44 207 437 3366
www.tombakerlondon.com

Welsh & Jefferies
20 Savile Row, W1
Tel: +44 207 734 3062
www.welshandjefferies.com

Budd Ltd
1a & 3 Piccadilly Arcade, SW1
Tel: +44 207 493 0139

Edward Bates
Hilditch & Key
73 Jermyn Street, SW1
Tel: +44 207 930 5336
www.bates-hats.co.uk

Geo F. Trumper
9 Curzon Street, W1
Tel: +44 207 499 1850
www.trumpers.com

G. J. Cleverley & Co.
14 The Royal Arcade,
28 Old Bond Street, W1
Tel: +44 207 493 0443
www.gjcleverley.co.uk

Hand & Lock
86 Margaret Street, W1
Tel: +44 207 580 7488
www.handembroidery.com

Hilditch & Key
73 Jermyn Street, SW1
Tel: +44 207 930 5336
www.hilditchandkey.co.uk

J. Floris
89 Jermyn Street, SW1
Tel: +44 845 702 3239
www.florislondon.com

James Lock & Co.
6 St. James's Street, SW1
Tel: +44 207 930 8874
www.lockhatters.co.uk

James Smith & Sons
53 New Oxford Street, WC1
Tel: +44 207 836 4731
www.james-smith.co.uk

John Lobb
9 St. James's Street, SW1
Tel: +44 207 930 3664
www.johnlobbltd.co.uk

Penhaligon's
16-17 Burlington Arcade, W1
Tel: +44 207 629 1416
www.penhaligons.co.uk

Swaine Adeney Brigg
54 St. James's Street, SW1
Tel: +44 207 409 7277
www.swaineadeney.co.uk

Truefitt & Hill
71 St. James's Street, SW1
Tel: +44 207 493 8496
www.truefittandhill.co.uk

Turnbull & Asser
71 & 72 Jermyn Street, SW1
Tel: +44 207 808 3000
www.turnbullandasser.com

ACKNOWLEDGMENTS

In addition to all of the ladies and gentlemen of Savile Row named in this publication, the author would like to thank Thames & Hudson and particularly my publisher Lucas Dietrich, editor Jennie Condell, production controller Jane Cutter and truly superb art director Samuel Clark. The principal photography for this book was executed with immense style by Guy Hills. Thanks are also due to *The Rake* magazine founder Wei Koh for permission to reproduce the exquisite work of staff photographer Munster. My readers Keith Levett, Helen Ball, Anda Rowland and Poppy Charles all improved the text with their comments. The Savile Row Bespoke Association has supported this project from the day in 2008 when Ozwald Boateng introduced me to Thames & Hudson. Tom Ford showed his characteristic generosity and class in giving us such an elegant foreword to *Savile Row: The Master Tailors of British Bespoke*. The book is dedicated to the late Judy Bennett and Rowland Lowe-MacKenzie.

James Sherwood
www.james-sherwood.com

BIBLIOGRAPHY

Amies, Hardy, *An ABC of Men's Fashion*, London: Newnes Key Books, 1964.

— *The Englishman's Suit*, London: Quartet Books, 1994.

Anderson, Richard, *Bespoke: Savile Row Ripped and Smoothed*, London: Simon & Schuster, 2009.

Aronson, Theo, *Prince Eddy and the Homosexual Underworld*, London: John Murray, 1994.

Botham, Noel, *Valentino: The First Superstar*, London: Metro, 2002.

Boyer, G. Bruce, *Fred Astaire Style*, New York: Assouline, 2005.

Bresler, Fenton, *Napoleon III: A Life*, London: HarperCollins, 2000.

Bret, David, *Valentino: A Dream of Desire*, London: Robson Books, 1998.

Buckle, Richard, ed., *Self-Portrait with Friends: The Selected Diaries of Cecil Beaton*, London: Pimlico, 1991.

Campbell, Una, *300 Years of Ceremonial Dress*, London: Ede & Ravenscroft Ltd, 1989.

Carter, Miranda, *The Three Emperors*, London: Penguin, 2009.

Charles-Roux, Edmonde, *Chanel: Her Life, Her World, The Woman Behind The Legend*, London: Quercus, 2009.

Clayton Calthrop, Dion, *English Costume Volume IV: The Georgians*, London, Adam & Charles Black, 1906.

Cohn, Nik, *Today There Are No Gentlemen: The Change in Englishmen's Clothes since the War*, London: Weidenfeld & Nicolson, 1971.

Cook, Andrew, *Prince Eddy: The King Britain Never Had*, London: Tempus, 2006.

Cope, Alfred, *Cope's Royal Cavalcade of the Turf*, London: David Cope Ltd, 1953.

Dance, Robert, *Glamour of the Gods: Photographs from the John Kobal Foundation*, Gottingen: Steidl, 2008.

David, Saul, *Prince of Pleasure: The Prince of Wales and the Making of the Regency*, New York: Atlantic Monthly Press, 1998.

Decharne, Max, *King's Road: The Rise and Fall of the Hippest Street in the World*, London: Phoenix, 2006.

De La Haye, Amy, ed., *The Cutting Edge: 50 Years of British Fashion 1947–1997*, London: V&A Publications, 1996.

Dobbs, Brian, *The Last Shall be First: The Colourful Story of John Lobb, the St. James's Street Bootmaker*, London: Elm Tree Books/Hamish Hamilton, 1972.

Flynn, Errol, *My Wicked, Wicked Ways*, New York: G. P. Putnam's Sons, 1959.

Foulkes, Nicholas, *Scandalous Society: Passion and Celebrity in the Nineteenth Century*, London: Little Brown, 2003.

– *Turnbull & Asser*, London: Brompton Press, 1997.

Gelardi, Julia, *Born to Rule: Granddaughters of Victoria, Queens of Europe*, London: Headline, 2004.

Gorman, Paul, *The Look: Adventures in Rock & Pop Fashion*, London: Adelíta, 2006.

Howarth, Stephen, *Henry Poole, Founders of Savile Row: The Making of a Legend*, Honíton: Bene Factum Publishing, 2003.

Jennings, Charles, *Them and Us: The American Invasion of British High Society*, Stroud: Sutton Publishing, 2007.

Kelly, Ian, *Beau Brummell: The Ultimate Dandy*, London: Hodder, 2005.

King, Greg, *The Duchess of Windsor: The Uncommon Life of Wallis Simpson*, London: Aurum, 2000.

Kobal, John, *The Art of the Great Hollywood Portrait Photographers 1925–1940*, London: Pavilion, 1980.

Laver, James, *Costume and Fashion: A Concise History*, London: Thames & Hudson, 1969.

Levinson, Peter J., *Puttin' On The Ritz: Fred Astaire and the Fine Art of Panache*, New York: St. Martin's Press, 2009.

Menkes, Suzy, *The Windsor Style*, London: Grafton Books, 1987.

Mrs Humphrey ('Madge of Truth'), *Manners for Men*, London: James Bowden, 1897.

Musgrave, Eric, *Sharp Suits*, London: Pavilion, 2009.

Norwich, John Julius, ed., *The Duff Cooper Diaries*, London: Phoenix, 2005.

O'Connor, Patrick, *The Amazing Blonde Woman: Dietrich's Own Style*, London: Bloomsbury, 1991.

Payne, Graham, and Sheridan Morley, ed., *The Noël Coward Diaries*, London: Phoenix Granta, 1982.

Pope-Hennessy, James, *Queen Mary: 1867–1953*, London: Phoenix, 1959.

The Rogers Collection, Auction catalogue, Sotheby's, London, January 28, 29, 30, 1998.

Schreier, Sandy, *Hollywood Dressed & Undressed: A Century of Cinema Style*, New York: Rizzoli, 1998.

Shawcross, William, *Queen Elizabeth: The Queen Mother*, London: Macmillan, 2009.

Summerville, Christopher, ed., *Regency Recollections: Captain Gronow's Guide to Life in London and Paris*, Welwyn Garden Cíty: Ravenhall Books, 2006.

Taylor, D.J., *Bright Young People: The Rise and Fall of a Generation 1918 –1940*, London: Chatto & Windus, 2007.

Titman, George A, ed., *Dress & Insignia Worn at His Majesty's Court*, London: Harrison & Sons Ltd, 1937.

Torregrossa, Richard, *Cary Grant: A Celebration of Style*, London: Aurum Press, 2006.

Vickers, Hugo, *Cecil Beaton: The Authorized Biography*, London: Prion, 1988.

Walker, Richard, *The Savile Row Story: An Illustrated History*, London: Prion, 1988.

Watt, Judith, ed., *The Penguin Book of Twentieth Century Fashion Writing*, London: Viking, 1999.

– *Dogs in Vogue: A Century of Canine Chic*, London: Little, Brown, 2009.

Weber, Caroline, *Queen of Fashion: What Marie Antoinette Wore to the Revolution*, London: Aurum, 2006.

Williams, Kate, *Becoming Queen: How a Tragic and Untimely Death Shaped the Reign of Queen Victoria*, London: Hutchinson, 2008.

Windsor, Duke of, *A King's Story: The Memoirs of HRH The Duke of Windsor*, London: Casssell and Company Ltd, 1951.

– *The Duke of Windsor: A Family Album*, London: Cassell, 1960.

Youssoupoff, Prince Felix, *Lost Splendor: The Amazing Memoirs of the Man who Killed Rasputin*, New York: Helen Marx Books, 2003.

Zeepvat, Charlotte, *The Camera and the Tsars: The Romanov Family in Photographs*, London: Sutton Publishing, 2004.

Unless otherwise indicated, quotations are taken from interviews and conversations with the author. Quotations from Douglas Hayward are taken from material stored in the Hayward archive.

Extracts from *Tailor & Cutter*, *Cloth & Clothes*, *Men's Wear* and *Man About Town* courtesy of the EMAP Archive held by the London College of Fashion. With thanks to LCF archives manager Katherine Baird.

The following publications were consulted: *Daily Graphic*, *Debrett's Peerage & Baronetage*, *The Field*, *Illustrated London News*, *The Sphere*, *Tailor & Cutter*, *The Times* (Gieves & Hawkes archive), *The Town* (Henry Poole & Co. archive), *Esquire*, *GQ*, *The Rake*, *The Telegraph*, *Vanity Fair* (Author's collection).

PICTURE CREDITS

p. 1: Guy Hills/2010; pp. 2–3: Guy Hills/2010; pp. 6–7: Jude Edginton/2009; p. 11: Munster/*The Rake*/2008; p. 12: Simon Perry/*The Rake*/2010; p. 14: Luca da Girolamo/Gieves & Hawkes/2009; p. 16: Henry Poole & Co. archive; p. 17: Guy Hills/Huntsman/2008; p. 18: Paul Manser/James Lock & Co.; p. 19: Author's collection; p. 20: Guy Hills/2010; p. 21: Guy Hills/2010; p. 22: Munster/*The Rake*/2010; p. 23: Getty Images; p. 24: Munster/*The Rake*/2009; p. 25: Guy Hills/2008; p. 26: Nick Knight/2005; p. 27: Munster/*The Rake*/2009.

p. 28: Author's collection; p. 30: Gieves & Hawkes archive; p. 31: © Stapleton Collection/Corbis; p. 32: Getty Images; p. 33: Lafayette Archive courtesy of Ede & Ravenscroft; p. 34: Author's collection (all images); p. 35: © Hulton-Deutsch Collection/CORBIS; p. 37: Tim Graham/Getty Images; p. 38: Tim Graham/Getty Images; p. 39: © Reuters/CORBIS; p. 41: Getty Images; p. 42 (clockwise from top left): Author's collection; Ede & Ravenscroft archive; Author's collection; Getty Images; p. 43: Ede & Ravenscroft archive; p. 44: Ede & Ravenscroft archive; p. 45: Monty Fresco/Getty Images; p. 46: Ede & Ravenscroft; p. 47: Lorenzo Agius/Ede & Ravenscroft; p. 48: Lorenzo Agius/Ede & Ravenscroft; p. 49: Lorenzo Agius/Ede & Ravenscroft; p. 50: Henry Poole & Co. archive; p. 51: Time & Life Pictures/Getty Images; p. 52: Henry Poole & Co. archive (all images); p. 53: Henry Poole & Co. archive (all images); p. 54: Getty Images; p. 55: Henry Poole & Co. archive (all images); p. 56: Henry Poole & Co. archive (all images); p. 57: Henry Poole & Co.; p. 58: Getty Images; p. 59: Henry Poole & Co. (all images); p. 62: (left) Huntsman; (right) Huntsman archive; p. 61: Getty Images; p. 63: Author's collection; p. 64: Author's collection; p. 65: (clockwise from top left) Roger Viollet/Getty Images; Everett Collection/Rex Features; Getty Images; Getty Images; Getty Images; p. 66: Huntsman archive (all images); p. 67: ITV/Rex Features; pp. 68–69: Huntsman archive (all images); p. 70: Guy Hills/Huntsman/2009; p. 71: Guy Hills.

p. 72: Tom Blau/Time & Life Pictures/Getty Images; p. 74; Getty Images; p. 75: (clockwise from left) SNAP/Rex Pictures; © Michael Nicholson/Corbis; Everett Collection/Rex Features; p. 76: Time & Life Pictures/Getty Images; p. 77: Author's collection; pp. 78–79: Author's collection (all images); p. 80: Gordon Anthony/Getty Images; p. 83: (clockwise from top left) My Fair Lady /Rex Features; c.Icon/Everett/Rex Features; p. 84: Agence Hoffman, Germany/ Madame Sfiri; p. 85: State Russian Museum, St Petersburg, Russia/ The Bridgeman Art Library; p. 86: (left) Getty Images; (right) Davies & Son archive; p. 87: (all images) Davies & Son archive (all images); p. 88: Guy Hills/2009; p. 89: Guy Hills/2009; p. 91: Hardy Amies archive; p. 92: Michael Murray & Associates/ Hardy

Amies archive; p. 93: (clockwise from top left) Hardy Amies archive; Peter Waugh/Hardy Amies archive; Hardy Amies archive; Chris Ware/Hardy Amies archive; p. 94: (clockwise from top left) Hardy Amies archive; Hardy Amies archive; Hardy Amies archive; Getty Images; p. 95: Hardy Amies archive; p. 96: Mark Weeks/Hardy Amies; p. 97: J. P. Masclet/ Hardy Amies archive (all images); p. 99: Guy Hills/ 2010; p. 100: Getty Images; p. 101: Patrizio Di Renzo/Mark Powell (all images); pp. 102–3: Andrea Baldrighi/Mark Powell (all images); p. 104: Everett Collection/ Rex Features; p. 105: Guy Hills/2007.

p. 106: National Portrait Gallery/The Bridgeman Art Library; p. 108: Gieves & Hawkes archive; p. 109: Apsley House, The Wellington Museum, London/The Bridgeman Art Library; p. 110: Lafayette Archive/ Ede & Ravenscroft; p. 111: Getty Images (all images); p. 112: Popperfoto/ Getty Images; p. 113: (left) Guy Hills/Norton & Sons archive; (right) Guy Hills/Gieves & Hawkes; p. 114: Gieves & Hawkes archive; p. 115: (top, all images) Author's collection; (bottom) SNAP/Rex Features; p. 116: Dege & Skinner archive; p. 117: Author's collection; p. 118: Henry Poole & Co. archive; p. 119: (clockwise from top left) Reginald Davies/Rex Features; AFP/Getty Images; AFP/Getty Images; Getty Images; p. 120: Jason Pietra/*Qvest*; p. 121: Jason Pietra/*Qvest*; p. 122: Author's collection; p. 123: Lafayette Archive/Ede & Ravenscroft; p. 124: (clockwise from top left) Getty Images; Gieves & Hawkes archive; Getty Images; p. 125: Gieves & Hawkes archive (all images); p. 126: (left) Author's collection; (right) Gieves & Hawkes archive; p. 127: The Crown Estate/The Bridgeman Art Library; p. 128: Gieves & Hawkes archive (all images); p. 129: Gieves & Hawkes archive (all images); pp. 130–31: Matthew Brookes/2009; p. 133: Guy Hills/*The Rake*/2010; p. 134: (clockwise from top left) Lafayette Studio/Ede & Ravenscroft; Getty Images; Getty Images; Getty Images; p. 135: Guy Hills/*The Rake*/2009; p. 136: (left) Guy Hills/2009; (right) Catwalking/Norton & Sons ; p. 137: Guy Hills/*The Rake*/2010.

p. 138: © John Springer Collection/Corbis; p. 140: Author's collection (all images); p. 141: © Sunset Boulevard/Corbis; p. 142: © Hulton-Deutsch Collection/Corbis; p. 143: © Sunset Boulevard/ Corbis; p. 144: (clockwise from top left) © JP Laffont/ Sygma/Corbis; © Bettmann/ Corbis; © Bettmann/Corbis; Getty Images; p. 145: Getty Images; p. 146: © Bettmann/Corbis; p. 147: © Sunset Boulevard/ Corbis; p. 149: © Sunset Boulevard/Corbis; p. 150: (clockwise from top left) © Gary Hershorn/Reuters/Corbs; © CinemaPhoto/Corbis; Warner Bros./ Getty Images; p. 151: Getty Images; p. 153: Munster/*The Rake*; p. 154: (top) Munster/*The Rake*; (bottom) Guy Hills/2007; p. 155: © Condé Nast Archive/Corbis; p. 156: (clockwise from top left) © Bettmann/Corbis;

Getty Images; © John Springer Collection/ Corbis; © Bettmann/Corbis; p. 157: Guy Hills/2008; p. 158–59: Ben Baker/Anderson & Sheppard; p. 161: Clive Arrowsmith/ www.clivearrowsmith.com; p. 162: Hayward archive; p. 163: Hayward archive; p. 164: (clockwise from top left) Hayward archive; Hayward archive; Everett Collection/Rex Features; Hayward archive; p. 165: Getty Images; p. 167: © David James/Sygma/ Corbis; p. 168: Guy Hills/London College of Fashion; p. 169: Nick Knight; p. 170: © Corbis; p. 171: Nick Knight; p. 172; Nick Knight; p. 173: Nick Knight; pp. 174–75: Guy Maineau.

p. 176: Glazier Design/Richard Anderson; p. 179: Nick Harvey/ WireImage; p. 181: (left) Pool Photograph/Corbis; (right) Ozwald Boateng; p. 182: Dave M. Benett/Getty Images; p. 183: James Devaney/ WireImage; pp. 184–85: Guy Hills/2007; p. 187: Ram Shergill/2009; p. 188: (top and middle) Jamie Morgan/Ozwald Boateng; (bottom) Scott Myers/ Rex Features; p. 189: Ozwald Boateng; p. 191: (clockwise from top left) Rex Features; Richard Young/Rex Features; Action Press/Rex Features; Ozwald Boateng; Matt Baron/BEI/Rex Features; p. 192: Michael Dunlea/ Rex Features; p. 193: Ed Reeves/2007; p. 194: Richard Anderson collection; p. 195: Glazier Design/Richard Anderson; pp. 196–97: Glazier Design/Richard Anderson (all images); p. 198: (left) Sipa Press/ Rex Features; (right) Venturelli/WireImage; p. 199: Glazier Design/ Richard Anderson; p. 201: John Spinks/Richard James; p. 202: John Spinks/Richard James (all images); p. 203: *John Spinks/Richard James*; p. 204: Dave Benett/Getty Images; p. 205: Jim Smeal/WireImage; p. 206: Richard James; p. 207: Guy Hills/2007.

p. 208: Christopher Tarling collection; p. 211: (clockwise from top left) Getty Images; Getty Images; Bill Zygmant/Rex Features; Bill Zygmant/ Rex Features; p. 212: © Hulton-Deutsch Collection/Corbis; p. 213: Christopher Tarling collection (all images); p. 214: Henry Poole & Co. archive; p. 215: Munster/*The Rake*/2009; p. 216: Guy Hills/2008; p. 217: Guy Hills/2009; p. 218: Edward Sexton collection; p. 219: © Norman Parkinson Limited/Corbis; p. 220: Getty Images; p. 222: (clockwise from top left) © Bettmann/Corbis; Getty Images; Getty Images; p. 223: Christopher Tarling collection (all images); p. 224: Christopher Simon Sykes/Getty Images; p. 225 Christopher Tarling collection (all images); p. 222: Munster/*The Rake*/2009 (all images); p. 227: Munster/ *The Rake*/2009; p. 228: David Nutter/Edward Sexton archive; p. 229: Seiji Kakizaki/Edward Sexton archive (all images); p. 230: Munster/*The Rake*/2009; p. 232: (top) Sue Barr/View Pictures/Rex Features; (bottom) Spencer Hart; p. 233: Spencer Hart; p. 234: Roger Rich/Aquascutum Ltd; p. 235: Erik C. Pendzich/Rex Features; p. 237: Munster/*The Rake*/

2009; p. 238: Munster/*The Rake*/2009; p. 239: Munster/*The Rake*/2009 (all images); p. 240: c.Focus/Everett/Rex Features; p. 241: Munster/ *The Rake*/2009.

p. 242: Munster/*The Rake*/2009; p. 245: Munster/*The Rake*/2009; p. 246: Guy Hills/ Huntsman/ 2009; p. 249 Junction Eleven/Turnbull & Asser; p. 250: Munster/*The Rake*/2009; p. 253 Munster/*The Rake*/2009; p. 254: Munster/*The Rake*/2009; p. 257: (top) Glazier Design/Richard Anderson; (bottom) Guy Hills/Huntsman/2009; p. 259: Samuel Clark/Chittleborough & Morgan; p. 260 Nick Knight; pp. 262–65: (numbered from left to right) Norton & Sons (1, 2), Henry Poole & Co. (3, 5, 6, 7, 10), Anderson & Sheppard (4, 11) and Richard Anderson (8, 9, 12); pp. 266–67: Dege & Skinner archive; pp. 274–75: All images supplied by and reproduced by kind permission of Dege & Skinner archive, Edward Sexton, Glazier Design, Guy Hills, Hardy Amies archive, Henry Poole & Co. archive, Huntsman Ltd, Munster/*The Rake*, Tony King; p. 288: Guy Hills/*The Rake*/2009.

INDEX

Page numbers in *italic* refer to illustrations.

Abbey Road 221
Abbot, Lemuel Francis *106*
Abercrombie & Fitch 16, 178, 184
Abyssinian Campaign 128
Adams, Thomas 40
Adeney & Boutroy 18, 88
Adjaye, David 192
Africa 132, 157, 186
Agius, Lorenzo 47
Alaïa, Azzedine *167*
Albany 181
Albemarle Street 63
Albert I of Belgium *111*
Albert, Prince 31, *32*, 35, 35, *124*, *125*, 126
Albert Victor, Prince (Prince Eddy) 29, *30*, *30*, 31, *32*, 35, 84, *112*, 122, 247
Alberta Ferretti *241*
Aldershot 118
Alexandra, Queen *42*, *43*, 43, 44, 84, 248
Alexandra, Tsarina 108
Alexei, Tsarevich 86
Alfie 150, *151*
Alfonso XIII 63, *65*, *111*
Alfred, Duke of Saxe-Coburg Gotha 60
Alice, Princess 108
Allan, Chris 46
Allen, Charlie 100
Alsleben, Gordon *184–85*
Althorp 47
Amanullah of Afghanistan, King 247
Ambassador 90
American Gigolo 148, *150*, 163
American in Paris, An 158
Amies, Hardy 38, 80,

90–97, *91*, 132, 206, 218, 272
Anderson & Sheppard 12, *13*, 19, 22, 23, *24*, 36, 38, *38*, 60, 66, 71, 135, 136, 140, 143, *144*, 145, 147, 150, *150*, 152–59, 168, 172, 184, *185*, 189, 190, *204*, 213, 214, 216, 238, 272
Anderson, Brett 233, *234*
Anderson, Per 152, 158
Anderson, Richard 25, *174*, *179*, *184–85*, *194–99*, 213, 256, 272
Andrews, Anthony 82, *83*
Annigoni, Pietro 124
Anthony, Gordon *80*
Anthony J. Hewitt 184, 272
Aosta, Duke of 25
Apple 210, 221, 222
Apsley House 18
Aquascutum 97, 234
Archer Street 98
Arctic Monkeys 233
Arena 206
Arena Homme + 180
Armani, Giorgio 25, 67, 150, *150*, 178, 181
Armstrong, John 181
Arnault, Bernard 192
Arrowsmith, Clive *161*
Arthur, Sir George Compton Archibald *117*
Asia 172
Astaire, Adele 63, *145*
Astaire, Fred 25, 64, *138*, 140, 147, 152, 154, *156*, 157, 168, 170, *170*, 223, 251
Atonement 215, *240*, *241*
Australia 124
Austria 50, 110
Avengers, The 148, *150*, 252
A–Z Revue 152

Baker, Andrew *176*
Baker, Ben *158–59*
Baker, Kenneth 180
Baker, Tom 273
Balanchine, Georges 157, 251
Baldrighi, Andrea *102–3*
Bale, Christian 148
Ballets Russes 157
Ballingall, George 23, 128
Balmain, Pierre 92
Balmoral *32*
Bamford, Lady 228
Bandwagon, The 152
Banton, Travis 140
barbers & perfumers 244
Barker, Christian *135*
Bashir, Martin 181
Bassano Studio 108
Bates Gentlemen's Hatter 247, 273
Bath 81
Batman 228
Batteson, Albert *44*
Beams 88, 136
Beatles, The 24, 210, *211*, 221, 222
Beaton, Cecil 72, 81, 82, *80*, *83*, 90, *125*, 126, 157, 168, 251
Beatrice of Saxe-Coburg, Princess 43
Beatty, Warren 160
Beau Brummell 75
Beauchamp Place 228
Beaverbrook, Lord 63
Beckham, David 53, *183*, 202, 214, 244, 251
Beckham, Victoria *183*
Bedford, Duke of 218
Belgium 35, 50
Bennett, Alan 6–7, 60, 87, 88, *89*, 95, 136, 170
Bennett, Joan 63
Bentley, Michael 92
Bercow, John 46

Bergen, Candice 165
Berkshire 230
Berluti 251
Bermans 97
Bespoke Couture 186, *188*, 189, 190, *191*, 192
Bettany, Paul 104, *104*, 190, *191*, 202
Biarritz 36
Bill (Hardy Amies commissionaire) *94*
Bismarck, Prince (Iron Duke) 56
Black, Cilla 165, 213, 221, 222, 223, 226
Blahnik, Manolo 158
Blair, Tony 190
blazers 35, 36, 95, 148, 163, 214, 216
Blitz 114, 126
Blow, Isabella 104
Boateng, Ozwald 24, 100, 148, 178, 180, 181, *181*, *184–85*, 186–93, *194*, 198, 214, 233, 236, 258, 272
Boca Raton 132
Boer War 116
Bogarde, Dirk 66, 160
Bonaparte, Jérôme 55
Bonar Law 252
Bond Street 16, 18, 60, 76, 114, 122, *125*, *128*, 158
boots: ankle 97; Queen Victoria's *238*; riding 76, *78*; Wellington 116
Borsi, Riccardo 181
Boss 181
Boulting, Ingrid *223*
Bowes-Lyon, Elizabeth *see* Elizabeth, Queen Mother
Bowie, David 100, *191*, 230, *235*

Bowles, Hamish 82, 181, 202
Boyd, Ann 97
Boyer, Charles 140
Boyle, Sir Richard 'the Rich' 16
Brandelli, Carlo 25, *26*, 135, 168–75, 206, 213, 214
Brazil 50
Breakfast at Tiffany's 170
breeches 60, 63, 71, 118, 136
Brewer Street 18, 100, 104
Brice, Jonathan 90, *92*
Bright Young Things, The 83
Brioni 140
British Fashion Week (1,973) 214
British Style Genius documentary 160, 162
Broadway Melody of 1942 156
Brockbank, Russell 114
Brodie, Sir Benjamin Collins 135
Brook Street 90
Brook's club 84
Brooks Brothers 158
Brown, Gordon 240
Brown, Peter 213, 221, 222, 224, 226
Browne, Lord *179*
Browne, Thom 210
Browns 178
Bruce, Ian 217
Brummell, George 'Beau' *19*, 19, 30, 74, *74*, 76, 81, 82, 84, 92, 186, 216, 244, 247
Brunswick Hotel 50
Bruton Place 238
Buchanan, Jack 140, 148, 152, 154, 157
Buckingham Palace 20, 40, 44, *45*, 110, *111*, *119*, 192

Buckingham, Duke of 128
Budd Ltd 248, 273
Burberry 135
Burke's club *162*, 165
Burlington Gardens 46, *46*
Burlington House 16, 18
Burstein, Joan 178
Burton, Richard 160, 166
Burton's 166
Butcher, John 248
Button, Jensen 190
buttonholes 157, 170, 256
buttons 60, 116, 211, 214
Byrne, Joshua 184
Byrne & Burge 272
Byron, Lord 76, 247, 251

Caen 76
Café de Paris 36, 104
Caine, Michael 26, 148, *151*, 160, *161*, 162, *164*, 165, 166, 248
Caine, Shakira *164*
Cairo 162
Calais 76
Cambridge 46, 81, 82
Cambridge, Duke of 43, 126, *126*, 128, 252
Cameron, David 240
Campbell Moore, Stephen *83*
Campbell, Miss 92
Campbell, Naomi 100, 104
Campbell-Walter, Fiona *see* Thyssen, Baroness
Canada 114
canes 97, *246*
Cannes 190
capes 214; Inverness *33*; matador *94*
caps 116, 120, 122, 126, 128; astrakan *110*; cloth flat *34*; fur *126*; plumed 108, *110*, *113*; smoking 18
Caraceni 140
Caraterroi 140
Cardigan, Earl of 56, 108, 128
Cardin, Pierre 90, 168

Carlyle, Mrs 81
Carnaby Street 24, 66, 86, 210, *211*, 214
Carnarvon, Lord 132, *134*, 135
Caroline of Brunswick *19*, 74
Carr, Garry 23
Carrington, Sir William 43
Carter & Co. *113*
Carter, Howard 135
Casino Royale 172
Castle, Irene *155*
Castlerosse, Lord 63
Catterick Camp 118
Cavendish, Lord Charles 63
Cerruti, Nino 148
Chalayan, Hussein 236
Chalk & Dawson 114
Chancery Lane 40, 43, 44, 46, *46*
Chanel, Coco 223, 248
Chaplin, Charlie 23
Charge of the Light Brigade 128
Charisse, Cyd 148, 152
Charles, Audie 160, 162, 166
Charles, Poppy 71
Charles, Prince 38, *38*, 43, 44, 46, 129, *204*, 244, 251
Charlot, André 152
Charlotte, Queen 18, 122
Château de Chantilly *167*
Cheshire Bespoke 184
Chester Barrie 230
Chesterfield Street 30, 76
Chittleborough & Morgan 170, 224, 227, 258, 272
Chittleborough, Roy 170, 213, 224, *226*
Chloe 228
Christian, Peter *93*
Christian, Prince 43
Christie's 56
Church Place 248
Church Street 95
Churchill, Winston 108, *111*, 136

City 120, 148, 244
Clarence and Avondale, Duke of *see* Albert Victor, Prince (Prince Eddy)
Claridge's Hotel *225*, 231
Clark, Ossie 210
Clark, Richard 238
Clash, The 98
Clayton Calthrop, Dion 76
Clifford Street 56, 104, 118, *162*, 165, 200, 206, 251
Clooney, George 140, 148, *150*
Cloth & Clothes *38*, 148
clothes rationing 114
coatees 21, 23, *56*, 88
coats 49, 83, 93, 95, *131*, 145, 147, *169*, *197*, 251; Flare Line 67; frock 34, 60, 66, 71, 77, *78*, 97, 104, 113, 148; full state coachman's *59*; full state footman's *59*; full state postillion's *59*; full state walking groom's *59*; greatcoats 97, 126; morning 34, 36, 60, *78*, *96*; pea 199; Royal Ascot postillion's *59*; tailcoats 67, *68*, 76, 154, 159, 170, 228; two-button *34*
Coburn, James 160
Codie, Lew 152
Coke, William 247
Coleridge, David 60, 71
collars 35, 57, 76, 97, 125, *163*, 198, 223, 238, 258; Nehru 213; shawl 67, *105*, 148, 232–33; stand 77; stiff 36, 46, 132; stud 100; tabs 46, 122; velvet 97; wing *32*, *34*, 62
Collingwood, Admiral Lord 108, 122
Collins, Wilkie 56
Colman, Ronald 140, 154
combat dress 120

Comme des Garçons 25, 88, 178, 202
Compiègne 55
Conduit Street 16, 18, 76, 114, 116, 118, 132
Connaught, Duke and Duchess of 43
Connelly, Jennifer *191*
Connery, Sean 248
Cooch Behar, Maharaja of 57, 63
Cook, Andrew 35
Cook, John *74*
Cook, Peter 160
Cool Britannia 190
Cooper, Diana 63
Cooper, Duff 251
Cooper, Gary 132, 140, *141*, *140*, 144, 147, 154, *154*, *156*, 157, 251
Cork Street 18, 53, 58, 76, 84
Cornwall, Duchess of 129, 251
coronation robes 40, *41*, *42*, 43–44, *45*
Correspondents, The 217
country attire 60
court dress 19, 23, *31*, 52–53, *52*
court tailoring 216
Coutts & Co. 52
Covent Garden 244
Coward, Noël 152, 154, 157, 160
Cowell, Simon 194
Cowes *86*
Cox, Patrick 202
Craddock Hartopp, Sir Charles *78*
Craig, Daniel 172, 202, 248
cravats *78*
Crawford, Joan *144*
Crimean War 108, 118, 122, 128
Crosby, Bing 132, 145, 199, 234
Crowe, Russell 190
Cruise, Tom 150, 202, *205*, 214, 240

Cubitt, Lewis 53, *55*
cuffs 35, *52*, 56, 67, *78*, 163, 238, 258; fishtail *105*; gauntlet 98, 104
Cukor, George 154
Cumberland, Duke of 252
Cundey, Angus 50, 56, 58, 67, 128, 228
Cundey, Howard 57
Cundey, Sam 56, 57
Cundey, Simon *184–85*
Curzon, Lord 252
Curzon Street 244, *245*, 273

D'Arblay Street 100, 273
Dahl, Roald 194
Daily Post 16
Daily Telegraph, The 92, 165
Daks 238
Dancing Lady 154
Dandy Fashions 210
Dash, Damon 233
Dashing Tweeds 88, *88*, *89*, 136, *136*, 214, 216, *216*, 218; 'Centre Point' designs *217*
Davies & Son 19, 23, *34*, 35, 84–89, 95, 110, 170, 184, 272
Davies, Thomas 84, *87*
Davis Jr, Sammy 160, *164*, 166
Day-Lewis, Daniel 150, 190, *191*
De Beers/Versace 'Diamonds are Forever' party *204*
Deacon, Giles 136
'Death's Head' Hussars 108, *111*
Dege & Skinner *17*, 19, 88, 114, 116–21, 135, 184, 248, 272
Dege, Arthur 116
Dege, Jacob 116, 118
del Toro, Benicio 194
Demsey, John 230
Denham, Sir John 16
Denman & Goddard 88, 184, 272

Denmark 35, 110, 126
Depp, Johnny 248
Derby 35
Desire 144
Devonshire, Duchess
of 90
Devonshire, Duke of 55
Deyn, Agyness *136*
di Frasso, Countess
Dorothy 154, 157
Di Renzo, Patrizio *101*
Diaghilev, Sergei 154
Diana, Princess of Wales
35, 95, *181*, 251
Dickens, Charles 56
Diesel 224
Dietrich, Marlene 23, 66,
140, *144*, 154, 248
Dines, George 110
Dior Homme 192
Dior, Christian 92, *205*
Dirty Rotten Scoundrels 162
Disraeli, Benjamin 56
Dixon, Sean 200, 202
Doherty, Pete 202, 228
Donaldson, Williams &
Ward 218, *225*
Donat, Robert 140, 154
Donna Karan 240
Dorchester Hotel *65*
Douglas, James 16
Douglas, Kirk 160
Dover *111*
Dover Street 210;
market 88
Drama 187
'drape, the' 158, 258
Drexel-Biddle Jr, Anthony
132, *134*
du Maurier, George 247
Dubai 172
Dublin *123*
Duffbffb, Rory *136*
Duke Street 110
Dunaway, Faye *149*
Dunhill 192
Dunkirk 114
Duran Duran 98, 233
Dutt, Robin 181, 200
Duveen, Joseph 125
Dylan, Bob 210

E. Tautz & Sons *113*, 132,
136, *137*
East End 98, 100, 114,
178,
236, 238
Eastwood, Clint 160
Ecclestone, Petra 228
Eddy, Prince *see* Albert
Victor, Prince
Ede & Ravenscroft 40–49,
108, 110, 118, 272
Ede, Joseph 40, 43
Ede, Rosa 43, *43*, 44
Edinburgh, Duke of *see*
Philip, Prince
Edward Green 251
Edward VII 30, 31, 32,
33, 35, 36, 43, *54*, 55,
57, 58, 60, 63, 71, 84,
110, 122, 135, 244,
247, 251
Edward VIII *see* Windsor,
Duke of
Edwardian cut 180, 181
Egypt 50; Khedive of
57–58
Elder Street 238, *238–39*
Elisabeth of Austria,
Empress 55
Elizabeth II, Queen 24,
38, 40, 44, *45*, 58,
90, 92, 97, 118, *119*,
124, 126, 192, 244,
247, 252
Elizabeth, Queen Mother
42, 44, 92
Ellis, Sean 171, 172
Embankment Gardens *94*
Embassy Club 36
English Patient, The 150
Epstein, Brian 248
ermine 40, 44, 46
Erroll, Countess Idina
of 64
Esquire 178, 180, 202, 251
Essex 98
Estée Lauder 230
Eton 74, 110, 184
Ettedgui, Joseph 230
Eugénie, Empress 55
Everest, Timothy 26, 82,
100, 148, 178, 180, 181,
183, 214, 215, 226, 230,
236–41, 254, 273
Everett Street 52
Everett, Rupert 202
Evisu 184

Face, The 100
Fair Isle *34*, 82
Fairbanks Jr, Douglas 25,
87, *142*, *144*, 145, 147,
148, 154
Faisal of Egypt, King 170
Far from the Madding Crowd 165
Farm Street Church 160
Farnes, Matthew 184–85
'Fashion in Motion' show
181
Fechter, Charles 55
Ferdinand I of Bulgaria
111
Ferry, Bryan 100, 104,
194, *198*, 251
Fields, Duggie 189
Fields, Patricia 247
Fiennes, Ralph 150, *150*,
157
Fife, Duchess of 43
Financial Times 135, *184–85*,
214
Finney, Albert 160
First World War 21, 63,
81, 108, 110, 113, 114,
116, 118, 125, 147
Fish, Michael 'Mr' *225*,
248
Fishburne, Laurence
190, *191*
Fitzgerald, F. Scott
248, 251
'Flare Line' cut 24
flash basting 57, 257, 270
Fleetwood, Ken *93*, 95
Fleming, Victor 157
Flights 18
Florence 25, 104, 120,
191
Floris, J. 244, 273
Flynn, Errol 100, 140
fob watches 98, 148, 163
For Your Eyes Only 162

Forbes, Bryan 166
Ford, Harrison 247
Ford, Tom *12*, *13*, 67,
104, 140, 158, 210,
238, 240
Form 228
Fortune 158–59
Foulkes, Nick 98, 181
Fox, James 64
Foxx, Jamie 190
France 18, 50
Franklin, Kate 225
Franz Ferdinand 233
Fraser, Angelica Patience
87
Fraser, Colonel James
Keith 78, 81
Fred's 104
Frederick VIII of Denmark
111
Freed, Arthur 157
French Revolution 18, 30
French, T. F. 168
Friend, Rupert 104
Frith Street 104
frogging *131*
Fryer, Elmer *142*
Furness, Viscountess
Thelma 63
Furnish, David 71, 202

G. J. Cleverley & Co. *250*,
251, 273
Gable, Clark 23, *65*, 66,
87, *140*, *143*, 145, 199
Gaekwar of Baroda,
Maharaja 57
Galliano, John 226, 236
Galt, Joseph 122
Gangster Dandy style 98
Gangster No. 1 98, 104, *104*
Garbo, Greta 23
Gardner, Ava 64
Garland, Judy *100*
Garlant, Ian 97, *97*
Garrard 247
Gaultier, Jean-Paul 25,
178, 202, 210
Gay, John 16, 18
George I of Greece 31,
111, 247

George III 18, 122, 244,
252
George IV 20, 21, 32, 33,
42, 74, 82, 120, 133,
239, 242
George V 30, *34*, 35, 36,
40, 42, 43, 44, *86*, 87,
110, *111*, 113, 116, 122,
123, 125, 244, 251
George VI 36, 42, 44, 87,
115, 125
Gere, Richard 150, *150*
Germany 50, 110, 132;
Grand Duchies of 110
Gershwin, George 147
Gertler, Mark 238
Gibb, Bill 225
Gibraltar 58, 110
Gielgud, John 160
Gieve, David 125, 126
Gieve, James Watson *113*,
114, 122, 125
Gieve, Robert James
Watson 129
Gieve, Rodney Watson
125
Gieves & Hawkes *6–7*, *14*,
17, 18, 20, 21, 23, *37*,
38, *39*, 60, *106*, 108,
108, 110, 113, *113*, 114,
115, 122–31, 171, 184,
192, 244, 272; Dress
Indicator 114
Gieves Ltd *106*, 108, 111,
114, 122, 125, 126, 128,
171
Gieves, Matthews &
Seagrove 125
Gigi 157
Gilbert, Alfred 113
Gillespie, Bobby 171
Gillroy, James *19*
Givenchy Homme 192
Gladstone, William Ewart
252
Glasgow 86
Gloucester, Duchess of 44
Gloucester, Duke of 87,
124, 244
gloves 81, 97, 145, 160
Godley, Georgina 184

Gold, Johnny 165
Gone with the Wind 143, 158
Gorman, Paul 98, 210
GQ 98, 180, 181, 216;
    Men of the Year awards
    191
Grafton, Duke of 18
Granger, John 132, 135
Granger, Nicholas 135
Granger, Stewart *65*, 66,
    75, 76, 145, 199
Granny Takes a Trip 210,
    211, 222
Grant, Cary 16, *23*, 132,
    140, *146*, 147, 147–48,
    150, 154, 170, 171, 248
Grant, Hugh 202, *204*
Grant, Patrick 6–7, 82,
    132, *133*, 135–36, 181,
    184–85
Great Depression 125
Great Exhibition (1851)
    244
Great Gatsby, The 162
Greenwood, Cox & Co.
    84
Grenson 251
Grey, Earl de 128
Grimshaw, Stewart 224,
    228
Gronow, Captain 74, 76
Grosvenor Street 92
Groucho Club 100
Guardian, The 98
Gucci 67, 104, 172, *198*
Guest, Montague John
    77, 81

Haakon VI of Norway *111*
Haies, William 145
Haig, Field Marshal
    Douglas 116
Haines, William *144*,
    154, *156*
Hall, Brian 194, 198
Hamad of Bahrain, King
    116, 120
Hamilton, George 160
Hammersmith 165
Hammick, Colin 66, *66*,
    67, 71, 87, 194, *194*, 198

Hammond & Co. 132
Hammond, Celia *165*
Hamnett, Katharine 178
Hamptons 132
Hand & Lock *21*, 22,
    157, 273
Hanover Street 18, 84,
    87, *87*
Happy Valley set 64
Hardy, Flag Captain 122
Harley Street 18
Harrison, George
    210, *211*
Harrison, Rex 66, *83*, *145*,
    148, 170, 199
Harrods 136
Harry, Prince 38
Hart, Nick 6–7, 25, 82,
    190, 206, 214, 230, *231*,
    233, *234*
Hartnell, Norman *41*, 92,
    97, 251
Harvey, David 92, 95
hats 145; Coke (bowler)
    31, 67, 97, 247; Hawkes
    Helmet 128; homburg
    31; Indiana Jones 244;
    top *34*, 113, 247; trilby
    147, 247; *see also* caps
hatters 247
Hawes & Curtis 38, 145,
    147, 210, 248
Hawkes & Co. 18, 108,
    108, 109, 114, *115*, 122,
    126, *126*, 127, 128,
    128, 244,
Hawkes Helmet 128
Hawkes, Thomas 18,
    122, 126
Hay *30*
Haynes, William 148
Hayward, Douglas 24,
    148, *149*, 150, *151*,
    160–67, 272
Head, Edith 140
Hebrides 135
Helman, Harry 88
Hemmings, David
    160, 248
Henderson, Mark 129
Hendrix, Jimi 210

Henry Poole & Co. 16,
    19, 31, 33, *33*, 36, *42*,
    50–59, 60, 66–67, 82,
    86, 87, 88, 108, 110,
    140, 145, 147, 158, 166,
    184, *206*, 214, 224, 236,
    262, 272
Hepburn, Audrey *83*, 170
Hepburn, Katharine 23,
    66, 199, 251
Hepworths 90
Hermès 251
Herron, Mark *100*
Heseltine, Michael 180
Hesse 108
Hewitt, Anthony J. 178
Heywood, Colin *158–59*
Hicks, Fanny 86
Hilditch & Key 247, 273
Hilfiger, Tommy 158
Hillier, Katie 136
Hills, Guy 6–7, *70*, 88,
    89, *136*, *184–85*, 214,
    216, *216*
Hirohito, Crown Prince
    60, *60*
Hitchcock, Alfred 132,
    144, 145, 147, 148, 170
Hitchcock, John 6–7,
    158, *158–59*, *184–85*,
    213, 216
Hitler, Adolf 113
Hockney, David 172
Holland, Hugh 206, 214
Hollywood 24, 60, 64,
    66, 87, 90, 132, 138–75,
    186, 190, 199
Honourable Corps of
    Gentlemen at Arms 128
Horsley, Sebastian
    194, 199
House of Boateng
    documentary 186
House of Holland 136
House of Lords 48, 86
Howarth, Russell *216*
Howarth, Steven 52
Howe, Admiral Lord
    108, 122
Huddersfield 171

hunting pinks *62*
Huntsman 19, 25, 60–71,
    76, 87, 92, 118, 140,
    143, 145, 148, 158,
    168, 171, 181, 184, 194,
    198, 199, 202, 205,
    213, 217, 236, 247, 248,
    257, 272
Huntsman, Henry 60, 64
Hurley, Elizabeth *200*
Hutton, Barbara 226
Hyde Park 53, 247

I Was Lord Kitchener's
    Valet 210, *211*
i-D 98
Illustrated London News 31
Iman 235
Independent, The 202
India 132
International Herald Tribune
    186
Irene 140
Irons, Jeremy *83*
Irving, Sir Henry 145
Islay woollen mill 63
Italian Job, The 148, 160,
    163, *164*, 165
Italy 50

jabots *52*
Jack the Ripper 31
jackets 132, *137*, 180, 202;
    256; dinner 31, 36, 56,
    167, *197*, *198*, 213; patrol
    110; racing 136; smoking
    22, 31, 56, *130*, 148, *157*;
    sports 38, *197*; William
    Morris 210, *211*
Jackson, Michael 20, 88
Jackson, Samuel L. 190
Jagger, Bianca 165, *212*,
    218, 223, *223*
Jagger, Mick 165, 190,
    210, *212*, 218
Jaipur, Maharaja of *65*
James & James 87
James Lock & Co. 18, 147,
    246, 247, 273
James Smith & Sons 252,
    253, 273

James, Richard *6–7*, 24,
    56, 82, 100, 135, 148,
    171, 178, *179*, 180, 181,
    184, *184–85*, 186, 194,
    200–207, 214, 218,
    229, 236, 238, 272–73
Japan 238
Jay-Z 233
Jazz Age 63, 248
Jermyn Street 118, 244,
    247, 248, *249*
JMH Group 172
jodhpurs *65*
John Lobb Ltd 242, 251,
    273
John, Elton 202, 210,
    219, 228
Johns & Pegg 87
Johnson, Herbert 247,
    252
Jones, John 118
Jones, Grace *167*
Joseph Starkey Ltd 125

Kane, Christopher 136
Kawakubo, Rei 88
Kelly, Grace 64
Kennedy, Joseph 87, 170
Kensington Palace, Royal
    Ceremonial Dress
    collection 40
Kent, Duke of 63, 64, 87,
    157, 244, 248
Kent, John 38, 135
Kenzo 192, 230
khaki uniforms 115
Khashoggi, Adnan 168
Kidman, Nicole 205
Kilgour 19, 25, *25*, 26,
    28, 38, 60, 88, 92, 118,
    135, 136, 140, 145, *146*,
    147, 148, 166, 168–75,
    182, 192, 206, 213, 214,
    223, 226, 233, 272
kilts *32*
Kind Hearts and Coronets 67,
    148
King's Road 24, 168, 210
Kingly Street *56*
Kitchener, Lord 114, 116
Klein, Calvin 157

Klein, Yves 189
knickerbockers 148
Knight, Nick 26, *169*, 171, *171*, *172*
Knightley, Keira *240*
Knightsbridge 228
Knize 140, 145
Knollys, Mrs *43*, 44
Kochno, Boris 154
Koh, Wei 170
Kray twins 98, *100*
Kubrick, Stanley 95

LaChapelle, David 171
Lachasse 90
Lafayette Studio 108, *110*, *112*, *123*
Lagerfeld, Karl 248
Lamb, Toby *202*
Lanesborough Hotel *179*
Langan's 165
Langtry, Lillie 55, 147
Lanvin 184
lapels 57, 95, *130*, *141*, 147, 160, 198, 210, 223, *225*, 228, 256, 257; double-breasted 104; peak 218, 259; shawl 226
Lauren, Ralph 158, 166, 178, 210, 228
Law, Jude 170–71, *182*, 190, 202
Lawford, Peter 160
Lawrence of Arabia 115, 158, 197
Lawrence, Gertrude 63, 152
Lawrence, Sir Thomas 84, *109*
Lawrence, T. E. 114
Layer Cake 172
Lebas, Boy 81
Led Zeppelin 233
Leeds, Duke of 18
Leibovitz, Annie 125, 126
Lennon, John *211*, 218, *222*
Lennox-Boyd, Mark 180
Leoni, Giacomo 16
Leopold of Belgium 126

Lesley & Roberts 140, 143, 145
Levett, James 184
Levett, Keith 58
Levitt, Martin 248
Lewis, Erin *88*
Lewis, Jerry 166
Liberty 234
Lichfield, Lord 162, 165
Lifar, Serge 154
'limp look' 60, 158
Linley, David 181
Lishak, Brian 64, 67, 194, 199, 213
Liverpool Daily Echo 95
Lloyd's Weekly London Newspaper 84
LMVH 192
Lobb, John 242, 247, 251
Lobb, John Hunter 251
Lodger 251
London College of Fashion 88, *168*
London Cut 36, 60, 140
'London Cut' exhibitions *2–3*, 25, *25*, 71, *105*, 120, *157*, 190
London Fashion Week 101
Look, The 210
Los Angeles 140, 170, 199, *218*, 233
Los Angeles Times 160
Louis IV, Grand Duke of Hesse 108
Louise, Princess 43
Louise, Ruth Harriet *156*
Lowe-MacKenzie, Rowland 226
Lowthorpe, Rebecca 190
Lucas, John *127*
Lumatwill ™ *88*
Lutwyche, Tony 181, 184, 272
Luxury Brands Group 97
Lyon, Ben 145

Maclise, Daniel *76*
Madame Tussauds 88
Maddox Street 18
'Made in Africa' foundation 186

Madonna 202
Magnus, Philip 55
Major, Dimi 166
make-do-and-mend initiative 114
Male W3 210
Malta 110
Mandarina Duck 230
Manuel II of Portugal *111*
Margaret of Connaught, Princess 43
Margaret, Princess *42*, 44, 165, 181, *225*
Margiela, Martin 236
Marie of Naples, ex-Queen 55
Marks & Spencer 158; Autograph collection 238
Marlborough House 55, 86, 244
Marlborough, Duke of 18, 244
Marshall, Herbert 154
Martin, Steve 162
Mary, Queen 35, *42*, 44, 64
mashers 35
Mason, Jem 53
Massive Attack 233
Matches 136
Matrix Reloaded 188
Matthews, Karl 158–59
Maurice Sedwell 19, 180, 226, 272
May of Teck, Princess *see* Mary, Queen
Mayer, Louis B. 154, 168
Mayfair 16, 18, 50, 95, 160, 234, 244, 252
Mayfair Hotel *41*
Mayfair Orphans Club 165
McAvoy, James *240*
McCartney, James 228
McCartney, Paul *222*
McCartney, Stella 228
McDougall, Kirsty 88, *89*, 214, *216*
McKellen, Ian 194
McNaughton, Colin 88

McQueen, Alexander 71
McQueen, Steve 24, 148, *149*, 160, 163, 230
McShane, Ian 165
Meard Street 210
Meet Me in St Louis 158
Men's Fashion Council 24, 67, 172
Men's Vogue 165, 172
Men's Wear 38, 171
Menjou, Adolphe 140, 148
Menkes, Suzy 186, 190
Menorca 244
Menswear Association of Britain 210
Merchant Taylors' School 116
Meredith, Melchizidec *106*, 122
mess dress 120, *120*
Mettrick, Guy 180
Meyer & Mortimer 18, 19, 76, 86, 114, 244, 272
Meyer, Jonathan 76
MGM 64, 145, 154, 157
Michael of Kent, Prince 38
Michael of Kent, Princess 97
Michael, George *100*, 230
Middle East 172
Milan 104, 181, 192, *198*
military tailoring 23, 107–37, 210
Miller, Rebecca *191*
Million Pound Note, The 67
Mission: Impossible 240
Mitchum, Robert 160, 163, 165, 170
Mod Male 210
Modesty Blaise 150
Mods 66, 168, 210
Mogambo 64
Monroe, Marilyn 158
Montagu of Beaulieu, 2nd Baron 113
Montagu of Beaulieu, Lord 213, 218, 228
Montgomery, Robert 63, 140, *140*, 145, *156*, *157*

Montrose, Duke of 40
Moore, Dudley 160
Moore, Jon 92, 97
Moore, Roger 160, 162, 165, *167*
Morgan, Jamie *188*
Morgan, Joe 213, 224, 226
Morgan, John 180, 181
Morley, Karen *65*
Morley, Robert 75
Morton, Cole 202
Moschino 158
Moss, Kate 158, 216
Mount Street 24, 160, *161*, *163*, 165
Mountbatten, Lady Edwina 63
Mountbatten, Lord Louis 38, 44, 63, 124, 248
Mouret, Roland 171
Moxon mill 233
Moy, Mr 18
Murphy, Patrick *6–7*, 60, 71
Muscat 119
Musson, Andrew *184–85*
Mutti-Mewse, Austin 97
My Fair Lady 74, *83*
Mysore, Maharaja of 57

Nairobi 64
Napier, Lord 128
Napoleon III 19, 50, *51*, 55, *55*, 265
Napoleonic Wars 52, 106
Nash, Beau 76
National Portrait Gallery 108
Naval Officer's Sea Chest 122
Navarro, Ramon *156*
Near East 132
Neasden 236
Nelson, Admiral Lord 84, *106*, 108, *108*, 114, 122, 247, 265
New Establishment 24, *100*, 176–207, 214, 233, 236
New Labour 190

New Look 92
New Oxford Street 252
New York 56, 64, 166, 181, *191*, 224, 228, *229*; Biltmore Hotel *228*; Metropolitan Museum of Art *234*; Plaza Hotel 64, *144*, *151*
New York Herald Tribune 95
New York Times 67
Nicholas II, Tsar 86, 247
Nicholson, Jack 98, 228
Nicodemi, Paul *136*
Nicoll, Richard 136
'Nine Kings' sitting 110, *111*
Niven, David 100, *132*, 248
Norman, Mabel 152
North by Northwest 147, *147*, 170
Northampton 251
Northamptonshire *47*
Norton & Sons 21, 82, 90, 92, 108, 132–35, 145, 181, 184, 248, 272
Norton, George James 132
Norton, Walter Charles 132
Norway 50, 126
Notorious Gentleman 145
Notting Hill 178
Novello, Ivor 63, *144*, 152
Nutter, David 228
Nutter, Tommy 24, 82, 87, 88, 95, 100, 165, 180, 189, 200, 206, *208*, 210, 212, 213, *213*, 214, 218, *218*, 221, 220–21, 222, 223, *223*, 224, 225, 226, 228, 236

O'Neill, Terry 165
O'Toole, Peter *115*
Obama, Barack *189*
Octopussy 162
Odette, Mlle 92
Old Burlington Street 52, 53, *153*, *158–159*, 192

Olivier, Laurence 66, *145*, *154*, 160, 199, 251
One Sunday Afternoon 156
Ono, Yoko 218, 223
Opening of Parliament 128
Orloff, Grand Duke 244
Orry-Kelly 140
Orsay, Alfred Count d' *76*, 81
Osborne, Royal Naval College 122
Outfitter, The 36
Oxford 46, 74, 82, 135
Oxford Street 166, *211*

Packer, Edward 66
Packer, Robert 64, 66, *118*, 199
Pall Mall 113, 166
Paltrow, Gwyneth *182*
Panges *102–3*
Paris 25, 84, 92, 104, 171, 178, 181, 192, 224, 251
Paris Fashion Week *174–75*
Paris Men's Fashion Week 189
Park Lane 18
Parker, Philip 57
Parkinson, Norman *219*
Patricia of Connaught, Princess 43
Pearse, John 210, 211, 272
Peck, Gregory 66, *67*
Peel, Sir Robert 84
Penhaligon's 244, 273
Peron, Eva 244
Persia, Shah of 57
Philip, Prince *37*, 38, 44, 46, 135, 210, 244
Philippe of Saxe Coburg, Prince 43
'Philwell lining' *121*
Picasso, Paloma 248
Piccadilly 18, 95, *102–3*, 128; Arcade 248
Pietra, Jason *120*, *121*
Pitt, Brad 148
Pitti Immagine Uomo foundation 25

Placebo 233
pleats 104; box 163; shooting 180
Plews, Malcolm 110, *184–85*
Polanski, Roman 160
Pont Street *91*
Poole, Henry 19, 50, 52, 53, 56
Poole, James 52, 53
Poole, Mary Anne 56
Poor Little Rich Girl 226
Pop 222
Porter, Cole 152, 251
Portland, Duke of 18
Portobello Road 189, 210, 211
Portsmouth 122, 125
Portugal 50, *94*
Potter, Cora 56
Potter, James 56
Powell, Eleanor 156
Powell, Leon *158–59*
Powell, Mark 25, 98–105, 180, 181, 272
Power, Tyrone 87, *145*, 251
Prada 172
Preston, Kiki 64
Price, Dennis 148
Prince of Wales check *33*
Princelet Street 236
Princes Street 18
Provans 224
Prussia 31, 108

Qaboos, Sultan of Oman 118, *119*, 120
Quant, Mary 160
Quantum of Solace 140
Queensberry and Dover, Duke of *see* Douglas, James
Queensberry House 16, 18
Quest 120, *121*
Quintino 170
Quirk, Hubert 125

Radcliffe, Daniel 104
Radziwill, Lee 165
Raft, George 100

Rajpipla, Maharaja of 63
Rajpipla, Prince 213
Rake, The 12, 27, 135, 170, *215*, 217, 226, 231, 237, 238, 240, 241, 254
Raleigh, Sir Walter 248
Ramroop, Andrew 180, *181*
Rankin 171
Rasputin 84
Rayment twins *188*
ready-to-wear 23, 25, 67, 82, 90, 92, 97, 100, 126, 129, 136, *137*, 178, 180, 199, 200, 206, 222, 228
Reagan, Ronald 66
Red Hot Chili Peppers 233
Reddish House *72*
Redford, Robert 186
Reeves, Keanu 190
Reeves, Vic 100
Regent Street 52, 56, 251
Rich, Roger *234*
Richardson, Tony 160
Richemont Group 192
Richmond Park 118
Richthofen, Baron Manfred von (Red Baron) 132, *134*
riding attire 60
Ritchie, Guy 202
Riviera, French 63
Robinson, Edward G. 170
Robot 98
Roger, Neil 'Bunny' 82, 87, 95, *95*, 216
Rogers 118
Rolling Stones, The 24, 233; 'Tour of the Americas' 224
Romania 125
Romford 98
Roosevelt, Elliott *156*
Ross, Jonathan 100
Rothschild, Baron Mayer de 52
Rotten Row 53
Rowland, Anda *6–7*, 152, 158

Royal Academy of Arts 16
Royal Arcade 251
Royal Ascot 35, 38, *83*, 247
Royal Geographical Society 128
Royal Mews 58
Rushmore, Mount 148
Russia 35, 50, 108, 110, 247
Russian Revolution 110
Rylands, George 81

Sackville Street 18, 76, 88
safari tailoring 132, 162, 216
Saint Laurent, Yves 50
Saks Fifth Avenue 228, *229*
Salter, William 18
San Francisco 199, *214*
Sander, Jil 236
Sandhurst, Lord 79
Sandhurst, Royal Military Academy 110, *111*, *119*, 120
Sandringham House *33*, 56, *134*
Sargent, Kathryn *6–7*, 129, *184–85*
Sartoria restaurant *101*, 104
Sassoon, Vidal 165
Savile Row *6–7*, 17, 46, 56, *59*, 65, 71, 92, 93, 94, *128*, 129, 135, *184–85*, 193, 195, 207, 214, 222
Savile Row Bespoke Association 24, 25, 126, 181
'Savile Row Street Party' show 182
Saville, Lady Dorothy 16
Saville, Peter 26, *169*, 171, *172*, *173*
Savoy Hotel 24, 67, *94*, 163
scarves 147
Schenck, Joe 158
Schiffer, Claudia 248
Schlesinger, John 223

Schmidt, Eddie 140
Scholte 34, 35, 36, 38, 87, 114, 140, 152, 158
Schweitzer & Davidson 18, 76
Scofield, Paul 160
Scott, Randolph 170
Sebastopol 122
Second World War 23, 82, 92, 108, 110, 114, 125, 132, 248, 252
Sellack, Miss 114
Sellers, Peter 160, 166
Sennett, Mack 152
Serov, Valentin 84
service dress 120
Sex and the City 247
Sexton, Edward 6–7, 24, 27, 168, 194, 199, 200, 210, 213, 218, 218–29, 258, 272
shako 126
Sharif, Omar 160, 199
Sheen, Michael 83
Shepherd's Bush 165
Sheppard, Eugenia 95
Sheridan, Richard Brinsley 92
Shields, Jimmy 154
shirtmakers 248
shirts 145, 147, 160, 163, 181, 189, 230, 233; bibbed 36; Marcella 230, 232–33; Mr Fish-style psychedelic 67; stiff collar 132; stud collar 46, 98
shoemakers 251
shoes 180, 200; Berluti 251; Church's 189; Cleverley 181, 250; cream 147; Cuban-heeled 224; Edward Green's 234; tobacco suede 35, 36
Shoreditch House 238
Shrimpton, Jean 165
Simpson, Wallis 30, 147
Sinatra, Frank 163, 226, 234, 248; Sinatra at the Sands 230

Sinclair, Clarence Bull 67, 141
Singin' in the Rain 157
Skinner, Michael 87, 114, 116, 118, 118, 184–85
Skinner, William 6–7, 116, 118, 120
Sky Captain and the World of Tomorrow 182
'Slim Line' cut 24
Smith, Paul 12, 178, 210, 224, 236
Smith, Peter 67
Smith, Will 190
Snowdon, Lord 67, 165
Soho 24, 86, 98, 99, 100, 104, 170, 178, 181, 210
Soho House 100, 184
Sotheby's 36, 82, 95
South Molton Street 178
Spain 31
spats 32; faux 97
Spelling, Lt Colonel 113
Spencer Hart 82, 206, 214, 230–35, 273
Spencer House 18
Spencer, Countess Raine 97
Spencer, Earl 46
Spencer, Oliver 158–59
Spencer, Victor 63
Sphere, The 42
Spiegel, Sam 157
Spielberg, Steven 247
Spinks, John 201, 202
Spitalfields 236, 238, 239
sporrans 32
sports clothes 36
Spy 35, 64, 76, 77–79, 81, 117
Spy Who Loved Me, The 162
St George's Street 184
St James's 16, 18, 84, 110
St James's Palace 58, 63, 247
St James's Street 18, 148, 242, 244, 247, 251, 252
St Martins College of Art 236
St Moritz 95
St Petersburg 84, 85

Stamford, Earl and Countess of 53
Stamp, Terence 24, 148, 160, 165, 166, 251
Stanbury, Fred 38, 87, 168, 168, 170, 171–72
Stanbury, Louis 87, 168, 170
Stanistreet, Michelle 190
Stanley, Henry M. 128, 132
Star, The 86, 87
Steiger, Rod 160
Stephen, John 210, 211
Sternberg, Josef von 140
Stockmar, Baron de 128
Stoke Newington 98
Stovel & Mason 143
Strachan & Co. 122
Strand 40, 132
strikers 57, 152, 170, 270
Strong, Roy 90
Stroud 125
studs, dress 46
Stultz 18
Suede 233, 234
suits 95, 97, 170, 171, 178, 181, 224, 225, 226; Bespoke Couture purple 188, 189, 190; business 145; chalk stripe 49, 162; checked 84, 213; cocktail 191, 231; dinner 46, 93, 130, 237; double-breasted 145, 196, 227; Flare Line City 214; houndstooth 27, 141; Loden shooting 31; lounge 35; Mr Fish 89; one-button 105, 196–97, 214, 230, 234; pinstripe 67, 100, 104, 148, 196, 226, 233; Prince of Wales check 213; riding 145; shooting 121, 214; single-breasted 141, 145, 160, 196, 226; three-piece 34, 132, 163, 183, 199, 213, 233; 'Utility' 114; Viceroy 47; white baste stitches 57

Sulka 192
Sullivan, Nick 178, 202
Sullivan, Wooley & Co. 74, 83, 145
Sunday Express 190
Sunday Telegraph 180, 181
Sunday Times 190, 192, 200
Swaine Adeney Brigg 247, 252, 273
Swallow Street 18
Swanson, Gloria 251
sweatshops 84–87
Sweden 50, 126
Sykes, Christopher Simon 224
Syon House 204

Tailor & Cutter 17, 23, 37, 50, 57, 66, 81, 140, 145, 148, 158
Tailor Made Man, A 145, 148
Tailor of Panama, The 165
Tailor, Ravi 184
tails: darting, padding and weighting 76; evening 36, 46, 82, 113, 148; morning 38
Talented Mr Ripley, The 171
Talley, André Leon 190, 198
Tarling, Christopher 208, 213, 224, 225
tartans 36
Tatler 81, 92
Tatsuno, Koji 184
Taylor, Elizabeth 75, 165
Taylor, John 233
Taylor, Kerry 95
Teck, Duke of 64
Teddy boys 66, 168
Tennant, Stephen 81
Tentis, Nick 104
Testino, Mario 39, 202
Thailand, King of 210
Thatcher, Margaret 180
Thewliss, David 104
This Charming Man 74
Thomas Crown Affair, The 148, 149, 163

Thomas, Philip 46
Thornton, Eleanor Velasco 113
Thurman, Uma 150
Thyssen, Baroness 41
tiepins 77, 100
ties 160, 189, 230, 233; black 77; kipper 67, 224; knots 32, 34, 36
Times, The 30, 67, 190
Times Luxx 6–7, 233
Todd, Dorothy 81
Tokyo 88, 157
Tom Ford International 140
Tong, Pete 171
Tonga, King of 23
Top Hat 147, 170, 170
Torregrossa, Richard 148
Town, The 16, 16
Trafalgar, Battle of 247
Travilla 140
Trickers 251
Trollope, Anthony 56
Trooping the Colour 116, 119
trousers 35, 36, 66, 76, 78, 79, 84, 86, 93, 104, 132, 147, 154, 156, 162, 178, 180, 210; flared 67, 212, 218, 223, 224, 251; Oxford bags 36, 104; turned-up 67
Truefitt & Hill 244, 273
Truman, Harry 87
Trumper, Geo. F. 244, 245, 273
Tuczek 251
tunics 2–3, 14, 23, 108, 116, 120, 122, 210
Turnbull & Asser 38, 224, 226, 248, 249, 273
Tuscany 27
tuxedos 14; 'cross-legged' 23
tweed 36, 135, 160, 196, 216, 212, 220, 257; Harris 133; see also Dashing Tweeds
20th-Century Fox 158
Twiggy 218, 222, 223

2001: A Space Odyssey 95
Ugogo 128
umbrella, whip & stickmakers 252
umbrellas 67
United Artists 154
United States 152, 172, 224, 226
Uomo Vogue, L' 100
US Men's Wear 213
Ustinov, Peter *75*

Valentine, Bobby 87
Valentino, Rudolph 23, 63, *144*, 152, 154, 251
Vallance White, James 221
Valley of the Kings 132
Vanity Fair 28, 31, *39*, 58, *64*, *77*, *78*, *79*, 81, *117*, 126, 157, 180, 181
Venice *212*
Versace, Gianni 50, 202, *204*, 218
Versailles 30, 82
vests 27, 120, 132, 256
VH1/*Vogue* Fashion Awards *191*
Vickers, Hugo 168
Victor Christian, Prince 43
Victor, Mr 92
Victoria & Albert Museum *89*, 118, *181*, 190
Victoria, Princess 43
Victoria, Queen 21, 32, 33, *33*, 34, 40, 43, 45, 52, 55, 57, 60, 81, 108, 113, *126*, 128, 135, 245, 247
View to a Kill, A 162, *167*
Vigo Street 186, 189
Villeneuve, Justin de 218, 222
Violet, Miss 92
Violet's club 100
Vogue 81, 82, *93*, *151*, 178
Vogue US 82, 181, 194, 198
Vogüé, Marquis de 132
Voyage 230

W 181
waistcoats 66, 76, 147, 148, 163, 256; Life-Saving *20*, 113; Melton *47*; white 31, 36, 53, *58*
Walker, Richard 64, 147
Wall Street 150
*Wallpaper** 214
Walsh, John 186
Walters, Catherine 'Skittles' 55
Ward, David 136
Ward, Leslie *see* Spy
Ware, Chris *93*
Waterloo, Battle of 122
Watson, Fargerstrom & Hughes 88, 95, 97, 168
Watson, Peter 157
Watson, Teddy 38
Watts, Charlie *224*
Waugh, Evelyn: *Brideshead Revisited* 82–83, *83*, 120; *Vile Bodies* 81, *83*
Weatherill, Bernard *119*
Weaving, Hugo *188*
Webb, Clifton 152, 154, *155*
Webb, Frederick 40
Webb, William 40
Webster's 248
Wellington, Duke of 40, 108, *109*, 120, 122, 265
Wells of Mayfair 87, 213
Welsh & Jefferies 19, 23, 38, 110, 184, 202, 223, 273
West, Kanye 233
West, Mae 23, 236
Westminster Abbey 44
Weston, John 18, 76
Westwood, Dame Vivienne *182*, *191*
White, Henry 128
White's club 84
Whitfield, James *158*–59
Wilde, Oscar 247; *The Picture of Dorian Gray* 79
Wilhelm I, Kaiser 108, 132
Wilhelm II, Kaiser *32*, 108, *111*, *134*, 247

Wilkinson & Son 118
Wilkinson, David 184
Wilkinson, L. G. 184
Willems, Frederik *6–7*, 129
William and Mary 40
William IV 31, 40, 135, 252
William, Prince 38, *39*, *119*
Williams & Co. 168
Williams, Robbie 214, 233
Willis, Bobby 221, 222, 223, 226
Willis, Emma 248
Willis, W. H. *78*
Wilson, Lambert *188*
Wimbledon 166
Windsor *38*; Castle 37, 44
Windsor, Duke of 30, 34, *35*, 35–36, 38, 55, *58*, *61*, 66, 67, *86*, 87, 88, *115*, 122, *122*, *124*, 125, 147, 157, 223, 247, 248, 251
Windsor knot 36
Windsor, Lord Freddy 38
Winkleman, Sophie 38
Winser, Kim 234
Winterhalter, Franz Xavier *31*, *51*
Wintour, Anna *198*
Wizard of Oz, The 157
Wodehouse, P. G. 168
Woolgar, Fenella *83*
Worth, House of 92

Yamamoto, Yohji 178, 202
York, Duke of (Prince George) *see* George V
Young, Robert *65*
Youssopoff, Prince Felix 84, *85*
Youthquake 24, 218
Yugoslavia 126

Zane, Billy *188*, 190, *191*

Overleaf: Anderson & Sheppard's Leon Powell removes a stray baste stitch before releasing the finished suit to the customer.